THERE'S NO PLACE LIKE HOME

THERE'S NO PLACE LIKE HOME

Anthropological Perspectives on Housing and Homelessness in the United States

EDITED BY
Anna Lou Dehavenon

Contemporary Urban Studies
Robert V. Kemper and M. Estellie Smith, Series Editors

BERGIN & GARVEY
Westport, Connecticut • London

Library of Congress Cataloging-in-Publication Data

There's no place like home : anthropological perspectives on housing
  and homelessness in the United States / edited by Anna Lou
  Dehavenon.
       p. cm.—(Contemporary urban studies, ISSN 1065-7002)
    Includes bibliographical references (p.   ) and index.
    ISBN 0-89789-484-7 (alk. paper)—ISBN 0-89789-661-0 (pbk.)
       1. Homelessness—United States—Congresses. 2. Homeless persons—
  United States—Congresses. 3. Housing—United States—Congresses.
  4. United States—Social policy—Congresses. I. Dehavenon, Anna
  Lou. II. Series.
  HV4505.T48   1996
  363.5'0973—dc20   96-10375

British Library Cataloguing in Publication Data is available.

Library of Congress Catalog Card Number: 96-10375
ISBN: 0-89789-661-0 (pbk.)
ISSN: 1065-7002

First published in 1996

Bergin & Garvey, 88 Post Road West, Westport, CT 06881
An imprint of Greenwood Publishing Group, Inc.

Printed in the United States of America

The paper used in this book complies with the
Permanent Paper Standard issued by the National
Information Standards Organization (Z39.48-1984).

10 9 8 7 6 5 4 3 2 1

For Janet M. Fitchen

whose untimely death deprived anthropology of
one of its most ardent, gifted fieldworkers.

Contents

Tables and Figures

FIGURES

Prologue: Azdak Lives

Kim Hopper

> "The housing industry trades on the knowledge that no western country can
> politically afford to permit its citizens to sleep in the street."
>
> Anthony Jackson, *A Place Called Home*, 1976

No doubt every age has its roster of "unbreakable" rules that some future era proves to be no such thing. When it comes to attitudes toward the poor in the United States, however, the cycle appears to be quickening. Jackson's study of low-cost housing in Manhattan is, after all, less than twenty years old but already it seems hopelessly dated, even quaint. The same applies to the "decent provision for the poor" that Samuel Johnson once put forth as the true measure of a civilized society. Five centuries of poor relief are enough to make one skeptical of the idea that any capitalist society (even one aspiring to the status of "civilized") has ever seriously followed that dictum.[1] Still, the moral legitimacy and force of the claim remain undeniable. Why else would the U.S. delegation have felt compelled to insist that footage of American homelessness be omitted from a 1987 United Nations film commissioned as part of the International Year of Shelter for the Homeless? The Reagan administration's objection? The film neglected to mention the distinctive "individual rights element" of homelessness in this country (*New York Times* 1986).

But embarrassment at our failure to keep the indigent off the streets at night is not just political posturing. Something much deeper is at stake, as a moment's consideration of the misery *not seen* will attest. Official relief aside, a vast make-shift array of "shadow shelter"—stemming for the most part from the claims of kinship and friendship—has traditionally made (and continues to make) the difference between a place on the street and a berth among familiar faces for most people on the margins. That being so, the scale of the visible homelessness apparent today is even more remarkable and the need for credible accounts of what went wrong more pressing. Violating core moral codes is customarily viewed as "unthinkable"; exceptions take shape not through the granting of dispensations but through reconsideration of whether an infraction has actually occurred (Edgerton 1985).[2] Elemental claims of belonging, of solidarity, may be one such value.[3] When kinship fails, the burden shifts to the modern state, and it is not one that can be denied or disposed of lightly. But complications may arise that effectively negate the burden. If potential objects of assistance "refuse" standing offers of help, for example, one can hardly say that they have been abandoned to their own devices. And if such refusals can be shown to be both habitual and commonplace, then little wonder our streets, alleyways, and parks are encamped with ersatz bedouins.

Now, a skeptic might be moved to wonder whether just such strategic logic might explain the extraordinary amount of resources and preachment devoted to depicting the street-dwelling poor as, alternatively, willfully self-destructive, hopelessly addicted, or hapless victims of pathology.[4] Among the merits of the reports and analyses gathered here is that they are further makings of an ethnographic corrective to such a view, which has been taking shape for a decade or so. Implicit throughout the volume (explicit in its recommendations) is the conviction that fundamental breaches of social contract will not be patched by local charity and informal assistance.

Rule-breaking is not only the precipitating occasion for a volume on homelessness; it is also, as its editor notes, a consistent theme in the anthropology of disorder it displays. Trespassing, squatting, misuse of public facilities, unauthorized doubling-up, misappropriation of properties not intended for habitation, illegal siting of trailers, misrepresentation of circumstances: in all of these we detect evidence of widespread contempt for the niceties of property rights when "necessity" demands otherwise. Coupled with these acts of disobedience are varieties of complicity making ordinary citizens (and some stray officials) accomplices to such crimes of poverty. This includes not only those who give direct aid and comfort to the scofflaws but those who quietly turn a blind eye and deaf ear to infractions of rules, who tolerate forbidden activities, who inject a little slippage into their rounds of surveillance. Such complicity warrants closer anthropological attention than we have given it up until now. Official apologetics and repressive measures notwithstanding, the stories recounted here make it clear that for some ordinary people the sense of moral failure provoked by visible homelessness continues to haunt them and prompt action.[5]

Take the account of the park dwellers in Orange County and, even more striking, that of the Mad Hatters in Atlanta. Like the shanty structures cobbled together by displaced urban dwellers elsewhere (Balmori and Morton 1994), their huts are *lumpen* constructions. An outlaw band of architects and builders, together with their homeless collaborators, manages to wrest habitable spaces into being using limited means, the necessary stealth, and energizing infusions of solidarity. Impressive as the accomplishment is, it is not entirely unprecedented. As Mike Robertson reminds us, religious organizations have been the mainstays of unofficial shelter for over a hundred years; some, like the Catholic Workers, share their own living space. Nonreligious groups, like ACORN, have successfully worked to merge active squatting with political organization. Rural makeshifts that fall far short of building codes, as the late Janet Fitchen spent a quarter of a century demonstrating, can be a way of life.

Such resourcefulness deserves note because more than a refusal to succumb to despair is at stake. There is counsel to stewardship. There is celebration of vernacular craft. There is hard work and genuine play. There are traces of pain (evident here in the continuing stories of the occupants of Mad Hatter huts). But above all, it seem to me, such efforts serve as gentle rebukes to those of us whose habit it is simply to pity their homeless creators.

None of this should be taken to suggest that the dirty, detailed work of politics can be circumvented. Structural change rarely comes from such fresh local experiments. And if some of the recommendations made here have already been overtaken by events, that says more about the depressing temper of our times than it does about the shortsightedness of those who made them.

In closing, let me admit to being tempted to view at least some of the species of insubordination chronicled here as contemporary versions of the "social banditry" that Eric Hobsbawm (1981) found at other times, in other places (specifically, peasant societies). Surely, there is at least suggestive evidence that some of these miscreant activities enjoy local popular support. But it would be a stretch to classify them as social banditry, if for no other reason than the pettiness of the crimes usually involved.[6] At the same time, these working affiliations and cooperative ventures do suggest alternative ways of doing what has traditionally been seen as "charity" work.

So, as a tribute instead to the *spirit* of social banditry that wafts through this volume, here is Bertolt Brecht's salute, in his fable *The Caucasian Chalk Circle*, to the mischievous judge Azdak. His tenure on the bench, riddled though it was with decidedly wacky interpretations of jurisprudence, had helped to inaugurate a new era of freedom for the local populace. Misrule may have been his element, but it had had a strategic purpose.

> And he broke the rules to save them.
> Broken law like bread he gave them,
> Brought them to shore upon his crooked back.

(Act IV)

That spirit lives and thrives in the acts of refusal documented here. And they, in turn, point to the need for a politics that would render them no longer necessary. Anthropologists have a role in both endeavors.

NOTES

1. As historians of social welfare policy from Elizabeth I through Chadwick, Bismarck, aid to widows and orphans, and the WPF and OEO (see Brennan's majority opinion in *Goldberg v. Kelly*, 1969) have repeatedly shown, the real question has been how stringently one can trim provisions and still pass them off as decent enough. Just as surely, common folk have traditionally proven quite suspicious of both poor relief and its official (often disciplinary) rationale (see, e.g., Kusmer 1987): owing to the elective affinities of uncertain livelihood, it is not hard for them to catch glimpses of their own possible future in the sorry spectacle of their neighbors' plight.

2. If permitting the poor to sleep in the street seems too ambiguous, think instead of historical debates over the worth of a slave for apportionment purposes, Roman Catholic deliberations over the grounds for annulment, or contemporary abortion debates about fetal viability. In each instance, whether an infraction is justified yields to the prior question of whether something counts as an instance of the alleged inviolate entity at stake—a person, a union, a life.

3. See Walzer (1983) on "membership," and Ignatieff (1984) on the claims of strangers.

4. A 1988 State Department memorandum on the subject concludes that public homelessness is "not a function of poverty but rather of disorientation and the toleration of American society for such aberrant behavior"—a tribute, as it were, to the rule of liberty. For further discussion and documentation for the case of New York, see Hopper (1991).

5. For a compendium of repressive local efforts, see National Law Center on Homelessness and Poverty, *No Homeless People Allowed: Anti-Homeless Laws, Litigation and Alternatives in 49 U.S. Cities* (Washington, D.C.: December 1994).

6. In a postscript to the revised edition, Hobsbawm is clear that while dodging customs inspectors or parking illegally carry little social opprobrium today, their practitioners are not—unlike social bandits—"people of whom their society could be proud" (1981:148). Admittedly, acts of solidarity undertaken out of compassion for the disenfranchised are less clear-cut. Clearing out illegal squatters, even when done for future public benefit, may generate protest by people with no direct stake in the property, as reactions to a recent eviction in New York City illustrates (Kennedy 1995; Sante 1995). Competing interests (and support for eviction) are more apparent when the outlawed use is suspect (alleged drug trafficking) and the local benefit is immediate (return of park space).

Acknowledgments

Preparing this book was a labor of love, but a long one. Without the encouragement and support of a number of people, beginning with my co-authors, it would not have been completed. I would also like to express my gratitude to Roy A. Rappaport. Under his guidance as president of the American Anthropological Association, Delmos Jones and I first convened the Association's Task Force on Poverty and Homelessness in 1988. Rappaport was convinced that anthropologists could make an important contribution to the greater understanding and amelioration of domestic social problems. The Task Force presented a number of panels at the Association's annual meetings. Some of the essays in this volume were presented first on these panels.

To Marvin Harris, my mentor and teacher, I owe a profound debt of gratitude for his teachings and his encouraging me to become an anthropologist. (Marvin, each of the co-authors had to listen more than once to my expounding on the critical usefulness of the emic/etic distinction in direct observation and collecting data on politically sensitive issues in one's own culture.)

I am also especially grateful to my friend, Estellie Smith, for her faithful—if sometimes cajoling—support. It was she who first suggested that the book be done and that I do it. (Estellie, I hope you were right and that it was worth it.)

In the political climate of 1995, it took time for housing as a human right to be revealed in the conclusion as the only logical framework for the summary analysis of the authors' policy recommendations. In general, Americans seemed to be growing less and less sympathetic to the deprived and destitute and more and more concerned about their own individual economic futures—not without reason. The comments of the experienced legal advocates, Steven Banks, Jane Sujen Bock, Andrew Scherer, and Justice Rajindar Sachar, helped reassure me that we were on the right track even though we might appear—for the moment—to be out of step. I thank each of them. I thank them all.

Finally, anthropologist Stephen L. Mikesell, Ph.D. deserves a gold medal for his work on the final editing and preparation of the manuscript. Once again, thanks Steve.

Anna Lou Dehavenon

Introduction

Anna Lou Dehavenon

This book shows that shelter—one of the most basic elements of human adaptation—is lacking for substantial numbers of people in the United States, the world's wealthiest, most advanced industrialized nation. That not all of a society's members realize that society's shelter norms shows that its social organization fails to meet a basic human need—for the shelter they require to live in aggregated rather than isolated, atomistic groups.

When a society's standard approaches to securing shelter fail, people with the fewest social resources are forced to break the rules in order to survive. These chapters explore some of the rules and behavior patterns that evolved after the middle 1970s when different groups of Americans could no longer secure stable housing for themselves and their families. Essentially, what these new rules and behaviors demonstrate is a conflict between human and legal rights. This book is also about health and disease, since many of those whom American society fails to shelter are failed first when their chronic medical problems are not adequately cared for.

The idea for this book emerged from two symposia organized by the Task Force on Poverty and Homelessness of the American Anthropological Association for the association's annual meeting in 1988. One of the primary goals of the task force was to look more closely than others had yet done at the causes of the poverty and low-income housing shortage associated with U.S. homelessness. It seemed to the task force members that the methods anthropologists use are particularly well-suited to examining the impact of the lack of stable housing on the daily lives of low-income people.

This book's chapters also reflect two other goals: documentation of the experiential and geographic diversity of U.S. homelessness and articulation of policy recommendations based on the analysis of primary data collected using ethnographic methods. As a result, this book examines the homelessness of both adults with children and adults without children in three different settings: rural, urban, suburban. Furthermore, each chapter includes its author's data-based recommendations on homelessness prevention.

Homelessness results when a household fails to maintain stable shelter for all its members. The reasons for this failure are found on the macro, middle, and micro levels of sociological phenomena. For example, on the macro level after the early 1970s, federal decision makers failed to confront major changes taking place in the world economy and the structure of U.S. society. These changes included slowed economic growth worldwide, the increase of speculative over-productive economic activity in the global market, deindustrialization, technological change, and the exacerbation of the cyclical crises of capitalism as more people than ever before became integrated into the global economy. The vulnerability of the United States to world economic cycles had never been so great.

During the 1970s and 1980s, these trends contributed on the middle level to cutbacks in federal funds for community development and the construction of subsidized housing and the failure of government to maintain the purchasing power of minimum wage and public assistance payments in the face of high inflation after the oil embargo of 1973. In the 1980s, other middle-level consequences included further federal cutbacks in subsidized jobs and job training programs, and the failure of local governments to maintain the low-cost rental housing they inherited through private landlord tax default and abandonment driven largely by inflated fuel costs. By the decade's end on the micro level, growing numbers of individuals and families lost—or could no longer afford—housing of their own because of increasing unemployment, low levels of public assistance and minimum wage payments, higher rents, drastic shrinkage of the livable low-income housing supply, rising discrimination, and drug, domestic, and other violence.

THEMES AND STRUCTURE

Four themes wend their way through the nine chapters of this book:

1. The inability of U.S. society to adapt effectively to the global socioeconomic changes that are increasingly linked to impoverishment and homelessness;
2. The need for the new behavior patterns the destitute and near-destitute develop to survive and the creativity of these patterns;
3. Public and private efforts to address the emergency needs of the homeless; and,
4. The development of the authors' data-based recommendations.

The conclusion summarizes the policy recommendations in the earlier chapters. This analysis reveals four specific categories of actions needed to prevent homelessness: providing emergency shelter, enabling people at risk to remain in their own housing, helping homeless people access existing housing, and increasing the stock of new low-income housing. The recommended actions in each category are presented as to whether they should be undertaken in the long-term, midterm, or short-term future and at which level of government. Also analyzed are a number of recommendations relevant to the stable income and good health needed for maintaining one's own housing once you have it. This chapter concludes with a discussion of some of the consequences for U.S. society if these kinds of actions are not taken.

In Chapter 1, Janet Fitchen shows that the problem of homelessness is not just urban, but rural too, and society-wide. She views homelessness in upper rural New York state as the result of inadequate resources and insufficient housing reserves. Both conditions are closely linked to poverty and lack of work. Irene Glasser conducted research sponsored by the U.S. Census Bureau in a small New England city. As she describes in Chapter 2, her experiences as a former social worker surfaced when she became a housing expert in order to fill a void left by local social agencies. She transported homeless individuals to important appointments and helped them apply for public housing and look for permanent housing. This chapter documents a wide range of adaptations to survival used by people with no shelter, from sleeping outside, living in shelters, living in marginal single-room occupancy hotels, to the ubiquitous doubling-up.

In Chapter 3, Rory Bolger explores history on a micro level. He explains how the urban crisis since the 1970s has affected Detroit, Michigan, a city well known for its strong blue-collar population and the once widespread availability of housing for it. His material on the rise of poverty and homelessness covers a longer time span than any of the other studies in this book.

In Chapter 4, Anna Lou Dehavenon focuses on doubling-up as the strategy that most homeless families in New York City pursue before asking the city for emergency shelter. She draws upon a cultural materialist approach to document the hardship these families face when they try to perform basic domestic functions in severely overcrowded, doubled-up housing conditions.

Andrew Maxwell also looks at the inner city, in Chapter 5. He views "squatting" in public housing projects as a response to the government's failure to provide "decent, safe, and sanitary housing" for people who cannot afford market-level rents. By keeping apartments empty when demand far exceeds supply, government avoids responsibility for people in need of low-income housing.

In Chapter 6, Amy Phillips and Susan Hamilton take up a low technology solution for homeless adults in Atlanta, Georgia. Social agencies give priority to sheltering homeless families with children, so there are few housing options for adults who do not have children with them. The "Mad Housers," a group of youthful volunteers with middle-class jobs, provide "huts" made of sturdy plywood to supply shelter for about $60 per person.

Like Chapter 6, Michael Robertson's Chapter 7 describes an attempt to solve some of the more immediate problems of the homeless. He finds that both fundamentalist and mainstream Christian groups who care for Albuquerque's homeless perceive poverty and homelessness in terms of food and shelter rather than the larger issues of inequality. Fundamentalists prefer to work with the "able-bodied" rather than the chronically homeless. Mainstream churches offer their volunteers personal religious growth through service to God in a ministry to the chronic homeless.

In Chapter 8, Talmadge Wright and Anita Vermund examine a marginalized population that resists institutional power and challenges mainstream definitions of the "proper" use of public space in southern California. The city government sees park dwellers as "out of place," "out of control," and a potential threat to other people's property. The workers at the neighboring welfare center view the homeless as the "undeserving poor," displacing the structural dimensions of homelessness onto individual responsibility and avoiding the larger issues of wealth and power.

In Chapter 9, Brett Williams views gentrification and displacement in Washington, D.C. within the broad context of the political economy. She sees baby-boomers as consumers rather than agents of gentrification. Williams sets out to correct a failure in her previous work—not seeing the brutality in the displacement of low-income African Americans in the gentrification process.

CONCLUSION

This book documents a lack of national will in the United States to confront and solve the low-income housing crisis, and, more broadly and fundamentally, its root cause, poverty. There is thus a lack of consensus and cohesion among Americans, even with respect to certain basic values. When social will is absent, social organization is more likely to fail at the margins—in an economic sense—where the homeless now live. When social will is present, as in most of the industrial nations of Western Europe, not as many people at the margins are forced or encouraged to behave illegally as many now are in the United States.

The "illegalities" described in the chapters of this book can be ascribed to both the homeless *and* the government. However, there is a substantial difference between the two. The illegalities of government are on a much grander scale, backed by physical force and usually hidden from public view. Examples cited by the authors include: political patronage (Maxwell, Williams); corrupt and inadequate management of public facilities (Maxwell); fraud in housing (Maxwell, Williams), nonenforcement of housing codes (Fitchen, Dehavenon), and illegal housing conversions (Fitchen, Williams); inadequacies in providing emergency shelter and permanent housing for the impoverished (Dehavenon, Phillips and Hamilton), and public health protection (Dehavenon, Fitchen); manipulation of the social service delivery systems depriving the homeless of the welfare and Supplemental Social Security Income to which they are legally entitled (Dehavenon, Robertson, Wright and Vermund, Robertson); unnecessary removal of children from the home (Dehavenon, Fitchen); racial discrimination and segregation (Bolger, Glasser, Williams); discrimination against families on welfare (Dehavenon, Fitchen); obstruction of the enumeration of the homeless and displaced (Williams); systematic and abusive police surveillance of the homeless (Wright and Vermund); and eviction, sometimes brutal, and theft by the police (Maxwell).

By comparison, the illegal activities of the homeless are largely public and controlled easily by a government which uses force. Illegalities include doubling-up (Bolger, Dehavenon, Fitchen, Glasser), working in the street-level underground economy (Bolger, Dehavenon, Fitchen), squatting (Phillips and Hamilton, Maxwell), petty theft (Bolger, Maxwell, Williams), use or street-level sale of drugs (Bolger, Maxwell, Williams), bathing in showers intended for tennis players and sleeping in park bushes (Wright and Vermund), and begging for food (Bolger, Robertson).

Few of the recommendations proposed by the authors would tap any private sector resource or initiate any new government program not already in place as a result of the public housing and Social Security laws enacted during and after the Great Depression of the 1930s. Therefore, they are not radical. What *is* radical is the notion of ensuring that the law and human rights protections pertain to all U.S. citizens.

We already know what is needed to end poverty and homelessness. What is lacking is national consensus about what to do and the political will to act upon this consensus. As Aidan Southall writes, this contemporary crisis of political will "is the product of material causes, the high level of collective consumption, and the net outcome of all the production relationships of those involved in it. . . . The most fundamental element of the crisis is inequality. . . . The essence of inequality—or the gross relative lack of access to resources—is coming to be seen as an injustice. . . . The injustice of inequality has now become scandalous. . . . The present crisis can only be solved by changes which have an ineluctably moral character" (1994).

As anthropologists have always done, the authors in this book searched for explanations of specific sociocultural phenomena, that is, impoverishment and homelessness, in the observation of low-income people's daily lives. We hope that this portrayal of their experiences researching the causes and consequences of these conditions in the world's wealthiest nation will contribute to building the political will needed to ameliorate them.

THERE'S NO PLACE
LIKE HOME

Poverty and Homelessness in Rural Upstate New York

Janet M. Fitchen

In rural upstate New York, changes in social organization as a result of the low-income housing crisis include an increase in single-parent families combined with a corresponding reduction in available employment opportunities. The result for many has been the removal of children to relatives or foster families when their parents become homeless. Needy families live in marginal housing, like trailers, with housing code violations, rats, polluted water, no sewers, and little or no code enforcement by the government until the families are forced to leave. Fitchen recommends preventive case management in public assistance programs and rent subsidies for families at risk of homelessness.

INTRODUCTION

Few people are aware that homelessness is a problem in rural America. Rural homelessness is conceptually "invisible" because it does not match our urban-based images and stereotypes. Rural homeless people are not seen sleeping on heating grates or in large congregate shelters, because there are few such places in rural and small-town America. Instead, people without homes are dispersed in temporary, inadequate sleeping arrangements, and since they usually have some sort of a roof over their heads, they are invisible to the public.

In the course of research in upstate New York I have found some rural residents who have housing problems severe enough to constitute homelessness. The roof that shelters them may be only a car or shed roof; it may be the leaking roof of a very old, dilapidated farmhouse or of an isolated shack with no running water; it may be the temporary roof of an old mobile home already fully occupied by relatives or friends, or of a borrowed camper-trailer parked off-season in a public campground. Families may have to move frequently from one such accommodation to another, remaining inadequately and insecurely housed for months or even years. People in these types of situations would surely qualify as homeless according to a more rural definition, such as that "their housing is both unstable and temporary . . . and they lack resources to secure adequate housing" (Patton 1988:188). In fact, they are seldom counted as homeless and rarely receive special homeless assistance.

The Limited Literature on Rural Homelessness

No clear agreement exists on how to define homelessness in rural areas. Even if an appropriate rural definition were developed, the "hinterland homeless" (Davenport, Davenport, and Newett 1990) would still be harder to find and count than their urban counterparts, because they are so dispersed. Since rural homelessness is often an episode or a series of episodes lasting only a few days or weeks, it is necessary to catch people during one of these periods if they are to qualify as homeless and be counted or studied.

In the late 1980s, reports from the Housing Assistance Council—a nonprofit organization in Washington, D.C. that deals with rural low-income housing needs—indicated that in several states, such as Minnesota and Arizona, where urban homelessness was recognized as a problem, the rural homeless population was actually growing faster. However, a state-by-state survey of homelessness made little or no mention of rural homelessness, even in chapters on rural states such as Alabama and Colorado, except to remark that counting the homeless in rural areas is even more difficult than it is in the cities (Momeni 1989). In New York State, rural homelessness "does not appear to be a major problem," a conclusion based on such sources as county welfare departments, which reported very few homeless families seeking assistance (Momeni 1989:135).

Among the few systematic studies of rural homelessness was a large project conducted in Ohio in 1984 and 1990 (Ohio Department of Mental Health 1985; First et al. 1990). The Ohio studies classified a person as homeless if she or he claimed to have no permanent residence and had spent the previous night in a shelter, mission, or cheap hotel, or in an abandoned or uninhabitable building such as a shed or barn with no utilities and which he or she neither owned nor rented. The studies found that the rural homeless differed significantly from the urban homeless. Rural homelessness is not as clearly associated with mental health problems or substance abuse as with family dissolution, conflict within doubled-up households, inability to pay rent, and unemployment (First et al. 1990:20–21). The more recent study, which interviewed 921 homeless adults in twenty-one rural counties, found that nearly 46 percent were staying with family members or friends; nearly 40 percent were in shelters or cheap hotels or motels; and less than 15 percent were literally without shelter or living in cars or abandoned buildings (First et al. 1990:13).

Other studies have found that rural homelessness is more closely associated with poverty than with mental illness, substance abuse, or life-style choice. Homeless people camping in national forests were not there out of preference for outdoor life (Southard 1993). The homelessness of school children in rural New Hampshire—whether "independent" teens or young children with a parent—was not caused by parental substance abuse or mental health problems, or by life-style choices, but by family poverty and upheaval (Luloff 1993).

One limitation in many studies of homelessness, both urban and rural, is that people without housing are studied as if that were their permanent condition. The anthropological emphasis on context is often missing, even where the research methodology is ethnographic. More attention should be focused on the strategies people use to prevent becoming homeless, as well as their strategies for surviving while homeless (see Bolger's chapter in this book, and also Greenlee 1991). Particularly in rural environments, where homelessness is apt to occur in discontinuous spells, I would suggest that we need to study "at-risk" people in their normal settings before they become homeless, or in between spells of homelessness by examining their vulnerability and discerning the interplay of forces shaping their lives. A more holistic, contextualized approach, which underlies this paper, may be especially fruitful for policy and program development, as it provides insight into what should be done to prevent homelessness, not merely how to shelter those who have already become homeless.

The Context of Rural Homelessness: Increasing Rural Poverty

Since rural homelessness is closely linked to poverty, the context of increased homelessness includes recent economic and social changes that have caused an increase in rural poverty and have transformed poverty into potential homelessness. Contrary to widely held assumptions, recent growth in rural poverty results less from agricultural decline or the farm crisis than from manufacturing decline. Downsized factories, increased overseas assembly, and shifts from manufacturing to low-end service-sector jobs have had a particularly devastating impact on rural America. Nearly 40 percent of the nation's rural population lives in counties where manufacturing constitutes the major share of local employment. The percentage of rural workers who earn low wages has grown from 32 percent in 1979 to 42 percent in 1987. In urban areas the figures are lower and have risen more slowly in these years, from 23 percent to 29 percent (Gorham and Harrison 1990:16). The inadequacy of rural employment as a contributor to poverty is revealed in the fact that in 1986 "about one-quarter of poor young adults in the rural labor force held two or more jobs" (O'Hare 1988:11). And still, they were poor.

Deterioration of rural employment has been compounded by an increase in single-parent families in rural areas. In the past, a large majority of poor rural households contained married couples. However, in recent years single parenthood has become increasingly common in the entire rural population and especially among the rural poor. By 1987, 39 percent of rural poor households were headed by women (Porter 1989:30). While this figure was still much lower than in central cities, single-parenthood has continued to increase in rural areas, even after having peaked and declined slightly in urban areas. The causes of this trend cannot be covered in this chapter, but its effects on rural homelessness are clear. In rural economies, where jobs are fewer and wage levels lower, single women with dependent children are at greater risk of poverty and are apt to stay poor longer than similar women in metropolitan areas (Ross and Morrissey 1989:65).

These major economic and social changes were clearly affecting the people in rural New York in the 1980s (Fitchen 1991a). Although poverty rates in rural counties varied from the low teens to the upper teens, in certain economically distressed communities they reached the upper twenties. At the start of 1990, some rural places were experiencing significant increases in poverty. For example, welfare rolls grew as much as 18 percent or more in a few rural counties in the year ending April 1990, while statewide in the same period they grew only 1 percent, and in New York City only 7 percent. In some rural counties, the April 1990 food stamp recipient numbers were 20 percent or more above the 1989 monthly average, which was nearly quadruple the growth in New York City.

The increasing incidence of poverty in rural New York comes from three separate sources, or "streams" (Fitchen 1991a, 1991b). First are the rural people who were raised in poverty or who have been poor for many years and, not having themselves escaped poverty, are now raising the next generation in poverty. The second are the rural people who had previously not been poor but have recently fallen into poverty as a result of employment deterioration or single parenthood. Third are the urban poor people driven out of cities by the high cost and deteriorated quality of life, moving to rural towns for cheaper housing and better living.

METHODOLOGY

Selection of Respondents

To explore the insecure housing situations that contribute to homelessness, I conducted unstructured but focused interviews with twenty low-income individuals and families living in rural counties of central and western New York, where I was already conducting research on poverty and other issues (Fitchen 1991a). To probe more deeply and systematically, I designed a residential history format that I had used as a guide for interviews with forty low-income women residing in the same counties. The main criteria for selection of respondents were (1) household income below or only slightly above the official poverty line, (2) dependent children, (3) willingness to be interviewed for this research, and (4) participation in some means-tested program such as Aid to Families with Dependent Children (AFDC), the Supplemental Nutrition Program for Women, Infants, and Children (WIC), a food stamp program, or Head Start.

Interview Content

Respondents were contacted through or at these or other programs and institutions and were interviewed at those sites or in their homes. The residential history format guided respondents through a series of questions about their present residence and several previous residences. For each residence, they were asked about the home (e.g., type of home and location, owned or rented, monthly costs, reasons for selecting it, duration of stay, distance from previous home, etc.); about the household (e.g., membership, sources of income, forms of assistance); and about temporary stays between residences. At the time of the interview, none of the forty respondents were actually without a place to live; yet, almost all of them indicated that they presently were or recently had been in a very precarious situation with regard to housing.

Focus Groups and Collection of Secondary Data

Interviews and residential histories were augmented in each county by focus-group sessions with low-income women. I also held group discussions and individual interviews with staff of schools and human service agencies, and I collected substantiating documentation from their records. From these disparate sources and separate places, all within the known context of poverty in rural New York, the precursors and patterns of rural homelessness emerge.

FINDINGS

Strategies for Avoiding Literal Homelessness

Most rural poor people I interviewed have used three principal strategies—alone, in combination, or serially—to keep a roof over their heads most of the time. While these strategies have generally enabled families to avoid literal homelessness, they constitute a "proto-homelessness" or "near homelessness," and when they are repeated over and over, they should be interpreted as homelessness.

Four individual case studies of precarious housing and homelessness are presented here to illustrate the range of family situations and housing problems I found. The case studies indicate some of the particularly rural aspects of homelessness. The cases all come from three adjacent counties in central New York, counties officially designated as rural, with mixed but faltering economies of manufacturing, services, and agriculture; with high poverty rates and per-capita incomes well below the state average; with recent suburbanization and second-home development; and with no large cities.

Case Study of Terry: Multiple Moves and Family Splitting

Terry and her children were still on the edge of homelessness after two years of "bouncing around" among several locations in her county. After her marriage suddenly broke up, she and her four children stayed with her sister in the village and then moved to a temporary residence in a rented trailer a few miles out of town. Because the trailer was too small and she had no reliable car, she decided to move back to the village and soon located an apartment above a vacant store. When Terry found this to be an unhealthy environment for her children she moved out again, to a two-bedroom trailer well out in the country. With a better car, the distance was not a severe problem, and at $250 the rent was cheap. However, because of the crowding in the trailer, she had to send her oldest child back to live with his father. After yet another move, Terry and three of her children are now back in the trailer cluster where she had lived a year earlier.

Case Study of Winnie and Danny: A Young Family with Marginal Income

Winnie and Danny had moved eleven times in the six years of their marriage, living in nine different communities, all within the county where both were born. They have circulated through a series of substandard apartments, trailers with leaking roofs and fire hazards, a place where inadequate air circulation exacerbated a medical problem, and places that were decent but too costly for Danny's marginal income. He was still earning only $4.45 an hour after three years in the same factory. Tomorrow they and their two preschool children would be moving again, but this would be "a good move" and an easy one, to an adjacent apartment in the same building in a small hamlet. The new place has the two bedrooms required by the department of social services if the family is to continue receiving support for a child with special needs. Their present apartment, where they have stayed only two months, is spotlessly clean, their possessions stacked and packed. Just four months after my interview, the family was again looking for a place to live.

Case Study of Mandy: Raising Children without Indoor Plumbing

After Mandy separated from her husband, she had a very difficult time finding a place for herself and two small children to live. She ended up in a rental trailer out in the country for $300 a month, plus utilities. The trailer had no water supply and no sewer, and the landlord, who lived in a house next door, told her to send her children to use the woods. Rats could not be kept out of the trailer. One day just after Mandy returned from the hospital with her new baby, the river behind the trailer overflowed its banks, coming right up to the doorstep, at which point she decided that two months in this place was long enough. She moved into the village to live with her boyfriend.

Case Study of Elvira and Fred: Camping, Doubling-up, and Substandard Housing

About five years ago, Elvira, her husband, their two older children, and the new baby lost the place where they were living, an old, rented farmhouse on a back road quite near where she had grown up. They were able to find another old house close by, but before they had been there two years the elderly landlord "sold the house out from under us." With no place to go, the family spent the next three months, in Elvira's words, "camping here and there." First they returned to her hometown and stayed with her brother and his wife in the village. But there were some difficulties in her brother's new marriage, and "although they were real good to us, we didn't want to overstay our welcome." They moved to a campground for two weeks, where the creek served as their bathing facilities. At this time, Elvira was working as a bartender and waitress, and her husband, who could find no farm labor jobs, stayed with the children. When everything they owned was stolen one day, they decided it was time to move out.

Some friends who lived in the country took them in. "They did the best they could to keep us all there, sleeping us wherever we could fit." Finally, Elvira found a house, or, as she called it, "a dump, a junkyard with rats" in a little hamlet, owned by the father of someone she knew. At $250 a month, the rent was low for a four-bedroom house, although the additional heating cost was high. They managed to cover their rent on her part-time work at a nursing facility nearby, combined with a meager income Fred was now making on a farm labor job, approximately $184 for a sixty-four-hour week. They spent weeks clearing the junk from the house and yard, and hauling it to the dump. Then Elvira became ill; she was finally diagnosed as having dysentery, which was traced to well water polluted from the old septic tank. When the landlord moved into a health care facility, his grown children took over the place and immediately raised the rent. So two years after they had moved in and cleaned up the place, Elvira and Fred packed up again. This time they found another place quite quickly, half of a house just at the edge of a neighboring hamlet, and they have now been in it two years. The place is small and inconvenient, but at $375 a month, Elvira reports that it is about the lowest rent around.

Doubling-up in Temporary Arrangements

As I found in earlier research (Fitchen 1981), when rural low-income people find themselves without a home, either because of marital violence, family breakup, or a house fire, the usual first recourse is to move in temporarily with parents or other relatives. Parents explicitly stated and frequently enacted their continuing obligation to their children: "You can always come home if you need to." Still today, as my residential history interviews indicate, families and individuals squeeze back in and live temporarily in doubled-up situations. Women who have recently separated from a husband or boyfriend, or who have lost or been evicted from an apartment, report in interviews that they turned first to their own families for temporary housing—staying for a few nights or even several months. Many claim that this assistance from a mother or sister is the only thing that saved them from becoming literally homeless when they lost the place where they had been living.

As the housing situation has tightened in recent years, doubling-up with relatives and friends has become more difficult. Relatives may be unwilling to take in an extra sub-family or be unable to keep them more than a few days. Cramming two families into a trailer or apartment that is already inadequate for one family often leads to friction; so the extra family soon moves to another temporary situation, and then to another. In some cases, the young family wears out the parents' welcome, perhaps because they have returned home too many times, stayed too long, or caused conflict and hard feelings over cost-sharing, housework, child care responsibilities, or drugs.

A more subtle form of doubling-up that may verge on, or lead to homelessness occurs when a woman with children moves in with her boyfriend simply because she has no alternative, even though she would rather not be living with him. More than one single mother has candidly commented that she would like to move out from an apartment shared with a boyfriend, or to kick him out of her own apartment, because of concern that the arrangement may not be good for her children, but rent-sharing with the boyfriend is the only way she can meet payments. Agency case-workers have confirmed in interviews that this situation is a common bind for low-income single mothers. While not literally homeless, women and children in such sharing arrangements lack secure and stable housing: a quarrel between the woman and her boyfriend may put one of them out of the apartment with no alternative housing arrangement in place.

Whatever their composition and however long they last, doubled-up situations are often a precursor to literal homelessness. In fact, when people do turn to small-town public shelter programs, in the majority of cases they report having spent the previous nights with relatives or friends. This pattern emerges clearly in interviews with staff of local shelter programs and in community human-service needs assessments.

Accepting Housing That Is Seriously Inadequate

Poor rural people have always had to put up with poor-quality housing because they could afford no better. Traditionally, poor rural families in central and western New York have owned their homes, and although many of their homes have serious problems in terms of structure, infrastructure, or size, owners have sacrificed quality of housing as a way to minimize cash expenses and remain independent of welfare (Fitchen 1981:96–98). Despite some improvements in the last two decades, much of the owner-occupied housing in the open-country pockets of poverty in upstate New York is still structurally unsound and lacks adequate wiring, running water, or plumbing.

Now, however, substandard conditions in the low-cost rental housing stock have become a problem of even greater concern, because a growing number of rural poor people are living in rented housing. With an inadequate supply of rental housing to meet the demand, low-income tenants have to accept whatever the market offers, paying ever-higher prices for lower-quality rentals. Many rental apartments created out of former houses and store buildings in small villages are not only deteriorating but are known to have code violations. However, inspection and enforcement may be minimal, in part because there is no alternative low-cost housing to which people could move. In some of the burgeoning trailer parks and in the new informal trailer clusters along back roads, water and sewer systems are unable to meet increased demand or state codes, and some of the rental trailers are seriously deteriorating. However, where local health authorities have closed down such trailer parks, the tenants are thrown into an even tighter housing market, and perhaps periods of homelessness.

Substandard conditions in themselves do not constitute homelessness by most definitions (Patton, 1988:188). However, deficiencies in a dwelling and its infrastructure definitely contribute to insecure tenancy and homelessness of the occupants. Residential histories gathered from families showed that the situation forcing them to double-up with others or seek emergency assistance often stemmed from a structural or operational problem that jeopardized health or safety, such as inoperable plumbing, major leaks, unsafe floors, fires caused by improper electrical wiring, bad drinking water, or a faulty furnace. However, as several residential histories revealed, when a family relocated to a better or safer dwelling, they might soon find the rent too much to manage and might again experience a spell of homelessness while trying to find a place with the elusive balance between affordability and quality.

The physical inadequacy of rural housing is especially evident in the temporary housing some families have had to accept during periods of homelessness. For example, they may have spent the entire summer in a borrowed camper-trailer in a state park or rented an isolated hunting cabin in the hills for the off-season—with no electricity, no running water, and no plowed road within a mile. These "roughing-it" arrangements are not described by mothers of small children as a rustic family vacation in the wilderness but as "the only place we could stay." As a worker in one human service agency observed, "Living in something not intended as a home—a shed, camper, or cabin with no facilities—rarely works out for long." However, because these families do indeed have a roof over their heads and are not going through formal institutional channels for assistance, they are not counted in estimates of the rural homeless population.

Moving Frequently among a Series of Cheap Residences

A housing pattern increasingly common among the rural poor is high residential mobility. Frequent residential moves are documented in the records of almost any agency or assistance program in communities with high poverty rates. School enrollment records and observations from school administrators and staff emphasize the mobility of some low-income families. Only a few of the forty low-income women in my questionnaire sample had "stayed put" for more than three years. Particularly stable were those who lived on farms (including both active operations and farms long since out of production), and those who were living in a trailer placed on land owned by their parents or grandparents, or in a house owned by these relatives who were charging no regular rent. Most others had moved quite frequently in recent years. Of the forty women, twenty-three had moved at least once in the last year, and twelve had lived in three or more residences in the last year. Highly mobile families tended to move suddenly as they circulated from one rented small-town apartment to another, from one village to another, from trailer park to trailer park, from village to trailer park and back to village, and from open country to village and back to the country. Most moves are short-distance, within a county or between adjacent counties, and frequent movers generally find their next home through networks of relatives and friends, many of whom have also been scrambling for housing.

The reasons most commonly given for moving away include: (1) threatened or actual eviction (most commonly due to falling behind in the rent, and to landlord complaints of property destruction by tenants); (2) inadequacy of the residence for family needs (due to physical problems in the building itself or to expansion of the family and consequent need for more space); (3) splitting up with a partner or fleeing an abusive situation; and (4) needing to leave a doubled-up temporary housing arrangement. Reasons for selecting the next residence include better quality, lower rent, and joining with or returning to a partner.

Factors That Transform Rural Poverty into Homelessness

In rural areas, as in urban, the most obvious factor pushing poor people into homelessness is inadequacy of the local housing stock, with demand for safe and inexpensive residential units exceeding supply. Other, less obvious, housing factors are also at work in rural areas to make low-income people more vulnerable now than in the past to becoming homeless.

Maldistribution of Low-Cost Rural Housing. On the whole, demand for inexpensive housing in rural New York has grown as rural incomes have deteriorated and as more single-parent families have formed. However, the supply has not grown commensurately.[1] The shortfall is essentially a problem of distribution and is shaped by the dynamics of local economies. In metropolitan fringe areas, communities that at one time had relatively inexpensive housing have become more costly as a result of suburban residential development and rural gentrification. Creation of public or publicly funded low-rent housing in rural communities has been quite minimal, with the exception of apartments for the elderly and some impressive but small-scale efforts by local nonprofit agencies using state rehabilitation and preservation funds. Waiting-list time for apartments in existing public housing is generally two years or more.

A major problem in the distribution of low-cost housing is its lack of correlation with employment opportunities. Inexpensive apartments and trailer parks are added to or generally available in only communities with weak real estate prices and sagging housing markets—that is to say, in areas with weak economies, which means marginal employment opportunities. When people with meager incomes— from employment, public assistance, or other transfer payments—move into a community because the housing is cheap, they may find that there are no adequate or appropriate jobs nearby and no public transportation to larger towns where jobs might be available. Maintaining a reliable car to commute to work can consume a significant portion of a worker's limited earnings. Conversely, the lack of a reliable vehicle may cause the worker frequently to be tardy or absent from work. Consequently, some people settle for poorly paid, part-time local jobs or for welfare. As their incomes remain low, even the relatively low rural rents strain many family budgets, and only the most frugal tenants will be able to keep up with their payments.[2]

Insecurity of Tenancy. Traditionally, most rural poor people have had the security and limited cash expense of owning a place to live, even if it was just a crumbling farmhouse, a tarpaper shack, or an old trailer encased in wooden additions. In most cases they had built their own homes or acquired them by inheritance or inexpensive purchase. Their homes were not mortgaged, and they carried a low assessment for property taxes. Indeed, home-ownership was a primary strategy used by families to minimize cash outflow and gain housing security (Fitchen 1981).

Currently in the densely settled Northeast, as well as elsewhere in the United States, home-ownership is becoming less possible, especially for low-wage earners.[3] With competition from more affluent exurbanite residents, urban vacationers, and retirees, access to old farmhouses and remote housesites has become limited, and poorer local residents have been unable to keep up with escalating housing and land prices, and property taxes. So, in some areas, a new generation of low-income rural families is no longer able to own even a very modest or substandard dwelling. Thus it becomes a generation of renters.

The low rate of home-ownership among the rural poor was evident among the forty low-income women interviewed for residential histories. Twenty-eight of them were currently living in a place they rent. Of the twelve who were not renting, only one family, a married couple, owned a home. Two more families were in rent-to-own arrangements, and in one case the woman's boyfriend owned the home. In the eight remaining non-renting cases, other family members owned the dwelling or the land where the woman and her family were living. Two single mothers were living rent-free with their parents in homes the parents owned. The renters in this sample were more mobile than the homeowners and also more likely to have lived in a doubled-up situation within the last year.

As the security of ownership gives way to the insecurity of tenancy, more rural poor people are at risk of becoming homeless. For low-income households, the problem with being a tenant is not only that rent payments take up so much of their income but that renting requires a cash outlay on a regular basis. Tenants are vulnerable to losing their rented home by eviction for failure to pay rent or by being squeezed out by rent increases. Rents paid by the families interviewed in this research varied greatly, ranging from $200 for a bad trailer in an undesirable trailer park and $250 in public housing, to anywhere from $250 to $450 for one or two-bedroom private apartments, depending on location and condition. In one trailer park, rental of a lot on which to place an owned trailer, not including charges for garbage collection, utilities, and water (which was inadequate and intermittent), went up in 1988 from $85 to $120 a month. Many of the families I interviewed paid well over half of their income for rent, and in some cases considerably more.

In 1989, workers in the department of social services in several rural counties reported that their clients, typically, were paying monthly rents around $100 above their welfare shelter allowance, squeezing the difference out of money intended for other household expenses. Only for people living in public housing or receiving federally funded Section 8 housing rental subsidies is there a rent ceiling limiting rent to one-third of their income. All other low-income tenants, unless their rent is paid directly by the Department of Social Services to the landlord or their budget is closely monitored by an agency case manager, are at risk of periodically falling behind in rent payments. Tenants in this situation get evicted, usually after thirty days' notice, and may experience a spell of homelessness before locating another place to live.

Poor people who live in trailer parks have an added risk of homelessness, because their housing is especially vulnerable to sudden changes in the local real estate market. If the park owner decides to upgrade his park or convert the land to condominiums or commercial buildings in order to earn a higher return on investment, park tenants who own their trailer but rent a lot for it are thrown into a unique—and uniquely rural—version of homelessness. They own a roof to cover their heads, but they have no place to put it. They may be closed out of other trailer parks because these parks are already at capacity, because the owners will not rent spaces for older, smaller trailers, or because rents in other parks are beyond what the family can afford. However, because of high land prices and mobile-home restrictions that increasingly blanket the open countryside, such displaced trailer owners do not have the option to purchase land where they might be able to set their trailer.

Curtailment of Informal, Family-Based Housing Strategies. In addition to marketplace forces, state building codes and local land-use regulations are apt to have a disproportionately negative effect on poor people, making it harder for them to build their own inexpensive housing. For example, used lumber is now strictly regulated in housing construction in New York state, and a certificate of occupancy now requires essential completion of a home before a family moves in. These restrictions, if enforced, eliminate or severely limit some traditional rural strategies for low-cost, do-it-yourself housing. Local municipal land-use regulations and building codes commonly associated with suburbanization and gentrification further reduce housing options of rural poor people. Municipal prohibitions and restrictions on mobile homes, such as large minimum lot sizes and large (expensive) trailer sizes mean that young local families are no longer free to set their own trailer on their parents' property. As state and local regulations have been promulgated and enforced, even low-income rural residents who do own their homes have lost a major set of strategies, such as incremental and intermittent construction with scrounged secondhand materials, that in the past had enabled them to expand and upgrade their homes as needed and whenever feasible. Consequently, poor rural homeowners are now less able to provide for their own long-term housing needs.

The availability of temporary emergency housing through social networks has also been curtailed. No longer can an old trailer or converted school bus be appended to a home for overflow housing and later be moved to a different home nearby to accommodate extra people there. Today, parents who are renters rather than owners may jeopardize their own housing situation by taking in grown children in need of emergency housing. The landlord may threaten eviction or may charge more rent on a per-person basis, even in trailer parks with owner-occupied trailers. If the host family is on public assistance, the welfare department may threaten to close their case for noncompliance with such regulations as overcrowding in bedrooms. This situation forces the extra household members to move on to someone else's place until they find one of their own. If the host relative or friend cannot take the whole family, a child or two may be sent to live with another relative for a while, or a young teenager may sleep in a car in the yard or go stay at the home of a girlfriend's or boyfriend's parents. In all these ways, reduction of informal emergency housing may push potentially homeless families into actual homelessness.

SUMMARY AND RECOMMENDATIONS

This research was conducted in a single state. However, my subsequent research on rural poverty in other states suggests that the etiology and forms of rural homelessness are quite similar elsewhere. Wherever significant rural poverty exists, rural homelessness must be addressed through the interweaving of three levels of remediation—emergency, intermediate, and long-term—and the interaction of three levels of government—federal, state, and local. The three levels of remediation are illustrated below, each with a few policy and program suggestions, some of which are already being tried in individual rural communities.

Level I: Emergency Assistance for Homeless Families and Individuals

A variety of housing remedies can be recommended for special situations that lead to homelessness.

Recommendation #1. Accept a working definition of rural homelessness that includes not only people turning to the few community shelters or sleeping in cars and barns, but also people frequently doubling-up with friends or relatives on an emergency basis or moving frequently from one temporary situation to another.

Recommendation #2. Fund and support more small-scale shelters and scattered-site, safe-home programs, which are particularly needed for women and children fleeing domestic violence and for lone teenagers who can no longer live at home.

Recommendation #3. Use homelessness funds to create revolving loan programs to help low-income people meet start-up costs of a residential move, such as security deposits or the first month's rent.

Recommendation #4. Fund and provide case management for proactive assistance to people on the brink of homelessness, particularly to families who have moved several times in a year, even if they do not actually have an eviction notice in hand.[4]

Recommendation #5. Provide financial reimbursement, food stamps, and supportive agency connections for host families in doubled-up arrangements in order to encourage and sustain these informal patterns of emergency housing assistance, where appropriate.

Level II: Intermediate-Range Efforts to Halt the Transformation from Poverty to Homelessness

Four basic types of recommendations are made to address the need for housing among the rural poor.

Recommendation #6. Address the maldistribution of rural low-cost housing. More specifically:

Recommendation #6a. Expand investment in public housing in rural communities, but only in small-scale, scattered-site housing projects suitable for families and appropriate to the social patterns and needs of rural communities.

Recommendation #6b. Expand loans and tax-abatement incentives for creating good quality private-sector rental housing for low and moderate-income rural residents.

Recommendation #6c. Allocate housing rehabilitation grants and loans on a community-by-community basis, not on the basis of aggregate county-level statistics, so that the smaller, poorer communities, with the greatest housing needs, can qualify even if located within relatively affluent counties.

Recommendation #7. Stem the loss of home ownership among low-income rural families in order to stabilize them residentially and socially, and to reduce their enforced mobility. More specifically:

Recommendation #7a. Challenge excessively negative and discriminatory local land-use regulations that may prevent home ownership among low-income people, including large-lot zoning and exclusionary restrictions on mobile homes.

Recommendation #7b. Arrange financing packages to enable modest-income families to purchase houses in economically depressed communities where population exodus has left a glut of inexpensive housing.

Recommendation #7c. Reexamine anti-homeownership policies of the welfare system, such as the standard practice of placing a lien on a home owned by a public assistance client, a practice that discourages home improvement and may push a family from ownership to tenancy.

Recommendation #7d. Protect vulnerable local residents from the market-driven effects of second-home development, i.e., bidding up land and housing costs in rural resort and vacation areas.

Recommendation #7e. Redesign homeowner loan and grant programs to meet more effectively the particular income and cash-flow limitations of poor people.

Recommendation #8. Increase the security of tenancy to reduce the frequency of eviction from rental housing. More specifically:

Recommendation #8a. Anticipate, monitor, and minimize the negative impact of rural economic development—such as a new factory or state prison, tourism, or recreation or retirement housing—in reducing the stock of inexpensive rental housing.

Recommendation #8b. Protect mobile-home park tenants from sudden displacement if the park owner decides to convert his or her land to more profitable uses.[5]

Recommendation #8c. Improve quality of apartments and mobile homes rented to tenants receiving welfare support or rent subsidy, by ensuring that local governments have adequate funds, authority, and political independence to make inspections and force improvements.

Recommendation #8d. Protect low-income tenants who might lose their rented homes as a result of either condemnation of unfit buildings or of major rent increases instituted by landlords to offset the cost of bringing their units up to code.

Recommendation #8e. Increase governmental rent subsidies, such as the HUD Section 8 subsidy program, allocated to rural areas and ensure that welfare rent allowances are realistic for the market.

Recommendation #8f. Modify certain welfare requirements, such as bedroom stipulations, that, if enforced, make it harder for low-income people to find and keep housing.

Recommendation #9. Encourage, rather than outlaw, informal family-based housing strategies that in the past have enabled people to cope with their housing needs on minimal incomes and have allowed them to remain more independent of public assistance. More specifically:

Recommendation #9a. Modify state building codes and land-use regulations that restrict cost-reduction housing strategies.

Recommendation #9b. Challenge excessive or inappropriate local housing and land-use regulations that inhibit people's ability to provide temporary housing for themselves and extra family members.

Level III: Long-Range Attack on Underlying Problems of Rural Poverty

Ultimately, reducing and preventing rural homelessness requires reduction and prevention of the poverty that renders some rural people homeless. Therefore, long-range recommendations include the following:

Recommendation #10. Implement a diversified, rural community development program that will improve employment opportunities. Specific recommendations for curing rural poverty are beyond the scope of this paper. However, research in rural New York confirms that a multifaceted community development approach is needed to improve rural employment opportunities through diversified economic development and other programs that rebuild communities and strengthen rural families—both two-parent and single-parent families. Because it attacks the underlying poverty, a concerted effort to improve local employment and strengthen community institutions would do more to eliminate homelessness in the rural area than would the construction of public housing. Similarly, strengthening the rural community as a social surround, and linking low-income families more securely within it, could be an essential, and uniquely rural, strategy to reduce poverty and combat homelessness.

Recommendation #11. Toward accomplishing these goals, more applied and multidisciplinary social science research is needed. Comparative studies in different rural areas could elucidate specific regional and local causes, patterns, and variations, and could enable more effective response. More research is needed especially on the informal strategies and social resources poor people employ to keep themselves housed, so that these strategies could be fostered and replicated rather than overlooked or outlawed. Finally, research is needed on connections and comparisons between homelessness in rural and urban places, with the aim of developing more effective programs to prevent and combat homelessness, both urban and rural.

CONCLUSION

In light of the generally weak economy of most of rural America, poverty will probably continue to grow, and with it the potential for rural homelessness. The cost of modest rural housing appears to rise, even as the incomes of poor rural residents fall. Meanwhile, the number of low-income rural residents grows. To dismiss rural homelessness as a less pressing problem than urban homelessness simply because it is less visible, less concentrated, and involves fewer people would be a grave mistake. On the other hand, to address rural homelessness with programs designed for urban areas would be a serious misuse of resources. Because rural homelessness differs from urban homelessness, and because the rural economic, social, and cultural context in which it occurs also differs, different approaches are needed.

NOTES

Research for this article was supported by the Ford Foundation through the Rural Economic Policy Program of the Aspen Institute. Portions of this chapter have appeared in earlier publications (Fitchen 1991b, 1992).

1. In the rural United States, the number of low-rent housing units diminished from 1979 to 1985 relative to the growing number of low-income renters, transforming a surplus of low-rent housing to a shortfall of 500,000 units by 1985 (Lazere, Leonard, and Kravitz 1989:11).

2. While rural rents are still lower than urban rents in most places across the country, rural incomes compared to urban incomes are even lower (Lazere, Leonard, and Kravitz 1989:20), leaving a rent burden at least as high in rural areas as in urban.

3. In 1985, only 55 percent of poor rural households owned their homes, which is well above the level of home ownership among poor metropolitan households (32 percent), but

low for rural Americans in general.

4. New York and some other states have allowed localities to set up homelessness-prevention programs, some of which have already proven the effectiveness of case management, counseling, and legal services in preventing high-risk people from being evicted. However, not all localities have developed such programs, and funding to assist people not actually homeless, which was seriously inadequate to begin with, has already been reduced or discontinued.

5. New York and a few other states have initiated special loan funds that give tenants an opportunity to purchase threatened trailer parks and operate them as cooperatives.

2

The 1990 Decennial Census and Patterns of Homelessness in a Small New England City

Irene Glasser

To protect themselves and ensure a certain amount of privacy and freedom of action, homeless single adults and families with children observe rules different from those of mainstream society. The creativity of homeless individuals in Glasser's small New England city is apparent, especially in their manipulations of surprisingly wide-ranging social networks. Glasser recommends increases in rent supplements and transitional housing, enforcement of antidiscrimination laws, and improvement in methods for enumerating different types of homeless and precariously housed individuals and families. (Pseudonyms are used for all proper names in her study.)

INTRODUCTION

I first noticed Brian in October walking down the highway coming into town each morning, carrying plastic bags. I approached him in the soup kitchen by asking him if he had a place to stay. He is a good-looking man who appears to be about forty, but later I learned he is really sixty years old. He seemed to have shaved. In a later conversation, I found out that he had been using the Legal Services bathroom to wash up, but they had told him not to. He was pacing and angry as he said, "I am organizing for the 4-H club—it is very important for youth to know about 4-H—to know about sheep." I said something about the shelter. He asked me, "Can you guarantee that it will be clean for the next ten years? For the next ten days?"

Two days later, Brian approached me in the soup kitchen. He said that he wanted a gift of a room a few blocks from the soup kitchen. He said again that he wanted a shower. I asked him if he got a check somewhere. He asked loudly if I was an Americanist or a Nationalist. I said I was born in the USA. He yelled that he didn't need money, just a room.

After this encounter, Brian was not around town for several months. In February I again saw him in the soup kitchen. He shook my hand and seemed to remember me.

He said that he was living like a king in his hotel room, that he no longer had to sleep in the woods. Brian told me that he had been taken by ambulance to the state psychiatric because he did not have a raincoat, but that now he had one. He pointed it out to me in his plastic bags, which he still carried with him. He told me that a social worker at the hospital helped him out and suggested he buy good shoes.

After the February conversation, Brian appeared to become more and more angry, eventually leaving his hotel room and returning to the woods. [Glasser 1991:16]

THE STUDY

Brian was one of 336 people, representing 156 households, who were followed by an ethnographic research project sponsored by the U.S. Bureau of the Census. The project was conducted during 1989 and 1990 in Centerville, a small New England city. The purpose of the research was to gather information that would result in refining methods for enumeration of the homeless for subsequent decennial censuses. We were to answer the questions: (1) Who are the homeless of a small city? (2) How might they be located? (3) Under what circumstances might they respond to the census? In addition to aiding the census effort, the study provided an opportunity to follow closely and describe a group of homeless people in their constantly shifting circumstances.

The Setting

At first glance, Centerville, with a population of 22,039 (U.S. Census 1990), is an idyllic small New England city nestled in the rolling hills of a countryside of homes and farms. However, on closer inspection, one sees a main street that has been devastated and nearly abandoned by new malls and by the closing of the local factories that had sustained the town. One could see an old hotel in the middle of town, now serving as a single-room-occupancy (SRO) hotel for single men (and some women), who spend much of their day standing outside on the street.

Centerville is poor by the state's standards: its median income for 1989 was $29,135, which was 70 percent of the state median income of $41,721. Although Centerville is only the forty-second-largest town in the state, in 1987 its average monthly General Assistance (GA) case load (for the state-funded welfare program for adults) was the seventh-largest for the state of Connecticut (1988).

Centerville is an ethnically diverse community that includes French Canadians, Eastern Europeans, Italians, Irish, and Hispanics. The latter make up 15 percent of the city's population according to the 1990 Census. Centerville has had a Puerto Rican population since the 1950s, when they were recruited from Puerto Rico by the now defunct textile mill (Boujouen and Newton 1984). Many Puerto Ricans have told me that they come to Centerville for the *tranquilidad* [tranquility] that they do not find in the larger northeastern cities from which they tend to migrate (Glasser 1988b). In addition to the Puerto Rican population there is also a growing community of Mexicans, who are attracted by the work offered by a local mushroom factory and a nursery, known as *los hongos* and *los palitos*, respectively.

The poor of Centerville are concentrated in the eight housing projects, the downtown area, and apartments in older frame buildings near the center of the city. There is also an eighty-five-room, single-room-occupancy hotel (SRO) and several smaller SRO buildings, which are usually without immediate toilet or cooking facilities. There is a sixty-bed shelter located thirty miles from Centerville and a thirty-bed shelter in town run by an order of nuns.

METHODOLOGY

Operationalizing Homelessness

The methodology for the study was to interview all the homeless within Centerville during a one-year period (1989) and to follow closely as many of the people as possible in order to describe their changing circumstances. The definition of homelessness used in the research included both the "literally homeless"—that is, "persons who clearly do not have access to a conventional dwelling and who would be homeless by any conceivable definition of the term" (Rossi et al. 1987:1136)—and the "precariously or marginally housed," who are "persons with tenuous or very temporary claims to a conventional dwelling of more or less marginal adequacy" (Rossi et al. 1987:1136).

In Centerville, the literally homeless are people who sleep on the street, in cars, hallways, the woods, or the homeless shelters. The precariously housed live in the welfare hotel or in the smaller SROs, or are doubled-up with other families. The precariously housed were included because they are likely to fall into episodic homelessness over a period of time (Glasser 1988b; Stefl 1987). In this study, the literally homeless and the precariously housed were often the same people at different times. For example, a person we met who was sleeping in the woods might get a room at the SRO, move on to a shelter, or stay with a friend; when that arrangement disintegrated, the person would move back into the woods. For the purpose of the study, a person's "place of sleeping" when first encountered was used in the quantitative analyses.

If an individual lived in the hotel, then his or her own self-definition determined whether the person was "homeless." For some residents, the hotel was their permanent housing. For others, it was termed "just a roof," "last resort housing," the step before sleeping outside. In the Census Bureau's homeless count, which took place on March 20, 1990, the hotel was canvassed because it was largely a residence for transients. The doubled-up families were precariously housed, since they typically lived with family or friends whose housing was marginal to begin with, or who were under threat of eviction if it became public knowledge that they were housing people outside of their household.

Research Team, Interview Tool, and Field Notes

The research team included ten people, male and female, four of them bilingual in English and Spanish, and two medically trained. I directed the team as an anthropologist. We met weekly in order to keep abreast of housing information and to compare notes on the people we had already interviewed. Once a team member had interviewed a person, that member maintained contact with the person.

The basic research tool was an interview schedule with which we tried to assess quickly the nature of the respondent's homelessness. Since we knew that some people would become irritated and leave the interview situation, we tried to establish essential information first, such as the state of their homelessness, and leave the more detailed questions for later. The interview provided a rapid assessment of our very first contact with the person. The answers to the interview questions were coded and entered into Statistical Analysis System (SAS) files for quantitative analysis.

Field notes became the way we followed the person's situation, and they were taken on almost all of the contacts. The research team members were urged to write their notes using the words spoken by the homeless people, and to note everything in the setting. In this way the world-view of the person could be uncovered (i.e., the "emic" view). There were eventually over one thousand pages of typed field notes. There were several instances when field notes were taken by more than one researcher on the same incident, illustrating the "Rashomon effect" (Heider 1988).

Research Approach

In the first months of the study, we let the health and social service community know of the study's existence, made frequent announcements in the soup kitchen about the study, and were present on all welfare check days.

The doubled-up families were probably least well represented in the study. Doubling-up was pervasive in Centerville among the poor, and there was no central place to encounter such families. We were aided in finding the doubled-up families by the fact that during the study period there were numerous efforts to evict people without a lease from public and U.S. Department of Housing and Urban Development (HUD) subsidized housing. People—often the host, rather than the guest, family—called the study staff to tell us about their situation.

We also quickly became experts in housing and filled a void in services for help with housing. Most of the social service agencies were very reluctant to help their clients with housing. This was in part because affordable housing was so scarce that their efforts were rarely rewarded. There was no agency that specialized in housing. Any agency that did help a client did so only as long as the client was willing to cooperate with them (for example, as long as a substance abuser was abstinent). Another factor that made housing help difficult was that the state and local programs to help the homeless were so fragmented, and the rules and administrative policies changed so frequently, that it was difficult to remain accurately informed.

As a final strategy for the study, the research team reentered the homeless community for several weeks before the March 20, 1990, Homeless Count (known as S-Night, the "S" standing for street and shelter), in order to observe the Census Bureau's efforts independently and to count the homeless in Centerville ourselves, to compare the Bureau's counts with our knowledge of who and where the homeless were.

FINDINGS

Types of Homelessness

The heads of 156 households were interviewed from October 1, 1988, through September 30, 1989. The households included 336 people, 145 of whom (43 percent) were children. The households were almost evenly divided between Anglos and Hispanics, and eighty-eight households consisted of people living in families. The age distribution of the heads of the households ranged from sixteen through eighty-four years, with a median age of twenty-seven. Almost half (43 percent) had one or more children under eighteen years old in the household, and 40 percent or more had children under fifteen years old in the household.

The major types of homelessness and the corresponding numbers of households were as follows: living on the street (nineteen, or 12 percent of households); living in the hotel or other SROs (thirty-nine, or 25 percent); living in a shelter (thirty-four, or 22 percent); doubled-up (sixty, or 38 percent); and evicted (four, or 3 percent). In the majority of cases, spouses were not present. The majority lived on some form of public assistance, including GA, Aid to Families with Dependent Children (AFDC), and Supplemental Security Income (SSI).

The primary locations for finding and interviewing the household heads in the study were the soup kitchen, the welfare office on check days, the shelters, and homes. In addition, six household heads were first interviewed in my office, in social service agency offices, or on the street. Each location had the advantage of allowing people to be met in a different stage of homelessness.

The soup kitchen was an ideal place in which to meet homeless people and to maintain contact with them. There are substantial numbers of social networks that form among the guests in the dining room. (See Glasser 1988b, for a full discussion of social networking in a soup kitchen.) The soup kitchen does not involve all of the poor of Centerville, but many of the people who are homeless or have marginal housing spend their mornings in the dining room and depend on the hot noontime meal as their main meal of the day. The soup kitchen was the point of first contact with most of the literally homeless in the study, with half of the residents of the single-room-occupancy hotel, and with one-fifth of the doubled-up.

The research team visited the soup kitchen for two to four days a week during the entire year. I would usually make an announcement inviting people who were homeless to come up to talk to me or a research assistant. The announcement would be made as lunch was about to be served at 12:30 P.M. The director would introduce me. The announcement was:

I am interested in talking to anyone who does not have housing. I am doing a study for the Bureau of the Census, and I have some housing information I would be glad to share with you.

And, in Spanish:

Estoy interesada en hablar a todo el mundo que no tiene viviendas. Yo hago un estudio por la «census» y yo tengo información sobre viviendas que yo puedo compatir contigo.

The use of the term "does not have housing" (*los que no tienen viviendas*) appeared to be less stigmatizing than "is homeless." On the first and sixteenth of each month, the GA checks were given out. (GA is the temporary welfare program for adults who are waiting for a state or federal welfare program or who are ineligible for any other kind of assistance.) The checks were ready to be distributed at 10 A.M., and by 9:30 A.M. there was usually a line of people waiting. Most of the check distribution was finished by noon. The routine for GA was for case workers to get clients with no housing who agreed to talk with us to sign permission slips. However, there were so many clients with no housing that the case workers quickly lost track, and the referrals were made to us on the spot.

"Check Day" was a good time to meet people coming into town, although it was necessary to follow people for several months to know if their lack of housing was a temporary situation or a long-term one. In the year of the study there appeared to be such a dearth of affordable housing that most people in the study went for months without housing. On Check Days we met forty-nine (31 percent) of the heads of households in the study, as well as members of almost half (twenty-nine) of the doubled-up households, almost one-third of the shelter households, and almost one-quarter of the hotel households.

Interviews in two of the shelters serving Centerville were the point of first contact for twelve households in the study. The shelters were an important place of first contact, because a number of the residents of the shelters neither received GA nor attended the soup kitchen.

Members of thirteen households in the study were interviewed by making home visits. Several families were found when the manager of the hotel told us about them; they were families whom he was eager to have leave. Some of the home visits were made to people referred by social workers, and several were to people who found the study on their own and left messages on my answering machine.

Patterns of Homelessness

One of the outstanding characteristics of the homeless population of Centerville, as documented by this study, is the pattern of change in terms of where the individual or family was sleeping. Whatever the category of homelessness of the person when first contacted and interviewed by the research team, the person's situation changed, sometimes several times, during the study period.

Another finding that emerges from the study is that the characteristics of the people are related to the types of homelessness. For example, the literally homeless, those who sleep outside, were the most disaffected and the least receptive to contact. The relationships we developed with the people who were literally homeless were nurtured only over several months. Even with such time invested, most of them did not want to tell us where they were sleeping. On the other hand, the doubled-up homeless, as a group, were eager to change their situation and would speak with us in hopes of receiving help with housing. Their homelessness was related to the dearth of low-income rentals available in the area. The lack of supply increased competition for the available housing, a problem that was compounded by the fact that the people in the study had various characteristics that made them undesirable to landlords (for example, ethnicity, poverty, lack of landlord references). The sheltered homeless were also easy to reach and in many ways resembled the doubled-up group. The residents of the hotel were accessible to the study staff, since we only interviewed those who had defined themselves as "homeless" and therefore wanted to speak with us.

Literal Homelessness

Members of the nineteen Centerville households who said that they were sleeping "nowhere"—including one elderly couple—were first contacted most often in the soup kitchen. It was clear that the homeless who slept in a car did not want us to know where the car was parked when they were asleep in it. The literally homeless had lost their housing (often a room in the hotel), and they had either been unsuccessful in finding new housing or had given up the search.

In analyzing field notes for the literally homeless, it appears that they were people who had severe drug or alcohol problems, or obvious mental illness. They were very independent and protective of their privacy. During the winter months of December, January, and February, the literally homeless were in cars and hallways; in the fall, spring, and summer months, they slept in the woods and parks. Since the study ended we have been made aware of the death of the only female among the literally homeless. She was the companion of Joe, and they both appeared to be intoxicated much of the day. The literally homeless constituted the group that most closely resembled the well-publicized homeless living on the streets of large metropolitan areas (see, for example, Baxter and Hopper 1981).

Representative of the literally homeless was Sam.

Literally Homeless: The Case of Sam

Sam was a black man in his fifties who was homeless for much of the study period. We came to know Sam and the extent of his problems when we became intermediaries in his quest for housing. Sam was a user of heroin, cocaine, and alcohol. He had chronic liver and other intestinal problems. He had been through much of the housing in Centerville and was *persona non grata* at the hotel. We had contact with Sam from December through August, and we have forty-five separate days of field notes about him. During most of this time he slept at various friends' houses, in the lobby of the hotel, and, briefly, at a shelter. He was hospitalized several times during the study period.

In December, Sam approached me in the lunch line of the soup kitchen after I made the announcement about the study. He said he could not live at Main Avenue (public housing owned by the city) any more. I gave Sam our housing materials. One week later, in the soup kitchen, Sam told me that he had slept on a chair in the lobby of the hotel but that he could not really sleep, because he was worried about people thinking he was drunk and was afraid of being robbed. He said that he had had a disagreement with L. (an owner of an SRO), who had received a check for a security deposit but had spent the money and put Sam's belongings on the sidewalk. Today Sam seemed quite stoned.

In order to apply for several housing projects, Sam needed a birth certificate. During the month of February, when Sam was still on the streets, we corresponded with a county in a southern state which had it. This took several letters, phone calls, and $10 because there was a discrepancy about the names on the certificate.

In early March, Sam moved into the shelter for one week. He slept there several nights, but on other nights he was gone. Although he got along well with the nuns, they said they needed his room if he was not going to use it all the time. He left and went back to the streets. In early July, Sam was able to move into a newly renovated room. The landlord had accepted a security deposit paid by a community agency. Although he was doubtful about Sam, he agreed to give him a chance. Sam still has this housing.

My last contact with Sam was in August, when I greeted him on the street on a Saturday; he crossed the street to shake my hand. He had a bottle of soda with him. At first he looked well, although rather drawn in the face, but then as we started to talk he slipped down a pole he was leaning on. He was nodding out; his eyes kept shutting except when I asked him a question, and then he would rouse himself out of sleep. I asked him how his health was, and he said that he was concerned, because twice he had found himself passed out on the sidewalk. He said that he had not been drinking or using a lot of drugs that day. He had called the doctor but was vague about what she had said. I suggested he go to the health clinic (Glasser 1991:25–27).

Single-Room Occupancy

Members of thirty-nine of the households in the study lived at the SRO hotel or one of the smaller SROs in Centerville. The hotel had a reputation as the place where drug addicts, alcoholics, and prostitutes lived. It was common to hear people say, "I am trying to stay sober [or straight], so I know I don't want to go to the hotel." The director of the methadone maintenance program said that she believed that "coke [cocaine] comes out of the faucets of the hotel." I noticed that when people are asked their address, they often say "____ Main," the street address, instead of "the hotel." The smaller SROs are sometimes referred to as "little hotels," a reference to the drug and alcohol use of the residents.

The hotel accepted almost anyone except people who had consistently failed to pay their rent. The minimum rent was $220 a month, which was the amount GA allowed. People paid the rent out of their income from a job or an assistance program (most often GA, AFDC, or SSI). People paid for one week at a time, although there were people who stayed for only one or two days.

It was easiest for the study staff to become involved with women with children living at the hotel. These people considered the hotel unsafe and too difficult a place to rear children, because of the large number of drug addicts and alcoholics living there and because of the lack of cooking and bathing facilities. A major factor for the women was also the threat of losing their children to foster care if the Department of Children and Youth Services/Protective Services knew of their situation and did not think that they were making efforts to leave. In reality, finding housing outside the hotel was difficult, in part because there was a stigma attached to having lived there. Most landlords did not accept a reference from the hotel manager, because they did not consider him a landlord.

SRO Residents: The Cases of Hilda and Sue

Hilda was a Puerto Rican woman of twenty-two, whom we came to know between March through September. She appeared to be representative of people who have spent all their lives living with someone else or in hotels or shelters.

The first day I met Hilda was March 14, 1989, at the soup kitchen. I had just made the announcement about being available to take people to public housing the next day (one of the only two days of the month that applications were accepted) when Hilda's boyfriend, Eduardo, approached me and said that Hilda needed a ride. Eduardo was at first glance a healthy-looking young man. I later learned that he was addicted to heroin. It was characteristic of our later contacts that he approached us first, rather than Hilda herself coming forward. She spoke a combination of English and Spanish; his English was more secure. I felt throughout my contacts with Hilda that although she asked us for rides to various places, she would have been glad not to talk to anyone outside of her social network. She was reluctant to go to the prenatal clinic or to apply for housing outside the hotel.

Despite her reluctance, over the next several months we gave her, at her request, rides to apply for housing and accompanied her on several visits to the hospital. Hilda "fell through the cracks" of most of the health and social service agencies, except for those like protective services, since she spent most of her time in her room at the hotel and most of the agencies were not looking for people to serve. We got to know Hilda as well as we did because we offered to help her with some of the things she wanted to accomplish or felt pressured to accomplish.

On March 15, I spent most of the day with Hilda. We met at the soup kitchen at 9:45 A.M. We then picked up three of Hilda's friends and went to the prenatal clinic, where Hilda made an appointment for herself. She had not been there in several months. After lunch at the soup kitchen, we drove Hilda and several more friends to the housing office to fill out applications. One problem was that while Ellen, a worker there, gave Hilda one point for substandard housing (i.e., the hotel), at the next desk another worker advised a new worker that Hilda could not get a point for substandard housing for the hotel, adding "She knew what it was like when she moved in!" [Glasser 1991:30–31]

In the months that followed, Hilda continued to stay in her room most of the day. In July we went to a HUD-subsidized project for an interview:

Alice, the manager's assistant, was not in a good mood. Hilda had no landlord reference except for the hotel, because the apartments had never been in her name. When Alice explained that the project would make a home visit to assess how she would be as a tenant, Hilda asked if she would know when it was to be. Alice said yes. Then Hilda asked if she, Alice, would be the one to do it. Alice said, "Oh no, I wouldn't go into the hotel!" After the interview, Hilda told me she had to get out of the hotel before the baby came, because the state had threatened to take a baby from her friend, who left for Puerto Rico before that could happen. Hilda seemed angry that she hadn't been able to get out of the hotel. Ricardo, a former shelter resident, came into the office, and I introduced him to Hilda. She asked him what the shelter was like, and he said, "Es bueno si comporte bien" (It's good if you behave yourself). Hilda made it clear that she did not want the shelter. [Glasser 1991:31–32]

In August, Hilda had her baby. Both she and the baby tested positive for cocaine, and her baby was removed from her custody. She moved into the shelter with her two remaining children. However, after about a month she was asked to leave because she was spending most of her time at the hotel with her boyfriend. The state eventually took her two remaining children from her.

Another woman staying at the hotel was Sue, whose situation we also followed for six months.

Sue was a woman in her thirties of Cherokee descent, who found herself and her son in the hotel after being dropped off by the traveling carnival she worked for, as it was finishing up its season. Sue presented a picture of a rather slow person, who appeared to get large amounts of money and then give it away. We were able to get to know Sue in part because she needed help in negotiating the welfare bureaucracy. Throughout the time of the study she dreamed of "going home to Oklahoma," where she was sure she would be accepted, although she had never been there. She later called one of the members of the team several times from Oklahoma, where in fact she appeared to be able to find housing much more easily than she had in this state. We saw Sue from November through March and received telephone calls from her from Oklahoma in April. [Glasser 1991:34–35]

Doubled-Up

The largest group of people in the study were doubled-up with other families. Their situations were precarious in that the host families often asked them to leave. In several cases the host family itself left the apartment. We tended to meet people whose doubled-up situations were soon to fall apart. Several of the calls we got to interview people came from the host family, anxious to have the guest family out.

When the heads of households of the doubled-up homeless were compared to those in the other categories, doubled-up homelessness was statistically correlated with being female, twenty-eight years old or younger, and Hispanic.

Maria was a Puerto Rican woman in her fifties who had raised fourteen children before she moved to Centerville with her three youngest and doubled-up with another family.

Maria and her three children moved to Centerville in the fall of 1988 and found affordable housing difficult to obtain. The research team had contact with Maria from November 1, 1988, through October 1989. Maria was a fifty-year-old Puerto Rican woman who had raised fourteen children and appeared to be an excellent mother. An adult daughter lived in one of the housing projects but felt that she could not risk her own housing by taking in her mother and three children. Maria ended up at the shelter in Centerville for one month, because the person she was living with had to move. During that time, she accompanied the shelter nuns to a Grange meeting in order to speak about the shortage of affordable housing, although she spoke very little English. [Glasser 1991:34–35]

Maria was one of the people in the study who would probably not have had a problem with homelessness had there been more affordable housing. However, she was homeless from November through the end of March. Landlords kept asking her for references that she did not have. It appeared that she had stayed with friends and relatives, in Puerto Rico and on the mainland, most of her life. One landlord wanted her credit references; she laughed and said that she was on welfare and did not have credit. Maria finally found a small apartment and was able to move out of the shelter at the end of March. I visited Maria in October 1989, in her cramped two-bedroom apartment, and found that in addition to her own three children, she had one of her adult daughters from Rhode Island and the daughter's two children staying with her for a while.

Centerville Shelters

Representatives of thirty-four households were interviewed who, at the time of their interviews, were living in one of the three shelters. We interviewed four of these households in a battered women's shelter—people who had nowhere to go, although they were ready to leave the shelter. We interviewed seven more households at the shelter in a nearby town, whose assistance was being paid for by Centerville, and the other twenty-three households at the shelter in Centerville. The

shelter in Centerville appeared especially compatible with the Hispanic female-
headed households, who constituted the majority of the residents of the shelter.
The women referred to the nuns as *las monjitas* (dear sisters) and generally had
more patience with the rules of the shelter than did the non-Hispanic residents.

Observations of the 1990 Homeless Census Count

As a final strategy for the study, the research team reassembled for the March
20, 1990, Census Bureau Homeless Count (S-Night). Our goal was to count the
homeless independently and then compare our findings with those of the Census
Bureau. The comparison was done for people living outside, for shelter residents,
and the residents of the hotel. We found that when the census takers visited the
shelters and hotel in person, they received a high degree of cooperation from the
management and tenants, and that the two counts were comparable. However, the
census enumerators found no one on the street. It appeared that without prior
relationships with the homeless living outside, there was very little likelihood of
finding them. Since the doubled-up population was not to be covered by the S-
Night count but by the regular April 1 census, it is difficult to know how many
doubled-up people were actually counted.

SUMMARY AND RECOMMENDATIONS

Two levels of recommendations emerge from this study: recommendations at the
federal level for improved methods of census enumeration for the homeless, and
recommendations at the federal and local levels for improved strategies for moving
people from homelessness to permanent housing.

Recommendations for Improved Methods of Census Enumeration

Recommendation #1. Improve the street-count methodology. Nationwide, it
appears that the homeless shelter count was reasonably accurate, due to a generally high degree of cooperation among shelter residents and managers. However,
the street count fell short of most estimates. (See Wright 1992 for an excellent
collection of articles evaluating the 1990 homeless count.) In Centerville, none of
the homeless sleeping outside were counted.

The 1991 census in India contrasted with the U.S. census count of the homeless.
The U.S. relies on sending out enumerators with no prior relationship with the
persons being counted, in the dead of night. In contrast, India required that enumerators spend three weeks learning all the places the homeless ("houseless," in
India) sleep within that enumerator's designated area of housed and non-housed
residents. As in the United States, the homeless were counted at night, when they
had bedded down on the pavement. The key difference was in the amount of
preparation and knowledge of the homeless that the enumerator had. (See Glasser

1994 for a discussion of counting the homeless cross-nationally.)

A further recommendation for the street enumeration is for a daytime count in public places, such as the soup kitchen. This would allow the homeless to preserve the privacy of their well-guarded sleeping spots. This strategy would have to be coupled with safeguards against an overcount, since many people who attend soup kitchens are, in fact, housed and will be counted in the regular enumeration effort.

Recommendation #2. Increase the categories of persons enumerated face to face. Since the hotel count in Centerville was accomplished by going door to door and appeared to be accurate, perhaps the smaller SROs should be counted in this way as well.

Recommendation #3. Improve the enumeration of doubled-up families. In 1990 the doubled-up homeless were expected to be counted as a part of the regular enumeration on April 1, on forms that households received by mail. Although it is not possible to know exactly how many of the doubled-up families were not counted, we suspect that many of these households were lost because the host families did not want to count them as "members of the household." (Each doubled-up family in which we were involved emphasized the temporary nature of the arrangement, even when the arrangement went on for months.)

In the years before the next census, pretests should be conducted of various wordings for the first question on the household census form, which now says: "List on the numbered lines below the name of each person living here on Sunday, April 1." Homeless doubled-up families are now supposed to be included in the category "Persons with no other home who are staying here on April 1." Technically, this includes the doubled-up family with the household; however, this may not be the householder's view of reality. Perhaps a separate question on the first page would allow the householder who answers the form to put the doubled-up person or family in a separate category, not to be confused with the rest of the family. Such questions might include the following: "Do you have anyone staying with you temporarily?", or, "Do you have anyone doubling-up with you?" Pretesting could be conducted in neighborhoods that previous research, such as this study, indicated had many doubled-up households. Improved promotional efforts within the poor communities where doubling-up is prevalent might increase the participation of these families. Promotional efforts by community organizations could urge people to answer the census in general, emphasize its confidentiality, and focus specifically on including the doubled-up guests of the householder.

Recommendation #4. Understand the limits of the sheltered homeless count. Enumerating people in shelters is one of the major methods of counting the homeless in the United States. This study's experience in the shelters shows that each shelter has its own official and unofficial screening devices. In other words, in counting the residents of a shelter, one is enumerating the "sheltered homeless" and not "the homeless." For example, we knew of situations at both shelters in Centerville in which residents were told to leave, at times with a police escort.

Recommendations for Improved Strategies to House the Homeless

The households included in the study were composed of people who were the most vulnerable in the very tight market of affordable housing. Most of the households were surviving on some form of public assistance, which, in relation to the current costs in the area, made renting an apartment extremely difficult. For example, a single mother and child, such as Sue and her son, would get a check for $450 a month. Most private landlords and all of the public and HUD-subsidized housing representatives insisted that they get a two-bedroom apartment—and most two-bedroom apartments rent for at least $450.

In order to increase the likelihood that homeless persons can afford housing and remain in it, the following recommendations are made.

Recommendation #5. Increase rent supplements. During the period of the study, some of the families and the elderly got relief from paying the full market rent, through public housing, Section 8, and a $50 monthly rent supplement from AFDC. However, both public housing and Section 8 required two-year waiting lists, and the AFDC supplement had very specific criteria that embraced few of the homeless families we encountered. The financial and psychological costs of maintaining a person or family in a shelter rather than providing them with a rent subsidy, appear obvious.

Recommendation #6. Increase the amount of transitional housing. There are several programs for transitional housing, which enable families who would ordinarily be denied entrance to live in decent apartments for up to two years in return for an agreement to work with a housing counselor. Often these programs work with mothers to make them economically self-sufficient, so that they can separate themselves from men in their lives who may be jeopardizing their housing (for example, living with a drug dealer). These programs also direct people to drug and alcohol rehabilitation if necessary.

Recommendation #7. Enforce antidiscrimination laws. The Hispanic population in Centerville was quietly impeded from obtaining housing because of the discrimination practiced by some landlords. For example, in one call I made for Ricardo, the landlord told me, after I told her his full name in the middle of the conversation, that the apartment had been rented, when at the beginning of the conversation it had been vacant.

Recommendation #8. Increase the number of "sweat-equity" programs. Throughout North America there are projects that involve homeless and doubled-up people in the physical renovation of deteriorated housing. In Centerville, a successful land trust project provided housing for several poor families who participated in the rehabilitation of traditional mill housing. Unfortunately, the pace of acquiring such properties is very slow, and they are not an immediate solution for a homeless person or individual. On the other hand, the housing is excellent, and the sense of community that emerges from the work is admirable.

CONCLUSION

The study was successful in locating many of the homeless people in the small city of Centerville, by entering into the social networks of the homeless themselves and of the service providers, and by becoming visible at the soup kitchen and on Check Day at the GA office. The process of entering social networks was helped by the effective communication within the substantial Hispanic population of Centerville. Most of the people contacted by the research team were willing to talk, in part because of the offer to exchange valuable housing information in the highly competitive affordable housing market.

Since the time of the study, there has been a recognition by social service providers of the seriousness of the lack of affordable housing for the poor in Centerville. The Centerville Homeless Coalition has met to advocate increased affordable housing in Centerville. A new program, the Centerville Housing Intervention Fund, has been created as a revolving loan fund to help with security deposits and back rent, as well as to mediate tenant-landlord disputes. There is also now a program of transitional housing, the Centerville Family Housing Program, which has agreements with public and private landlords to take in "high risk" tenants in exchange for a promise to work with the clients on their responsibilities as a tenant.

Homelessness is perhaps the most visible manifestation of poverty. Whereas people may find various ways to increase their supply of food, paying rent depends on a reliable supply of cash. Lack of a stable home means that every area of a person's life, health, education, and employment, is in disarray. The study in Centerville was able to document these effects on a cross-section of one city's homeless population.

NOTE

This research was conducted under a Joint Statistical Agreement 88-22 sponsored by the Center for Survey Methods Research, Bureau of the Census, Washington Plaza, Room 433, Washington, DC 20233. The author thanks Dr. Matt T. Salo for his assistance in this research. The findings, recommendations, and conclusions are those of the author and are not endorsed by the government.

3

Doubling-Up: A Strategy of Urban Reciprocity to Avoid Homelessness in Detroit

M. Rory Bolger

Bolger explores the housing consequences of the decline in Detroit's auto industry. His analysis reveals a reliance on the extended family and the reciprocal exchanges within it, especially on a neighborhood level. Bolger's homeless gain resources from families and friends, from the underground economy, and from begging, borrowing, and stealing. Bolger recommends increasing federal subsidies for jobs and job training, and the construction of more subsidized, low-income housing.

INTRODUCTION

Today there are more poor people in Detroit than in the 1970s. The median household income fell from $18,333 in 1974 to $13,455 in 1985, and the median rent rose from $333 in 1974 to $365 in 1985, as adjusted for inflation.[1] The total number of housing units declined dramatically (Lynch and Leonard 1991:17), and there were fewer affordable housing units. Figure 3.1 shows the loss of housing between 1940 and 1990 in the working-class community known as Jefferson-Chalmers, in which my research was carried out. My substantive focus is homelessness viewed within the context of Detroit's experience of the urban crisis from the 1970s into the 1990s. Homelessness is now conspicuous in a city formerly known for high blue-collar wages, individual home ownership, and widespread housing availability. What happened in Detroit, and why? How do those at risk of homelessness respond to these changes?

Lynch and Leonard conclude that "although the affordable housing crisis is national in scope, it is particularly severe in the Detroit Metropolitan area" (1991:xii). While 62 percent of poor renters nationwide spent at least half their income on housing in 1985, 80 percent of the poor Detroit renters did. Whereas 46 percent of poor homeowners nationwide spent at least half their income on housing that year, 72 percent of the poor Detroit homeowners did (Lynch and Leonard 1991:17).

Figure 3.1
Housing Units in Jefferson Chalmers (Selected Years)

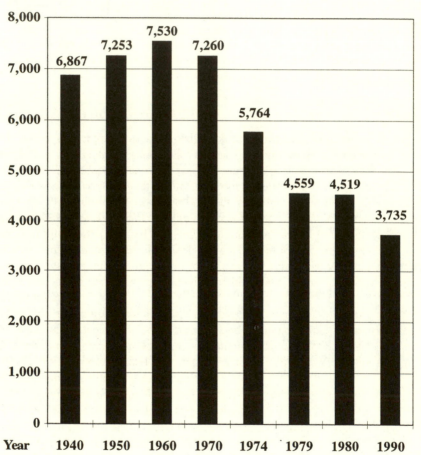

Sources: 1940, 1950, 1960, 1970, 1980, 1990—U.S. Census; 1972 Urban Collaborative (1974); 1977 Bolger (1979).

Over the past several decades, the causes of Detroit's urban crisis, and of homelessness as one of its key manifestations, have been discussed from two perspectives. One views the problems of cities as caused and perpetuated primarily by the
values and behaviors of the poor (Banfield 1958, 1970; Lewis 1959, 1961, 1966a,

1966b, 1968; Breckenfeld 1977; Wirth 1938; Merton 1968; Frazier 1939; Drake and Cayton 1945; and Johnson 1941). The other perspective views the problems of cities primarily as the result of structural factors in the socioeconomic order (Domhoff 1967; Ewen 1978; Ryan 1976; Piven and Cloward 1971; Valentine 1968, 1971, 1973; Wilhelm 1971; Hannerz 1969; Liebow 1967; Rodman 1971, 1973; Tabb 1977; Rubenstein 1970; Altshuler 1970; Eames and Goode 1968, 1977).

In the research for this chapter, I found the socioeconomic perspective the more useful of the two. The residents in my community of study have a generalized understanding—based on collective experience—that the relatively disadvantaged socioeconomic status of Jefferson-Chalmers is a product of conflicting interests between "haves" and "have-nots." To approach a community study from a "victim-blaming" perspective is tantamount to psychological reductionism, which holds that the ills of the neighborhood are simply the ills of the individual and family writ large. This approach would have closed many interviewees' doors and yielded precious little usable information for the community organizers who sanctioned my work and received my final report.

Cultural ecologists emphasize research that interprets people's behavior as adaptive strategies. Many studies of urbanites have focused on the strategies that families in stressed situations adopt as reasonable responses to extrinsic factors. Graves and Graves (1974) identified strategies related to migration, while Lebowitz et al. (1973) have charted those of people seeking counsel and assistance in an urban community. Among these strategy-oriented works, Stack's works (1970, 1974) have been of great use in the present study of families, networks, and their reciprocal and cooperating behavior. Stack provided firsthand insight into the child-keeping, goods-circulating, and kin-reliance behaviors that pull many black families through from the day that their money and food run out.

Detroit's Jefferson-Chalmers

The research for this chapter focused on the one–square-mile, blue-collar, Detroit community known as Jefferson-Chalmers (see also, Bolger 1979). Many of today's homeless were gainfully employed in the early 1980s, just after my 1977 fieldwork was completed. Some still have ties in this and other lower east-side neighborhoods.

In the late 1970s, Jefferson-Chalmers was a community of ninety-six blocks and fifteen thousand people, seventeen churches, four schools, eight recreation areas, three grocery stores, nine small markets, four islands, one citizens' district council (CDC), and one river—the Detroit River, which forms the international boundary with Canada. The river, the islands, and the CDC remain. The population was down to 9,290 in 1990, and all the other numbers except of the blocks have dropped since the 1970s.

By the 1990s, the millions of Community Development Block Grant (CDBG) dollars that had been spent on Jefferson-Chalmers had eliminated much of the blight evident in the 1970s. New housing—some of it for low-income people, some of it for moderate and higher-income persons—was built on vacant urban renewal lands. CDBG dollars were also spent in the acquisition of land and improvement of the infrastructure for the Chrysler Corporation's new Jefferson North Assembly Plant.

Jefferson-Chalmers remains a community, insofar as most of its people's day-to-day needs can be met within the one–square-mile area. It is a community also because people think it is. Its name derives from two main cross streets. To leave the community, one must either cross a river, a canal, a city limit, a factory, or a major traffic artery. The city government approaches it as an area worth saving. The city has received federal monies for loans to homeowners in the specific census tracts composing the community.

The People of Jefferson-Chalmers

The community has been shaped by the auto industry. The lure of relatively high wages for unskilled labor during the two world wars produced profound changes in Jefferson-Chalmers' ethnic mix. The city's prewar industrial workforce of Irish, Germans, and Poles became progressively more African American. The community evolved from a white-majority community hosting a black enclave, to one that was half white and half African American. By 1970, the community was predominantly black.

At the time of my 1977 Jefferson-Chalmers community study, about two-thirds of the population was African American, and one-third was Anglo. The 1990 census counted 85 percent of the population as African American. There has been a decline of housing units from 4,559 in 1977 to 3,735 in 1990—a decline of 18 percent in thirteen years.

The original auto plant of the Chalmers Motor Car Company and the dozens of others that operated in the first half of this century historically provided Detroiters, such as Ulysses (described below), with high, blue-collar wages negotiated by the United Auto Workers (UAW) union. Abundant, flat land suitable for development led to extensive construction of single-family housing units before and after World War II—housing that was affordable to many Detroiters.

A result of the prolonged economic dislocation of the late 1980s and early 1990s has been that the highest economic return is no longer found in the central cities of the United States' industrial heartland—hence deindustrialization (Newman 1985). Left in the wake of departing industry and eroding tax bases are people, such as those in the Detroit community of Jefferson-Chalmers, who still have basic needs for shelter, food, and employment, but who are increasingly unable to meet their needs in the present socioeconomic order (Bolger 1979:4–8).

METHODOLOGY

Participant Observation

Participant observation in Jefferson-Chalmers was aided by my wearing the many different "hats," which connected me with diverse networks of Jefferson-Chalmers residents: in-law, neighbor, volunteer, musician, parishioner, customer, teacher, researcher, block club activist, photographer, and food co-op member. My informants for the Jefferson-Chalmers community study numbered in the dozens before either they or I knew they would be informants.

Through my wife, a Jefferson-Chalmers native, I gained easy entrance to a long-standing network of neighbors. Living in the neighborhood made for a natural, "front yard" relationship with neighbors who shared the kinds of quality-of-life problems our block club would address: trash pickup, crime prevention, stray dogs. As a supporter and inaugural member of the community food co-op, I learned plenty about "working together" and heard much conventional wisdom about politics and economics during a recession.

Working as a church organist in a community striving toward ecumenism provided me with enough "notoriety" among church congregations that my "ethnographic nosiness" was tolerated and even welcome. I was a known commodity. My work as an anthropology instructor at the community college that Jefferson-Chalmers and other lower east-siders attended opened up almost daily discussions of local life, problems, and solutions.

Providing volunteer work for the citizens' district council as a newsletter reporter, photographer, and liaison to retailers exposed me to a broad cross-section of the community. I was accepted in a variety of locales where people would talk. I would listen, unencumbered by note pads or tape recorders, and would later compile anecdotal information based on these encounters.

Four key informants were invaluable in reading the pulse of the community: (1) a white school teacher and playground activity leader who is a lifelong community resident, civil rights activist, and my father-in-law; (2) an African-American woman, a newcomer to the community, fellow parishioner and musician who rode public transportation every day; (3) an African-American man, whose family was one of the first black families to move into the community and who spent most of his nonworking hours building school and community organizations; and (4) an Anglo woman who established an innovative day care program that successfully reached both children and parents.

These four informants provided a sounding board for my research ideas and, in general, were not surprised by the quantitative findings of my 235 face-to-face interviews. Our relationships were comfortably reciprocal, in that my primary data were often useful for or applicable to furthering their various efforts and initiatives.

During a four-year period following my move into the community, I absorbed and compiled a limited oral history of its families. In developing historical reconstructions, I accrued the greatest asset from having married into a family that, at that time, had sixty-year roots in an eighty-year-old community. My wife taught in a neighborhood elementary school. Another valuable asset was membership in a church that presided, for better or worse, over much of the community's history and had passed through transitional crises comparable to the city's and community's. Fifteen years after my move to Jefferson-Chalmers, the church was closed and consolidated with a nearby parish.

The familial and ecclesiastical experiences of the four research years created the deepest ties to the Anglo community of Jefferson-Chalmers. My own employment experiences and those of my wife also provided ties to the African-American community, which made up two-thirds of the population.

As a community college instructor, I frequently taught anthropology classes at instructional centers close to or within the community. The community college student body was predominantly African American and mainly women in their thirties—almost a profile of the interviewees in my survey. My familiarity with community people and problems led to a general acceptance of my role as interviewer, although I was of different race from the majority of interviewees.

Census, Sampling Method, and Survey Instrument, 1977

I designed a 5-percent random-sample survey of community households that amounted to 235 interviews. The sample was drawn in proportion to the number of housing units in the community's four census tracts. (With population declines, there were only three census tracts in 1990.) It took several weeks to complete a "windshield survey" of all the housing units on the ninety-six blocks constituting Jefferson-Chalmers. This entailed the systematic recording of the addresses of all occupied housing units.[2] Data were analyzed by computer, using the Statistical Package for the Social Sciences (SPSS). The frequencies and cross-tabulations generated from the data analyses formed a major part of the study. By the end of a three-month interviewing period, Labor Day to Thanksgiving 1977, the 235 interviews were completed. The twelve-page questionnaire was given face-to-face and took an average of twenty-five minutes to complete, in the interviewee's own residence.[3]

FINDINGS

The Setting: Deteriorating Socioeconomic Conditions in a Deindustrializing Community

Detroit's dependence on the auto industry is largely responsible for the boom and bust cycles that Detroiters have faced for the better part of this century. Detroiters' wage income disappears as recession recurs. In the early 1990s, the city remained mired in a recession that some pronounced to be over elsewhere in the

United States.

While Detroit is still some years away from experiencing the degree of homelessness existing in New York, Washington, or Los Angeles, the continuing deterioration of the economy suggests that Detroit's future can now be read on the streets of those cities. Real income has fallen 27 percent between 1974 and 1985, and the real cost of rental housing has simultaneously risen 9 percent (Lynch and Leonard 1991:17). In Jefferson-Chalmers, there were 48.5 percent fewer housing units in 1990 than in 1970, as shown in Figure 3.1, and most of the units that disappeared were low-income rentals.

A symbol of the community's dependence on the auto industry can be seen in the new Chrysler Corporation auto assembly plant, constructed alongside the ruins of the plant that first anchored the community in 1907. In the late 1970s, 35 percent of Jefferson-Chalmers workers drew their paycheck, pension, or unemployment compensation from General Motors, Ford, or Chrysler; 26 percent were affiliated with Chrysler Corporation alone.

Finding #1: Housing Loss. The windshield survey house-count provided some astonishing information. Whereas, the 1970 census reported 6,602 households in the four census tracts that constituted the community, my 1977 count discovered only 4,675 units remaining in the wake of urban renewal. Thirty percent of the community's housing stock had been bulldozed, burned, or abandoned in those seven years.

The attrition of housing units continued through the 1980s. Multiple family buildings in Jefferson-Chalmers—providing some of the least expensive rental housing—declined from 529 units in 1980 to 299 in 1990, a 43 percent loss. Another low-income housing alternative was endangered, the community's 160-site trailer park. It is one of only two trailer parks in Detroit, and it sits on prime riverside acreage that the city hopes will be redeveloped into higher-density, higher-income housing.

Finding #2: Interviewees and Their Housing. More than half the 1977 survey respondents were female; and 69 percent were African American. Forty-one percent worked in manufacturing, and 47 percent worked in service occupations. A majority of respondents lived in single-family dwellings; 25 percent were part of extended families. Thirty-four percent lived below the poverty line, and 45 percent of the households included an individual who had been unemployed during the three years preceding the survey.

Finding #3: "The Disappeared"—Jobs and Affordable Dwellings. One interviewee, Ulysses, a thirty-three-year-old African American, was a foundryman for Chrysler who in 1977 lived with his family in a brick duplex on a tree-lined street. By Jefferson-Chalmers standards, Ulysses was prosperous, earning wages bargained by the UAW that were higher than the typical salaries of the professional workers living in his same community. With inflation, his paycheck did not go very far even then to meet the needs of his family—a wife, two teenagers, and a preschool youngster.

Today, householders like Ulysses are on the "endangered species list." His house sits on a block pockmarked by vacant lots, high weeds, and derelict structures. Only 45 percent of the 1977 dwelling units on Ulysses' block remained standing in 1993. In 1977 he was among the 36 percent of survey respondents who lived in duplex housing, but in 1990 only 20 percent of the Jefferson-Chalmers housing stock was two-family dwellings.

Not only is much of the housing stock gone that Ulysses knew, but the very foundry in which he worked closed in 1977. Thousands of Chrysler jobs, both hourly and salaried, disappeared. A thirty-three-years-old Jefferson-Chalmers resident with a high wage factory job is something of an anachronism in 1993. The average age of the Chrysler worker laboring in the new Jefferson North Assembly Plant adjacent to the Jefferson-Chalmers community is fifty-one years; the average worker's seniority exceeds twenty years (*Automotive News* 1991:12).

Finding #4: Single and Two-family Dwellings as "Double-ups." Unlike other cities, many of the poor live in, or own, homes or flats where the costs are relatively low and space is large enough to absorb homeless, or soon-to-be-homeless, kin. These are "double-ups." In 1990 only about half (1,617 of 3,189) of Jefferson-Chalmers' occupied housing units were renter-occupied. This was true in spite of the devastation of Detroit's housing stock in the previous twenty years and the dramatic fall in household income, which was tied to the disappearance of good factory jobs. The remainder of the units were occupied by owners.

Notwithstanding the construction in recent years of luxury condominiums and a completely new subdivision of higher-income, single-family homes, Jefferson-Chalmers is still a very affordable place to live. Median contract rent was $190 per month in 1990 (see Table 3.1). Few of the Jefferson-Chalmers rental units are apartments; rather, they tend to be two-story houses and duplex flats. Many landlords are simply other older, working-class Detroiters, or former Detroiters, who were able to buy a second home. Often, the second home is rented out to family or friends.

Between 1974 and 1985 the number of low-income renters in Detroit increased from seventy-four thousand to 107,000. Yet the number of low-income rental units decreased from what was a slight surplus of seventy-six thousand to sixty-three thousand in the same period, creating a deficit (Lynch and Leonard 1991:xiv).[4] In 1990, the median housing unit value in this private-home community was a modest $24,852 (Table 3.1). While this is relatively affordable housing, it is still inaccessible to the public assistance recipient whose monthly check from the Department of Social Services was cut off or seriously eroded by inflation.

National policy has abandoned the construction of new, subsidized, family housing. At the same time, the number of unsubsidized low-rent housing units in the private market dropped by 39 percent between 1974 and 1985 (Lynch and Leonard 1991:18). These trends result in fewer shelter choices for very-low-income Detroiters. Particularly vulnerable are young women with children who have very low incomes and who have never had their own homes.

Table 3.1
Selected Demographic, Economic, and Housing Characteristics for Jefferson-Chalmers Community, 1980 and 1990

Community Characteristic	1980 Census	1990 Census	Change (%)
Total Persons	12,580	9,290	-26.1
White	2,578	1,396	-45.8
Black	9,833	7,807	-20.6
Median Household Income	$12,119	$15,659[a]	+29.2[a]
Manufacturing Jobs (%)	42.4	33.5	- 8.9
Households	4,016	3,189	-20.6
Families Below Poverty (%)	28.0	40.7	+12.7
Housing Units	4,519	3,736	-17.3
Persons per Housing Unit	2.64	2.91	+10.2
Housing Units Vacant (%)	11.2	14.6	+ 3.7
Median Value	$18,088	$24,852	+37.4
Median Contract Rent	$150	$190	+26.7

Source: U.S. Census Bureau

[a]Not adjusted for inflation.

Finding #5: Recession, Reciprocity, and Doubling-up—The Case History of Kendall Tyler. For those most vulnerable to recessions, reciprocity could make the difference between being homeless and being sheltered. For the extended families of auto workers like Kendall Tyler, reciprocity came in the form of co-residence, or doubling-up.

Kendall Tyler lost his job at Chrysler in 1973, just before the recession hit. He remained out of work for eighteen months. Unemployment compensation and supplemental benefits totalled $188 every two weeks, which did not fully provide for his wife, two children, and a stepchild. In 1975, Tyler eventually found non-auto, non-union work, and his wife was hired for an experimental program at a Cadillac Motor Division Plant. Their economic situation improved, but the plight of their kin did not. Kendall's mother and sister were facing homelessness because of their poverty. Like thousands of Detroiters, Tyler made room for his relatives in his own home. Although the extra people in the household provided valuable assistance with child care, Tyler's wife and mother often found themselves at odds over running the house and raising the children. Tyler and his wife, Mary, as wage-earners, were easy marks for cash-poor friends and relatives who regularly had to borrow money to get by.

Within a year, the five-person household of Kendall Tyler grew to seven and then fragmented under the strain. Mary and the children moved to another part of Jefferson-Chalmers; Kendall moved into an upper flat above a friend; and his mother and sister each moved to different homes. Mary and Kendall shared parental responsibilities through the week from their separate homes. A year after they broke up, Mary asked Kendall to take the children, so he moved to a new flat near a close friend before the winter set in. He lived with the three children, the oldest of whom came from an earlier marriage of Mary's. The children frequented the house of Kendall's close friend for meals, care, and temporary fosterage. Tyler's domestic network reached across the community to his sister's new residence, and up to where his mother had moved. Contact among them increased because of his added responsibilities with the children.

In 1993, Kendall Tyler reflected about himself and his peers who once worked for high wages in the plants. Of them, only one still works for Chrysler; others are doing drugs, in prison, or dead. Still others work for only a fraction of their factory wages, as gas station attendants, jitneys, mechanics, private security guards, or landscaping and snow removal laborers.

Twenty years after leaving Chrysler, Tyler is only now earning the same amount that he earned in 1973, and this only because his unionized employment as a corrections officer includes mandatory overtime, which boosts his wages. Kendall Tyler says that he went eleven years before getting a good job again, and that the corrections job was largely due to having some college education. His ex-wife remarried and remains on the payroll of the General Motors Cadillac Division, although she is currently "on disability."

The families of friends, Kendall observes, seem to have disintegrated over the years. Most of the people he works with as a corrections officer come from broken families. Kendall Tyler sees job training and retraining as the best way to save Detroiters, especially the young, from joblessness and the risk of homelessness.

Finding #6: Recession, Reciprocity, and Doubling-up—General Trends. Following the mid-1970s recession, I discovered widespread reciprocal exchanges among individuals, families, and households in Jefferson-Chalmers. In many instances, reciprocity was the difference between having enough money to pay the rent and going homeless. Among households closely related by blood, generalized reciprocity, in which a service or gift would be offered without any immediate expectation of a return, was common. For example, payback for child-keeping may not have been "in kind," but its eventual reciprocation helped cement kin and fictive-kin ties. These persons recognized each other as "those you can count on." Down the line, the child-keeper's own children are sure to be fed a full meal or two, perhaps just at the time that her refrigerator is barest.

The case history of Kendall Tyler illustrates that poor households often cannot cover major monthly bills, such as rent and utilities, and also place food on the table each day. For Tyler's friends and relatives, watching his kids meant more than making sure they did not get in trouble; it meant having enough money to buy food to feed three extra mouths. Some day, he reasoned, the shoe would be on the other foot.

Kendall Tyler's experience with family size and composition fluctuating in response to fluctuating resources was repeated in scores of other households in the Jefferson-Chalmers community during the recession of the mid-1970s. In 1972 only

8.7 percent of the community's households were composed of extended families under one roof (Urban Collaborative 1972). By 1977, this rate had doubled to 17.9 percent. If a broad definition of "extended family" is used that includes persons related as a family even though they live under different roofs, then the 1977 Jefferson-Chalmers rate for extended families was 25.1 percent (Bolger 1979:216). The increase in extended family formation was observed throughout Jefferson-Chalmers, in neighborhoods with substantial white populations as well as in all-black neighborhoods.

Finding #7: Recession, Reciprocity, and Doubling-up—General Principles. Reciprocity can make the difference between having enough money to pay the rent and going homeless. A pivotal strategy of Detroiters, who are thoroughly accustomed to the boom and bust cycle of the auto industry, involves the giving and receiving of goods and services without the use of money—what Sahlins identifies as "reciprocity" (1972:188–96).

Extended families and expansive networks are crucial social resources in an environment of fluctuating economic resources. Persons at risk for homelessness use the resources available, among them the telephone and the freeway, to maintain support and rely on their networks. Unemployment, rather than income level, influences people's readiness to reciprocate and cooperate. Unemployment was a factor which, regardless of income or station, could be anxiety-provoking. Those who shared that experience of vulnerability and marginality would be more likely to "help each other out."

The type of family in which one lives can also have an important bearing on reciprocation and cooperation. Households with children reciprocate and cooperate with the greatest frequency. Households with children have more different kinds of needs that stimulate informal exchange arrangements between kin and neighbors.

The unemployment experience in Jefferson-Chalmers is a levelling mechanism. It is an agent of humility that disposes the recently unemployed to share, reciprocate, and cooperate more often, regardless of race, family type, socioeconomic class, or income. The recession of 1975 officially left 14.5 percent of Detroit's workforce unemployed. By 1978, the rate had fallen to 8.3 percent. In 1982, the Michigan Employment Security Commission (MESC) counted 20.3 percent of the workforce as officially unemployed. The rate then declined, to 16.5 percent in 1992. None of these figures includes "discouraged workers," who no longer go to the MESC offices to seek work.

Great fluctuations in employment show no signs of dampening. The old Chrysler Jefferson Assembly Plant was closed and demolished in 1990, in response to the flagging sales of the Dodge Omni and Plymouth Horizon models that were produced there. The plant's 3,700 workers waited two years for the new Jefferson North Assembly Plant to open. In the new high-tech plant, 206 robots, aided by only 2,100 of the former workers, began assembling the Jeep Grand Cherokee in early 1992 (Plumb 1991:34).

Finding 8: Increase in Household Density. The density of persons per household in Jefferson-Chalmers increased in 1990 by 10 percent to 2.91 persons per household, as compared to 2.64 persons in 1980. This increased density, at a time when overall birth rates were declining, is a predictable result of doubling-up.

SUMMARY AND RECOMMENDATIONS

Summary of Adaptive Strategies

To "stay afloat," Detroiters in Jefferson-Chalmers, and other Americans like them, select and combine a variety of survival strategies. These may involve: (1) wage-work in the mainstream economy, as enjoyed by those Chrysler workers who were called back to assemble the Jeep Grand Cherokee at the new Jefferson North Assembly Plant; (2) public assistance, such as aid to dependent children, which is collected by many single parents; (3) poverty-wage work or involvement in an "underground economy," such as year-round windshield washing near freeway entrances and other busy intersections, criminal activity related to drugs or alcohol, and reciprocity—all typically unreported to tax authorities.

The rate of household experience with unemployment can be very high in communities like Jefferson-Chalmers. The aggregate unemployment rate in that community appears to be the chief factor in promoting helping-behaviors among all residents. For example, 45 percent of all households in the Jefferson-Chalmers random sample experienced unemployment during the three recession years preceding the 1977 survey.

An oft-repeated strategy in Jefferson-Chalmers and similar communities is the commencement of low-paying, service-sector employment after the disappearance of higher-paying union-shop employment. Low-seniority, unskilled industrial workers who never regained the jobs from which they were laid off in years past can now be found working for minimum wage in fast-food restaurants near those same industrial work sites, or working as "rent-a-cops" at nearby clinics and check-cashing stores.

An emerging pattern of repeated deindustrialization, unemployment, and racial discrimination can decimate a community's stock of affordable housing. After 1970, for example, bulldozing, burning, and abandonment reduced Jefferson-Chalmers' housing stock by 30 percent. Almost all of this demolition took place in the census tract closest to the Chrysler factory—the part of the community that had housed African Americans the longest. Once set in motion, these processes increase the risk of poverty and homelessness for everyone in the community. Low-income housing, public transportation, and child care are unprofitable and are relegated to the margins of any for-profit economy. Yet deficiencies in these areas, as in primary health care, consign many of the poor in Jefferson-Chalmers to joblessness, poor health, and homelessness.

A pivotal strategy for Detroiters, who are long accustomed to the fluctuations caused by the auto industry, involves reciprocity, or the giving and taking of goods and services without exchanging money. In many instances, reciprocity makes the difference between being able to pay the rent and going homeless. For those most vulnerable to poverty and recession, reciprocity in the form of doubling-up, or rent-free co-residence, makes the difference between being sheltered and being homeless.

Recommendations

Recommendation #1. The federal government should restore federal funding for subsidized jobs and job training programs to 1980 levels.

Recommendation #2. The federal government should restore federal funding for housing programs for low-income persons to 1970 levels.

The HUD section 8, housing construction program of the 1970s provided Detroit with a substantial inventory of safe, sanitary, and affordable rental housing. The success of this program was due in large part to effective involvement of, and underwriting by, the Michigan State Housing Development Authority (MSHDA). The 180-unit MSHDA development in Jefferson-Chalmers is testament to the potential of well maintained very-low-income housing. Federal abandonment of this program consigns many of Detroit's poor to substandard housing and eventually to emergency shelters for the homeless. Unlike in some other cities, many poor Detroiters live in, or own, a home or flat where the costs are relatively low and the space is large enough to absorb homeless or soon-to-be homeless kin.

Recommendation #3. The federal government should increase Section 8 subsidies, support the state's restoration of public assistance payments for adults without children, and increase the welfare shelter budget for families to the median rent level so that they can afford to rent suitable housing.

In Jefferson-Chalmers, as in Detroit as a whole, housing has become scarcer, more expensive, increasingly substandard, and more crowded. The positive side of the reciprocity is clear: one person rescues a kinsperson or friend from homelessness by allowing them to double-up. However, the negative side is equally clear. A primary tenant can lose his or her rental housing because of overcrowding, or the emotional toll of doubling-up can fracture an extended family, as in Tyler's double-up arrangement.

The relative affordability of Jefferson-Chalmers housing was recently undercut by executive action at the state level. In the summer of 1991, Michigan's new Republican governor announced the elimination of General Assistance welfare benefits for able-bodied individuals without children. As a result, forty-five thousand heretofore eligible Detroiters lost $160 per month that they had previously received. This amount came close to covering the cost of a typical Jefferson-Chalmers rental.

Recommendation #4. The federal government should support the state's public assistance shelter budgets for single adults and families, which would enable them to pay to remain in the double-ups—when they want to stay and when there is enough space.

CONCLUSION

In Detroit, the existence in homes of adequate square footage—in addition to a sense of generosity and commitment to one's kin and friends—has enabled people to double-up and to take in others who are close to homelessness. Yet ownership or tenancy in a three-bedroom, freestanding house has become a thing of the past for thousands of Detroiters. Problems of homelessness more often associated with large coastal cities are becoming commonplace in Detroit.

Reciprocity continues to be part of everyday life in communities like Jefferson-Chalmers, particularly among those who have experienced job loss. Doubling-up is the most common way of avoiding immediate homelessness. Resoluteness and resilience go a long way toward helping families compensate for the havoc visited on their lives by budget-cutting at all levels of government. Nevertheless, the disappearance of housing resources that staved off homelessness for decades is now bringing thousands of Detroiters close to an absolute minimum of family security.

Compensatory education, manpower training (as illustrated in the Kendall Tyler case history), and community action programs are all important. However, any presumption that these alone will redress the poverty that now virtually guarantees homelessness for many, rests on the premise that poverty is a product of the poor themselves. On the contrary, the inevitable conclusion to be drawn from this chapter is that the cure for homelessness lies more in increasing the availability of low-income housing and narrowing the progressively widening chasm between the poor, those who work, and those who control society's resources, than in changing the values and behaviors of the poor.

NOTES

1. According to census data on Jefferson-Chalmers, the median family income in 1970 (in 1990 dollars) was $18,966.61; in 1990, it was $17,906.29.

2. At the beginning of the survey, the 1970 census was seven years old and calculably misleading due to the unexplained omission of 10 percent of the community. In 1972, the Urban Collaborative (1972) carried out a survey of the Jefferson-Chalmers community that proved valuable in plotting the change of the community in the two post-census years. A 1 percent sample of a 1975 Citizens' Survey offered some indications of demographic trends in the community, but not the exact information needed to conduct a community study.

3. Fortunately, the success rate in completing interviews was very high; 87 percent of those approached granted an interview. However, not all the information desired was offered. For example, in 9 percent of the cases, respondents declined to provide information pertinent to income size and its sources. The refusal rate was highest among older, white women, who were reluctant to allow entrance to any stranger.

4. At the same time, some of the very cheapest housing, namely subsidized public housing, is vacant and unavailable. The Detroit Housing Department has been criticized by the U.S. Department of Housing and Urban Development (HUD) for having 42 percent of its housing units, 3,600 units in all, vacant in 1990. The Detroit Housing Department cannot fill the rental units in old housing projects that are available and has preferred to demolish rather than rehabilitate many units needing repair.

4

Doubling-Up and New York City's Policies for Sheltering Homeless Families

Anna Lou Dehavenon

Homeless families, like other families in the United States, need stable living space in which to socialize and enculturate children, store food, cook and eat, care for clothing, receive mail, use the telephone, and engage in adult sexual intercourse in accordance with the mainstream culture's rules of privacy. The author documents the search for the stable housing homeless families in New York City need to keep together, attend school, and work. However, the city government assumes that the housing standard for very-low-income families should be lower than for other families and that poor families should opt for living doubled-up, no matter how crowded, rather than using the public shelter system. Dehavenon recommends increasing rent subsidies for low-income families, the construction of more subsidized low-income housing, and the U.S. government's support of the United Nations' effort to recognize housing as a universal basic human right.

INTRODUCTION

Homelessness has many faces, some more visible than others: the single adults who stay in public places and the adults and families who stay in public shelters. These two groups make up most of the official homeless count. A third group, those who stay doubled-up in other people's living space because they cannot afford their own, is much less visible. The individuals and families in all three groups have one thing in common: the lack of shelter over which they have stable, legal control. This is the salient feature of the operational definition of homelessness used in the research on which this chapter is based. Furthermore, a "double-up" is defined as a living arrangement in which two or more families share the same space, for which the host family pays the rent to the landlord and the guest family does not.

As a strategy for obtaining shelter, doubling-up enables those who employ it to avoid the degradation of public shelters and being included in the government's official homeless count. Doubling-up also gives the housed individuals who are in the personal networks of the homeless an opportunity to share an important resource with them (see Bolger, Chapter 3). Since the doubled-up homeless are less visible than the other two groups, they have received much less attention from researchers and the general public. However, in order to understand fully the more conspicuous manifestations of homelessness on the streets and in public shelters, it is necessary to understand the instability of "invisible" double-ups. This chapter's first goal is to explore how well—in spite of many difficulties—families living doubled-up in New York City in 1991 were able to fulfill the basic functions of family life and why so many double-ups fall apart. The research on which this chapter is based has shown the fragility of overcrowded double-ups as a solution to homelessness (cf. Action Research Project on Hunger, Homelessness, and Family Health 1989, 1990, 1991, 1992, 1993, 1994, 1995, 1996).[1] Poor families throughout the United States have adopted the double-up strategy for a number of reasons, the primary one being the decreased supply and exponentially rising cost of low-income housing in many regions of the country after the middle-1970s. In the late 1970s there was a dramatic rise in family homelessness. After 1980, the resulting housing crisis was a predictable outcome of these developments as well as of changes in the political economy and of decisions by policy makers at all three levels of government (see page xviii of the Introduction; HUD 1994).

In New York City, doubling-up became a live issue in 1990 when the city released a new plan to discourage families from entering the public shelter system. An important element of the plan was based on the assumption that city welfare workers could "divert" many shelter applicants back to the double-ups they had just left. This chapter's second goal is to examine briefly how well this strategy worked.

Theory

The research presented here is based on a cultural materialist approach that employs the "emic/etic" distinction in all aspects of data collection.[2] Research methods include participant observation and the use of structured questionnaires (Dehavenon 1995; Harris 1964, 1983; Lett 1990). This approach is incompatible with the view that the personal weaknesses of poor families are the primary cause of their impoverishment and the homelessness which is one of its symptoms. Furthermore, this approach presupposes that an empirically based analysis of the behaviors of poor families and the socioeconomic context in which they occur can provide a more reliable understanding of the causes of their impoverishment and its impact on their capacity to perform basic domestic functions.

This work draws on three aspects of anthropological theory.

- *The theory of the family*: Domestic structure and functions adapt to diverse economic, political, and social conditions. In the domestic sphere, there are culturally patterned activities that include eating, sleeping, adult sexual intercourse, and the enculturation of children. These activities are performed within a stable physical context that includes shelter (Adams 1960; Bender 1968; Yanagisako 1979).

- *The theory of community*: To ensure the continuity of culture, people form stable group-ings, larger than the family but smaller than the entire cultural group (Arensberg and Kimball 1965).

- *Theory of the organization of complex societies*: This includes, for example, the notion that relationships between macro and micro levels of social organization exist in "linkages between local level events and forces operating in the larger society" (Dewalt and Pelto 1985).

These theories ground the observation and analysis of the behavior of impover-ished homeless families empirically, and establish the findings as a legitimate basis for public policy. Recommendations related to legislative and administrative rem-edies for homelessness and doubling-up at the local level are relevant also to remedies at the state and federal levels. Currently, nowhere in the literature is there a focus on doubling-up per se. However, since 1985 a number of books and reports refer to it as an aspect of homelessness (Action Research Project on Hunger, Home-lessness, and Family Health 1989, 1990, 1991, 1992, 1993, 1994, 1995, 1996; Barak 1992; Dehavenon 1987; Knickman and Weitzman 1989; Rossi 1987; Stegman 1993; Task Force on Homelessness of the Manhattan Borough President's Office 1987; The New York City Commission on Homelessness 1992; U.S. Department of Hous-ing and Urban Development 1994; Wright 1989).

New York City's Response to Increased Pressure on Homeless Shelters

In the 1980s, the number of homeless families in New York City swelled. State law required the city to provide needy families with emergency shelter, but city govern-ment discouraged homeless families from asking for help by providing substandard shelter. Mass shelters were created to accommodate large numbers of strangers, men, women, and children, who slept side-by-side in huge open rooms. By 1991 almost six thousand families were staying in the city's shelter system, and the waiting time for permanent housing was at least eighteen months for families offi-cially registered in the shelters. Many other homeless families were not officially part of the system. At least thirty thousand households lived doubled-up in New York City Public Housing Authority apartments. Hundreds of thousands of others with incomes below $25,000 a year had difficulty finding their own housing because they could not afford an apartment in the city's high-cost private rental market (Action Research Project on Hunger, Homelessness, and Family Health 1991, 1992, 1993, 1994, 1995).

For many people, doubling-up was the only alternative to asking the city for emergency shelter. Litigation over the unwholesome conditions for homeless fami-lies in the unwelcoming mass shelters compelled the city to create a second set of shelters which gave them more privacy. Because the city's supplies of emergency shelter and subsidized housing for low-income families fell far short of the demand, many families were forced to stay overnight (illegally) in the city's after-hours welfare offices or Emergency Assistance Units (EAUs). The EAUs' original purpose was to provide a place where families could come for help and acquire safe, stable shelter; however, the city's diversion program, other administrative barriers, and overcrowding in the shelter system distorted that purpose.

New York state law requires that emergency relief be available to needy families around the clock. Initially, a single EAU in lower Manhattan provided shelter placements for families who became homeless outside regular business hours. However, as the number of homeless families rose, the city's welfare centers could not place them during the day and were forced to send them to the EAU in Manhattan to wait for nighttime placements after 5:00 P.M. Eventually, EAUs were opened in the three other boroughs with high rates of poverty: the Bronx, Brooklyn, and Queens.[3] By 1990, the shortage of emergency shelter and low-income housing and the city's failure to meet its construction goals had resulted in massive bottlenecks at the EAUs, where hundreds of families were forced illegally to sleep overnight on tables, chairs, and floors. The shelter crisis deepened throughout 1990 and 1991 and continues today.

Double-ups became the center of a major public policy controversy in 1990. The number of families seeking emergency shelter rose steeply in August, although the rise was well within the historic precedent previously set for that month. (With hot weather and no school, the stresses on overcrowded double-ups increase, and every year since 1986 more families sought emergency shelter in July and August than in other months). Nevertheless, the city argued that a "sudden influx" of "not truly homeless" doubled-up families was striving to enter the shelter system to obtain city-owned apartments. This argument provided the rationale for the city's new policy of trying to divert families back to the double-ups they had stayed in most recently. Nevertheless, in spite of stiffened eligibility requirements and the diversion effort, families routinely waited overnight at the EAUs for emergency shelter placements.

In response to increasingly dangerous and unhealthy conditions at the EAUs in 1991, the Legal Aid Homeless Family Rights Project brought the first of five contempt-of-court motions against the city in the New York State Supreme Court. These motions challenged the city's practice of illegally denying shelter to homeless families, placing them in unlivable hotels and "overnight" shelter beds, and forcing them to stay at the EAUs overnight.[4]

Almost all the families waiting for shelter at the EAUs with their children in 1991 were African American or Hispanic, reflecting the ethnic profile of the city's low-income population. Most of the parents were born in the city and had worked, or were still working, at low-paying, entry-level jobs. Seventy-three percent included a single parent, three of whom were male; in 26 percent, both parents were present. Two percent included extended family members. The median age of the mothers was twenty-six; the median age of the fathers was twenty-seven. In 82 percent of the families, one or two children waited with the parents. In 14 percent of the families one or more other children were separated from their parents because of the family's lack of permanent housing. The same reason separated 8 percent of the families from their husbands, fathers or both.

METHODOLOGY

On twenty-five Monday nights between January 7 and August 26, 1991, I observed and documented the experiences of families waiting for shelter placements at the Bronx, Brooklyn, and Manhattan EAUs.[5] I chose Monday nights because on that night a larger proportion of these families than on other nights of the week had already gone to their welfare centers for help earlier the same day. As a monitor for the Coalition for the Homeless, I also observed the degree of the city's compliance with relevant court rulings related to the administration of welfare and the emergency shelter system.

The EAU ambiance resembled that of waiting rooms in welfare centers and prisons. The entrance was flanked by uniformed guards with metal detectors. Families were first searched and then told to "go sign in at the window." It was often difficult for them to find a place to sit down because of the severe overcrowding and shortage of chairs.

Each Monday night, the fieldwork was carried out in three phases. Arriving at 5:00 P.M., I first counted the families who already waited at the EAU. Thereafter, I recorded the times when other families arrived and when all families left the EAU to go to shelter placements. Between 5:30 P.M. and 10:30 P.M., I completed a structured, long-form questionnaire with a randomly selected sample of eight families. After 11:15 P.M., I completed a structured short-form questionnaire with all the families I had not yet interviewed. Each Monday night, I stayed at the EAU until after midnight or until I was able to record the time at which each of the eight families I had interviewed with the long-form questionnaire received a shelter placement and could tell me where it was and for how long.[6]

The first time I went to each of the EAUs, I observed the layout of the waiting rooms to identify the natural seating areas to be used as sampling zones. In both the Bronx and Manhattan EAUs, there were two of these areas, both oriented toward television sets. In Brooklyn there were also two areas, one facing a TV set and the other the Plexiglas windows through which families communicated with the workers. On subsequent visits, I divided my time between the two areas at each EAU and used the following procedures to sample the families for interview with the long-form questionnaire.

- I chose the chair as near the center of the first area as possible and sat down.
- After a brief period of observation, I spoke with and then interviewed families seated nearby in the following sequence: the families seated to my immediate right, to my immediate left, directly in front of me, and directly in back of me.

- I moved to the second seating area, where I repeated the same procedures.
- To reduce any bias associated with family choice of seating area, on successive Monday nights I alternated the area where I started.
- I only interviewed families who arrived before 9:30 P.M. and did not include those who spoke to me first and those who fell outside the study's sampling frame.

Before starting each interview, I introduced myself to the family as an EAU monitor for the Coalition for the Homeless. I told them I was doing a study of the services families receive at EAUs and welfare centers as well as of some of their income, housing, and health problems. I gave them my card, told them that I do not work for the city, and that I would not take their names. I also told them that although I am not an expert on EAU services, I would try to answer any questions they might have during the interview, or later if they called me collect at the number on my card.[7] The long-form questionnaire documented the age and gender of all family members, where they had slept the night before, their brief work and housing histories, the conditions in the most recent double-up in which they stayed for at least a month, any professionally diagnosed medical problems, and pregnancy. In 1991 I interviewed 202 families using the long-form questionnaire. Analysis of this interview data is the basis for the findings in this essay.

FINDINGS

Findings from my 1991 research are summarized here according to different types of domestic functions.

Domestic Function 1: Providing Family Subsistence. Ninety-four percent of the homeless families in the 1991 study were receiving or applying for public assistance. In one-third of the double-ups, both the host and guest units were on public assistance. If the parent(s) in the guest units were over twenty-one and did not do all of their food shopping and preparation with the host units, they were eligible for full benefits and a claim case of their own (Table 4.1). Nine percent of the guest units in double-ups were put on the host unit's welfare case incorrectly and therefore received lower basic welfare grants than they were entitled to. Twenty-seven percent did not have their own food stamp cases. Half were added to their hosts' cases incorrectly. Twenty-seven percent did not receive the public assistance shelter allowances they were eligible for and that would have enabled them to contribute to the rent their hosts paid the landlord. Nevertheless, most of the guest units gave their hosts money for rent (92 percent), and 45 percent paid more than half the rent paid to the landlord. Only 64 percent of the guest units who received public assistance and paid rent had a room of their own in the double-up.

Domestic Function 2: Providing Stable Family Shelter. In 1991 only 29 percent of the EAU families were asking the city for emergency shelter for the first time; the others had all asked at least once before. Figure 4.1 indicates where families who were new to the system had slept the night before I interviewed them; most had

Table 4.1
Benefits for 45 Homeless Guest Families, Where Both the Guest and Host Units in Double-ups Receive Public Assistance

Benefit	Yes (%)	No (%)	N.A.	Family Did Not Know (%)	Total
Public assistance basic grant for food and other	87	13[a]	0	0	100
Food stamps	73	27[b]	0	0	100
Public assistance shelter grant	44	27	11[c]	18	100

[a]Nine percent received lower benefits than they should have, because they were put on the host unit's basic grant incorrectly; that is, the guest unit parent(s) were over 21, and the two units' families did not food shop and cook together. Four percent of the guest units were put on the host's cases correctly because they did food shop and cook together.
[b]Half were put on the hosts' cases incorrectly for the reasons given in *a*; half were put on the hosts' cases correctly.
[c]Inapplicable because the host family's shelter grant paid the entire rent.

slept in double-ups (78 percent), and fewer families than in 1989 and 1990 had ever had apartments of their own (Action Research Project on Hunger, Homelessness, and Family Health 1989, 1990, 1991).

More than half had stayed in double-ups two or more times before first seeking emergency shelter from the city; the range was one to five-or-more times. These

Figure 4.1
Where 100 Homeless Families Slept the Night before They Sought Emergency Shelter in 1991

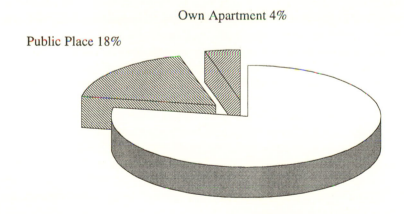

Own Apartment 4%

Public Place 18%

Double-up 78%

findings show how critical and unstable a resource double-ups were for families trying to avoid the shelter system. Of the families who came back for the second or more time, greater than half came from the double-ups where they had previously sought to escape the discomforts and deprivations of the shelter system (Action Research Project on Hunger, Homelessness and Family Health 1991; Newman 1991; Powell 1991). Other returnees slept in short-term hotel or overnight shelter placements or in public places—for example, abandoned buildings, subway cars, parks, hospital waiting rooms, public offices, railway and bus stations, hallways, or in the street. As one mother recounted, "We rented a room in a friend's apartment, but they needed the space. Our baby was crying, and they had to go to work." Another young mother described her dilemma: "At my grandparents' there were seven people in three rooms. They let me and the baby stay, but my husband had to sleep in the hallway. Two people on the 13th floor gave us blankets and a pillow, and I brought him half of my dinner when they fed me." The hosts in more than half the double-ups were relatives; one-third were friends; almost one-tenth of the families rented rooms in the apartments of strangers (Table 4.2).

Domestic Function 3: Adult Sexual Intercourse. The EAU families were asked if they had a room of their own in the double-up, if the parent(s) had their own bed, and if the mother's mate could "stay over" (Table 4.3). Less than half the families had their own rooms (40 percent), and less than half the parents had their own beds (45 percent). Those without rooms usually slept on the living room couch or floor. Almost half the parents slept with one or more of the children (45 percent). Slightly more than half the mothers with mates were able to include them in the doubled-up living arrangement (56 percent). However, several volunteered the following explanations: "Sometimes he could come"; "He could visit but not spend the night"; "We had to go in the hallway"; and, "I preferred not to have him visit."

Domestic Function 4: Providing Family Nutrition. A further perspective on domestic life is gained by examining the ability of doubled-up families to meet their

Table 4.2
Primary Tenants for Doubled-up Family Guest Units

Primary Tenant	n	%
Friend	49	33
Relative		
Mother	47	32
Other[a]	40	26
Rented room	13	9
TOTAL FAMILIES	149	100

[a]Aunt (N=12), grandparent (N=8), mother-in-law (N=5), sister (N=5), brother (N=4), cousin (N=3), father (N=2), uncle (N=1)

Table 4.3
Privileges for 145 Doubled-up Family Guest Units

Activity	Yes (%)	No (%)	Total (%)
Family had own room	40	60	100
Parent(s) had own bed	45	55	100
Mother could include mate	56	44[a]	100

[a]27 percent of the mothers did not have mates.

Table 4.4
Cooking and Eating Privileges for 129 Doubled-up Family Guest Units

Activity	Yes (%)	No (%)	Total (%)
Able to store own food	80	20	100
Able to cook	86	14	100
Able to eat together as a family	74[a]	26	100

[a]Fifteen percent of guest units cooked and ate with the host unit who in almost every instance was a relative.

members' nutritional needs (see Table 4.4). Most of the families could cook (86 per cent), but some only with difficulty. The mother of a two-month-old son reported that each time she had to ask the host: "Can I use your stove? Can I use the refrigerator?" Another mother responded, "She's funny about people in her kitchen. She might let me heat the baby's formula, but nothing for me." Somewhat fewer families were able to store their own food (80 percent), and fewer still could eat meals together as a family (74 percent). As one mother of two observed of her own mother with whom they lived, "She takes something of mine, but she doesn't like it if I take something of hers." The mother of a five-month-old daughter reported, "There was never a question of 'my own food.' If she was hungry, she took what she wanted. She has an addiction, so she doesn't buy food. I was buying for everyone in the house." These findings suggest that doubled-up parents often had difficulty fulfilling their families' nutritional needs.

Domestic Function 5: Interactions with the Outside Community. Doubled-up families were asked if they could receive mail and use the telephone—that is, carry out two important activities associated with maintaining sources of income in a complex society (employment, unemployment benefits, public assistance social security, supplemental security income, etc. [Table 4.5]). More than one-fifth of the doubled-up families could not receive mail. Others had problems keeping their mail private, reporting: "Sometimes they opened it"; "She'll look at it before I get it"; "Yes, but they go into it. My mother said she sent me some money, but I didn't get it." Only 40 percent of the families could count on using the telephone. They

Table 4.5
Communication Privileges for 144 Doubled-up Family Guest Units

Activity	Yes (%)	No (%)	Sometimes (%)	Had own (%)	Total (%)
Able to receive mail	77	23	0	0	100
Able to use the telephone	38	52	7	2	99[a]

[a]Total does not equal 100 because of rounding.

reported: "I could use it if I asked"; "I could've, but I didn't"; "I didn't even try to use it"; "It was a problem. They said I used it too much for $40"; "Only at night, so I couldn't call my welfare worker"; "She makes sure she answers it, so she knows who's calling me. We had arguments about it"; "I could use it but not give the number out."

Of the primary reasons families gave for leaving the most recent double-up in which they had stayed at least a month, overcrowding was most frequent (61 percent) (Table 4.6). One mother with two adolescent children had been staying in her mother's three-room apartment with eight other people. She remarked, "Mothers always want to be there, but I didn't want to take her out of her own bed." A couple with four children stayed a month in the father's aunt's three-room apartment where four other people also lived. They reported, "When her husband came home, we had to take the kids out until he went to sleep. Sometimes he just stayed home and we couldn't go back." In 27 percent of the overcrowded double-ups, the arrival of a new baby increased the stress of overcrowding to the breaking point. The mother of a newborn who had lived with five other people in four rooms also reported, "The house looked dirty; it was not a place I wanted to keep my baby in." In 7 percent of the double-ups, drug use exacerbated the overcrowding.

In 1989, 74 percent of the doubled-up families studied by the Action Research Project lived in "very crowded" conditions, defined by the city as 1.5 or more persons per room (Stegman 1993). Two years later, in 1991, 88 percent of the double-ups in the same research had 1.5 or more persons per room. These findings supported the city's 1991 Housing Vacancy Survey finding that severe crowding in New York City housing had increased: by 69 percent since 1987 and 144 percent since 1978!

Families also left double-ups for other reasons than overcrowding. Forty-six families (26 percent) gave equally substantial reasons for being unable to remain in them. Only 12 percent gave reasons that might have been reversed by financial assistance or mediation, as suggested by the following: "We could not pay"; "There was a conflict and the threat of violence"; "They put us out"; "She was mentally ill"; "We can't impose." Only two families volunteered reasons which suggested they were seeking emergency shelter as a means of obtaining a city-owned apartment. These findings show that the doubled-up families suffered severe hardship

Table 4.6
Primary Reasons Guest Unit Families Did Not Stay in Double-ups

Reason	n	%
Too crowded[a]	106	61
(2 or more persons per room	[50]	
3 or more persons per room	[43]	
Also new baby	[29]	
Also drugs)	[7]	
"The landlord said we couldn't stay."	16	9
Primary tenant evicted	9	5
"We could not pay."	7	4
Conflict/threat of violence	6	3
Primary tenant moved	5	3
"They put us out."	5	3
Drugs	5	3
"They have relatives coming back."	3	2
Fire	2	1
"CWA[b] will take her children if we stay."	1	
"She's getting her kids back from foster care."	1	
"I could get my other kids back if I had my own place."	1	2
Member of host family mentally ill	1	
No gas or electricity	1	
Alcoholism	1	
"We can't impose."	1	
"I want my own place."	1	3
TOTAL FAMILIES	172	99[c]

[a]In many of the households there were two or three persons per room (N=50 and N=43, respectively). Included are households in which the reason secondary to crowding was the arrival of a new baby (N=29) or the presence of drugs (N=7).
[b]The Child Welfare Agency which administers foster care.
[c]Total does not equal 100 because of rounding.

trying to provide their children with adequate, stable shelter before they sought emergency help from the city.

The doubled-up families were also asked what would have to be different for them to stay in their most recent double-up (Table 4.7). Only twenty-three families (14 percent) might have remained if, for example, the following had occurred: domestic disagreements had been successfully mediated (fourteen families); they had received public assistance (seven families); if there had been a stove (one family); and if the electrical services were restored (one family).

The above findings support the conclusion that the city's policy of trying to send homeless families back to double-ups was not a permanent solution to their problem; analysis of the data in Tables 4.6 and 4.7 suggests *why*. The research also

Table 4.7
What Would Have to Have Changed for 159 Guest Unit Families to Remain in the Double-up

Required Change	n
If there had been more space	68
(If I had my own room.	
If my sister hadn't come back with her five children.	
If we had our own room and been able to cook.	
If she didn't have family coming to stay.)	
If it had not been impossible.	15
If I hadn't had the baby.	12
(If my baby didn't cry so much.)	
If the landlord had let us stay.	7
If we had received all our public assistance.	7
If they had not been evicted.	5
If we got along.	14
(If she had wanted us to stay there.	
If she had let me be a woman.	
If my mother were not there.	
If I got along with my mother.	
If she hadn't wanted my whole check.	
If he had wanted me to stay.	
If we could have gotten along.	
If my brother were out. We fight over the food stamps.)	
We're all on the same case.	
(If there hadn't been all those men around my daughter.	
If my stepfather had not tried to rape me.)	
If they weren't using drugs.	5
(If only it were me and her and the kids and no drugs.)	
If they hadn't moved.	4
If my name was on the lease.	4
If my mother was off alcohol.	3
If CWA[a] had not said we had to leave or they would take the children.	
If there had not been a fire.	2
If CWA hadn't been checking on her.	1
If my mother had not been so ill.	1
If my grandmother had not died.	1
If there had been a stove.	1
If there had been electricity.	1
If it wasn't only temporary.	1
If I could have had privacy.	1
If I had wanted to live in somebody else's home.	1
If I did not want my own apartment.	1
If there were some other way to get an apartment.	1
TOTAL	30

[a]Child Welfare Agency

showed that diverting families back to double-ups did not work, except temporarily when families applying to the system for the first time accepted a modest food allowance as an incentive to remain doubled-up for one or two weeks longer before entering city shelters. The city also failed to comply with the law that families be placed in shelters by at least 8:00 A.M. the day after they applied and in the same neighborhoods where they had lived before so as not to disrupt their personal networks and school, work, and clinic schedules.

SUMMARY AND RECOMMENDATIONS

Recommendation 1. The U.S. government should support the United Nations effort to recognize housing as a basic human right.

Recommendation 2. Federal and state governments should adjust public assistance payments to the Consumer Price Index, as with other forms of entitled income. This recommendation arises from the finding of this study that most homeless, doubled-up families were subsisting on a basic public assistance grant for food and all expenses other than rent and medical costs, a grant that had increased only 56 percent between 1969 and 1991. This modest increase could not keep pace with the almost 300 percent rise in the Consumer Price Index for the New York metropolitan region during the same time period. In addition, the public assistance shelter allowance was only half the amount needed to rent an apartment in the very expensive private market in New York City.

Recommendation 3. Federal and state governments should better fulfill their responsibility to oversee the administration of local public assistance programs, and local administrators should provide families with all the entitlements for which they are legally eligible. Findings from this study show that almost half of the doubled-up guest units did not receive the correct basic public assistance grants, food stamps, or shelter allowances. Almost all of them gave some money to their host units for rent, often more than half the monthly amounts these units paid to their landlords. In return, many did not even have their own room in the double-up.

Recommendation 4. Homelessness prevention programs at all levels of government should recognize unstable, doubled-up living as a form of homelessness. Section 8 rent subsidies should be available to all who are eligible, and federal funding for the construction of new, subsidized, low-income housing should be restored to previous levels. This study supports these recommendations. Most of the families in this research had never had their own apartments, and more than half had stayed in two or more double-ups before applying to the city for emergency shelter.

Recommendation 5. Public health and housing authorities at all levels of government should evaluate the significance for family health and child development of the overcrowding and lack of privacy experienced by homeless families who live doubled-up. Findings from this study show that less than half the doubled-up families had a room of their own. The mates of more than half the doubled-up mothers were also present, but less than half had their own beds.

Recommendation #6. Public health officials at all levels of government should assess the impact on family health of inadequate nutritional provisions for over-crowded, doubled-up families. In the present study, many of the homeless guest units had difficulty cooking or could not cook at all. Others could not store their own food or eat together as a family. The federal government should also enact a system of universal health care and immediately undertake a national assessment of the prevalence of malnutrition among the homeless. This should include those who live doubled-up, those on public assistance, and those working for the mini-mum wage.

Recommendation #7. Federal and state governments should exercise their over-sight role more effectively by helping welfare recipients obtain the postal and phone services they require to maintain work, school, clinic, and other appointment schedules in a complex society. This recommendation follows from findings in this study that more than 20 percent of the doubled-up guest units could not receive mail and 30 percent lacked access to a phone.

Recommendation #8. Public housing and public health authorities at all levels of government should enforce existing health and housing codes in public and private housing. Local governments should develop and employ a risk profile based on these codes to determine in home visits which individual double-ups are ad-equate for healthy family life and for how long. They should also provide public assistance payments, food stamps, and support services to the other families living in the same double-up when the assessment process finds them eligible. This study revealed that it was sometimes the inability of both the guest and the host units to pay, or pay enough, that forced them both to leave their double-ups and seek emergency shelter from the city.

CONCLUSION

The findings from this study demonstrate that many impoverished homeless families forced to stay in overcrowded doubled-up conditions are unable to act in the domestic sphere in accordance with the prevailing norms of mainstream U.S. society. They cannot afford to rent their own homes because the purchasing power of the minimum wage and public assistance payments have not kept up with infla-tion. Regardless of family size and the ages of their children, doubled-up guest units have no, or at most one, room of their own in which to live. Many parents lack their own beds, and most slept with their children whether or not the husband or father was present. A substantial proportion of doubled-up families can not store their food, cook, or eat their meals together as a family.

Overcrowding was by far the most frequent reason families are forced to leave double-ups, and almost all their other reasons for leaving were similarly nonnego-tiable. Many doubled-up families have no access to the accepted forms of commu-nication for interacting with the outside community of work, school, health care, and their personal networks.

In response to prevailing economic, social, and political conditions, doubled-up homeless families were forced to develop alternative domestic structures and modes of functioning that they could not sustain permanently. Furthermore, doubled-up families were unable to maintain the other stable groupings and relationships required to ensure their continued participation in mainstream American life. Also because of the city's faulty administration of social services and the emergency shelter system, families who request emergency shelter are not placed in their former communities where they could maintain their previous ties as required by law. As a result, families who lack stable housing of their own are unable to sustain the social relationships and groupings on which their participation in mainstream American life would have to be based.

The recommendations that flow from this study are based in part on the social theory of vertical linkages in complex societies between forces operating both in the larger society and in local events. For example, federal policy and actions, or non-actions, related to the minimum wage and to public assistance and subsidized housing programs influence the behavior of homeless and doubled-up families in New York City. The absence of federal support for low-income housing and inadequate federal oversight of the administration of social programs can strongly affect the conduct of those programs and the personal decisions of impoverished families at state and city levels.

NOTES

1. The Action Research Project on Hunger, Homelessness, and Family Health is supported by the Foundation for Child Development, the Edna McConnell Clark Foundation, J.P. Morgan & Co., Incorporated, the New York Community Trust, the Olive Bridge Fund, and the 1990 Josephine Shaw Lowell Award of the Community Service Society.

2. The cultural materialist approach distinguishes between mental and behavioral events and usually involves two kinds of methods: one capturing the perspective of the informant, the other that of the observer. In the first, or "emic," approach, the observer uses logical concepts and distinctions that are meaningful and appropriate to the informants; in the second, "etic," approach, the observer uses concepts and distinctions suited to the community of scientific observers (Dehavenon 1995; Harris 1983; Lett 1990).

3. The Bronx, Brooklyn, and Manhattan are the boroughs of New York City with the highest rates of unemployment, poverty, and family homelessness.

4. In 1991 I testified as expert witness in two cases brought on behalf of homeless families by the Legal Aid Society in the Supreme Court of New York State. First, in *Jiggetts v. Perales*, findings from my research were introduced in support of an increase in the public assistance shelter allowance. As of March 1996, the court's subsequent favorable ruling had enabled 30,000 families to remain in apartments from which they would have otherwise been evicted for nonpayment of rents above the allowance. In the second case, *McCain v. Koch*, other findings from the study were credited with having contributed substantially to the same court's ruling New York City in contempt of court in 1992 and 1996—when the

Project's annual report on the experiences of homeless families was entered into the court record—for denying homeless families emergency shelter and leaving them overnight at the EAUs. As a result of the first of these rulings, these families eventually received more than 5 million dollars in court ordered fines.

5. Twice I substituted Tuesdays for Mondays: on Martin Luther King's Birthday in January, and in August when a hurricane struck.

6. January through March, I left the Bronx EAU by 12:30 A.M. April through May, I stayed at the Brooklyn EAU until 1 A.M. By July and August, the system was so backed-up in the Manhattan EAU that I remained there until between 6:45 A.M. and 11:35 A.M. the next morning to fulfill the requirements of the research methodology.

7. Before beginning the questionnaire, I completed a public assistance budgeting worksheet developed by Legal Aid with each family I interviewed to ascertain if they knew about and were receiving the following: (a) the correct public assistance grant for a family the size of theirs, and (b) the special grants for families in the shelter system. New York state's public assistance payment consists of two grants: one for basic needs (for example, food, clothing, furniture, utilities, transportation and so forth) and one for shelter. The federal food stamp allotment is designed as a supplement to the food budget in the basic needs grant. Upon finishing the budgeting form, I gave it to the family, along with a copy of the Legal Aid Homeless Family Rights Project's booklet, *Homeless Families: Know Your Rights.*

5

A Home By Any Means Necessary: Government Policy on Squatting in the Public Housing of a Large Mid-Atlantic City

Andrew H. Maxwell

Maxwell demonstrates the coercive but ineffective approach of a highly urbanized, East Coast government housing authority toward squatters in public housing. The government views squatters as violating the sanctity of property and thus as "pathological" and a threat to the existing social order. The police vandalize squatters' belongings when they make evictions, and they engage in other brutalities as well. Behind these actions lie poor management, political patronage, and the fiscal advantages of maintaining empty apartments that remain subsidized by the federal government. Maxwell recommends that the federal Department of Housing and Urban Development (HUD) stop allocating public housing subsidies on a per-unit basis, subsidize only occupied units, and not evict squatters automatically.

INTRODUCTION

This chapter explores aspects of municipal and federal government policy that contribute to squatting in the public housing projects of a large mid-Atlantic city. The "Mid-Atlantic Redevelopment and Housing Authority" (MARHA)—a pseudonym—is the agency responsible for constructing and managing "Mid-Atlantic City's" public housing. It is bound by the basic HUD requirement of providing "decent, safe, and sanitary" shelter for people who meet specified income qualifications. MARHA has been unable to fulfill this requirement. It has consistently ranked among the worst local agencies in providing adequate shelter. For example, MARHA's public housing ranks behind Detroit and East St. Louis, with roughly a third of the apartment units vacant. The dimensions of the vacancy problem come into even sharper focus when Mid-Atlantic City's estimated thirteen thousand homeless people are taken into account.

There is a cruel irony in the relationship between HUD and MARHA. Ironically, federal policy encourages local authorities to keep apartments empty. The housing shortage precipitated by the HUD policy—combined with such political and economic factors as increased unemployment, a rise in home foreclosures, and the crisis in low-income housing—have contributed to the emergence of squatters throughout Mid-Atlantic City's public housing.[1] Some people circumvent MARHA procedures by squatting. Unlike many people, squatters fail to follow the legal route of adding their names to a waiting list, to procure housing.

This chapter describes several forms of squatting as adaptations to the low-income housing crisis in Mid-Atlantic City. It discusses how and why MARHA systematically deprives people of housing by maintaining vacancies when the demand for apartments far exceeds the supply, and it offers recommendations for changes in public housing policy.

A Public Housing Population Profile

Most MARHA public housing tenants are working-class people with very low incomes, and members of either racial or ethnic minority groups. The majority are African-American. Of this group, most are native to the United States, primarily "Mid-Atlantic State" but also some southern states. A minority of the African-American tenants come from various parts of the Caribbean. There is a sizable Spanish-speaking population, the majority of which are U.S.-born Puerto Ricans. The Spanish-speaking group includes recent immigrants from Puerto Rico and smaller numbers of Dominicans. European ethnic groups, such as Italian, Greek, and Irish, constitute a minority in public housing.

Family types include the nuclear family and (most commonly) the single-parent, female-headed family. Although rare, there are also male-headed, single-parent families. Extended family households might be expected to be more common, given the low incomes of project residents, but federal housing policy dictates that elderly persons should be housed in separate projects. Roughly one-quarter of the tenants are working poor people who pay rent that MARHA considers reasonable, i.e., a rent based on a sliding scale matched to income. Depending on the amount of their incomes, some employed residents can pay market-level rents.

Approximately 73 percent of all tenant families rely on some form of public assistance as their only income. In many instances, assistance payments are augmented by informal, sometimes illicit, economic activities. For example, the destruction of project property that MARHA officials point to as wanton vandalism is often actually a source of income. On a number of occasions I observed teenage boys stealing appliances and copper tubing from vacant apartments or brass fire hose fixtures from standpipes in the hallways; they promptly sold these items to nearby appliance stores and salvage yards.

Squatting Strategies

Some of the strategies for occupying apartment units in Mid-Atlantic City conform to the standard criteria of "squatting" in that they involve the illicit seizure and occupation of public living space by individuals or groups. Squatting most often occurs in societies undergoing industrialization and the resulting processes of urbanization and migration of rural peasants to the cities for jobs. Under such circumstances squatting is a solution to the problem of people's need for shelter in new urban settings. Following a takeover of open spaces—in some cases through accretion, in others through highly orchestrated mass invasions—the process of squatting typically entails the construction of homes on the newly occupied sites (e.g., see Brown 1977 on Columbia; Epstein 1972 on Brazil; Mangin 1967b on Peru; Leeds 1969 on Brazil and Peru; Leeds and Leeds 1970 on Brazil and Peru, and 1976 on Brazil, Peru, and Chile). As Mangin points out in the Peruvian case, "Police forces, . . . middle-class and upper-class observers, . . . politicians, . . . conservatives, . . . city planners and architects, . . . newspapers, . . . [and] . . . social workers" (1967b:21) share the view that squatters are disorganized and reprehensible and that the entire process is an aberrant threat to the existing social order.

Squatting occurs periodically in advanced industrial societies and not necessarily as a function of rural-urban migration. However, labor is still a factor in the sense that squatters are typically working-class. They are either unemployed and therefore homeless, or underemployed and therefore unable to obtain housing that meets basic, socially defined human needs. Compared to developing societies, squatting in the United States is now less common and the seizures of property more transient. This was not always the case. Our country's history offers compelling examples of squatting. For example, in Borgos' (1986) discussion of the ACORN squatters movement, he reminds us that squatting on the U.S. frontier was common and accepted. The Homestead Act of 1862 represented government approval of squatting and was an attempt to control it, in that it granted land to people who occupied a parcel of land for at least five years. During the Depression era, there were "Hoovervilles." The 1974 Housing Act contained a homesteading provision. In the 1980s, following the widespread abandonment of private dwellings in inner-city areas and foreclosures on FHA-insured mortgages in the 1970s, working poor people formed the Association of Community Organizations for Reform Now (ACORN). Their members started squatting in vacant structures in cities across the United States (Borgos 1986).[2] During the 1980s and 1990s, as homelessness has grown, so too has squatting by individuals and families. For example, the homeless have formed encampments on heating grates in Washington, D.C., in and around the New York City Port Authority, and in tents in national and state parks. For unemployed people, squatting is still a solution to the fundamental human need for shelter.

The currently illegal status of squatting seems to confirm assumptions held by MARHA officials—who share the views of officials in Peru, Brazil, Columbia, and Chile—that squatters exhibit "pathological" behavior that can be attributed to their lack of mainstream values.[3] Such behavior is therefore claimed to be "disorganized," behavior that violates the sanctity of property. The official bureaucratic view of squatting ignores most studies of squatters, which present evidence of a high degree of organization and internal structure in the establishment of squatter settlements. However, the bureaucratic view is consistent with common social science conceptions of poor people in general (for example, the so-called "underclass" as a recent analytical subset of "the poor") and of homeless people as a sub-subset of the underclass. The stress in these studies on asserted normative versus disorganized behavior is evoked in notions of the "deserving" versus the "undeserving" poor. This conceptualization of the poor is evident in Wirth's notion of urbanism (1938), Lewis' (sub)-culture of poverty (cf. for example 1959, 1970), and Wilson's notions of "underclass," "social isolation," and "concentration effects" (cf. Maxwell 1993).

Theoretical Issues

Convention assumes that poor people lack mainstream values, but they are not thought to have no values at all. Rather, the twofold assumption is (1) that poor people's values, while initially adaptive in dire economic circumstances, subsequently become isolated from initial conditions and serve to keep poor people impoverished—another version being that "pathological" values and behaviors perpetuate poverty (cf. Lewis 1970); and, (2) that poor people's values are fundamentally distinct, stemming as they do from a traditional, folk, or rural context. Both of these assumptions suggest the isolation of poor groups. Epstein has referred to the emphasis on values and rural origins in the squatter literature as the "pathologist-dualist viewpoint" (1972:52).

I will argue that the reasons for inadequate shelter and, therefore, squatting in Mid-Atlantic City are to be found in institutional constraints on individuals and families, specifically the failure of a public bureaucracy to achieve its objective of providing housing for those who cannot afford it in the market. The view taken here is that squatting cannot be explained simply by the motives of those who do it. Squatting is not wholly, or even primarily, an autonomous act. It is systemic. Squatting in Mid-Atlantic City, in particular, flows from and is perpetuated by the policies and actions of local and federal housing officials. Moreover, it is organized behavior, in the sense that it is purposive (Buckley 1967), not random. For people who squat, the goal is shelter.

METHODOLOGY

The gist of the theoretical debate about squatting, and also of the related poverty debate, involves the causal importance of structural, institutional forces of an economic and political nature versus that of individual behavior. My assumption that squatting is caused by institutional forces dictates a methodology that focuses on, for example, bureaucratic policies and procedures that affect impoverished people and which, therefore, may foster squatting. In the final analysis, sociocultural phenomena should be understood as systemic, relational processes and events. Categories like the "underclass" and even "squatters" impede the development of systemic conceptualizations if they are not seen in relational terms. Therefore, the findings presented in this chapter exemplify and emphasize institutional constraints as opposed to the behaviors and attitudes of the individuals and families who squat.

Most of the data contained in this chapter derive from (1) analyses of internal agency documents—for example, memoranda on HUD audits of MARHA, MARHA policy statements, and computerized records of tenant financial and demographic characteristics—and (2) observations made while I was employed by MARHA.

The fact of my employment at MARHA allowed me to witness firsthand the generally deplorable conditions in its public housing, and in particular the vacancy problem and consequent squatting. However, working for MARHA also made it impossible for me to use standard anthropological field techniques to gather information on squatting. For example, I was unable to select informants or develop a relationship with key informants and thus did not have "informants" in the usual sense of the term.[4]

My encounters with individuals and families who were squatting in MARHA apartments occurred in two ways. First, I became aware of people who were squatting as a member of a team from the MARHA Central Office management staff charged with developing an accurate inventory of occupied and unoccupied apartments. The Authority's top management did not know the exact status of the units, partly because project managers were careless, as was MARHA management generally, in keeping track of tenants in their respective projects. As a result of bad publicity in the press and pressure from HUD, MARHA management decided to look more closely at its property.

It was during the inventory that I first encountered people who were illegally occupying apartment units. The team's procedure entailed going from door to door to confirm that people living in an apartment were listed on the Authority's tenant register. Many were not, and they were not alarmed by our discovery of them. For example, a man revealed not only that he was squatting but that he knew of people who had traveled from a nearby city in order to squat in vacant MARHA apartments. His demeanor and casual attitude suggested that the practice was common and sensible. Once the inventory was complete, apartments were categorized as either legally occupied, vacant and welded shut, vacant and open, or occupied by squatters. The MARHA then moved in to evict squatters from illegally occupied units, but not necessarily in order to enable legitimate tenants to occupy the units.

Eviction was my second and most emotionally and physically difficult type of encounter with squatters. During an eviction, the MARHA teams were reconstituted to include two Central Office management staff persons and the project manager; a plumber to turn off the water and cap the pipes and radiators to prevent further use; an electrician to disable electrical outlets; a welder to remove locks, doorknobs, and on our exit, to weld the steel doors to their frames; and usually two uniformed Mid-Atlantic City policemen. In such circumstances, the use of a questionnaire or other formal data gathering tool was out of the question. I relied primarily on on-site, qualitatively grounded observations and non-intrusive questions. Legal tenants in neighboring apartments and project maintenance personnel responded to questions about squatters. Their answers, especially those of maintenance personnel, tended to be biased, often displaying hostility toward squatters. Sensitive to the situation, I also questioned squatters themselves. As one of at most two people in the group who displayed empathy toward the squatters, I was able to engage them briefly in conversation as they watched the eviction process unfold. However, our exchanges took place under conditions of extreme duress.

FINDINGS

Conditions of Public Housing in Mid-Atlantic City and Elsewhere

Conditions in Mid-Atlantic City's public housing projects were at their worst for most of the 1980s. The seven-to-thirteen-story high-rise buildings in most of the projects were improperly maintained. They were structurally sound, but many other problems existed. The exteriors and grounds were in disrepair, the interiors needed paint, elevators did not work, and trash chutes were backed up with garbage—sometimes as high as twelve or thirteen stories! Even trash compactors did not work. Hallway lights were missing; mailboxes, windows, and toilets were broken; and apartments were infested with rats and roaches. With densities as high as a hundred apartment units or 250 bedrooms per acre, these conditions were intolerable for tenants. Fires were rampant. Lacking a workable system for garbage disposal, tenants (especially those on upper floors) gradually started to deposit their trash and garbage in vacant apartments. Either by design or by accident trash-strewn apartments would be set ablaze, covering hallways with soot. MARHA's vacancy rate was the highest in the country one year, approaching 50 percent in some projects, so there was ample opportunity for fires. In that same year, as in the preceding several years, eleven thousand families were on a waiting list to get an apartment. In 1992, approximately 6,500 families were on the waiting list. According to a coalition for low-income housing, many of the families on the authority's list had been waiting for a decade.

It is important to note here that these conditions are atypical of public housing, per se. Although print and television journalists would have us believe that disrepair is the norm—for example, the much-televised Cabrini-Green projects in Chicago, or St. Louis' infamous Pruitt Igoe projects—the reality of public housing in general is quite different. Similar projects in another nearby city are well maintained. In fact, the record for public housing nationally is quite good (cf. Bratt 1986).

In contrast to most cities, where public housing constitutes less than 5 percent of the total housing stock, public housing in Mid-Atlantic City makes up 10 percent of the city's housing stock—the highest proportion for any city in the country. A total tenant population of about twenty-two thousand is housed in two hundred buildings located in twenty-seven separate projects dispersed throughout the city. The projects contain about thirteen thousand apartment units (Table 5.1), over half of which are in high-rise buildings for families. The rest are equally divided between high-rise buildings for the elderly and low-rise buildings for families.[5]

Types of Squatters

Squatting is not a uniform process in Mid-Atlantic City's public housing projects, and squatters are not a unified group. In general, there are two categories of squatters: (1) those who never bothered to follow any of the required procedures to secure public housing, and (2) those who at one time were legitimate tenants. The first group, which I call "hardcore" squatters, is the smaller of the two. They could potentially occupy all or most of the Authority's roughly four thousand vacant units (Table 5.1).[6] However, many of these units are uninhabitable because of extensive damage caused by vandals, or because they are filled with garbage or have been set on fire. The distribution of occupied and unoccupied apartments in a typical project composed of high-rise buildings is nearly equal (Table 5.2).

To some extent the first, "hardcore" group fits the generally accepted image of squatters, and it, in turn, is composed of several subtypes. One subtype consists of people who squat not only, nor even primarily, to secure shelter but to find anonymity in the high-rise buildings. These are people who engage in criminal activities of various kinds; they are mainly petty criminals and drug users, both heroine and crack cocaine addicts.[7] Two other subtypes are unemployed homeless men, and employed people who, victims of deception, believe they are paying rent

Table 5.1
MARHA Totals

Units	1	1 Bedroom	2 Bedrooms	3 Bedrooms	4 Bedrooms	5 Bedrooms	Total
Vacant	324	753	1833	671	250	117	3954
Occupied	687	2501	3499	1823	289	141	8949
Total	1011	3254	5332	2494	539	258	12903
Paying max.	28	292	481	281	32	6	1120
Avg. rent	$81	$94	$105	$123	$129	$128	$105

Source: Mid-Atlantic City Redevelopment and Housing Authority.

Note: The rent figures of course only pertain to occupied units, and they are averages. If these amounts seem low, they must be understood relative to 1983–84, the years in which the statistics were compiled. More important for perspective is that rents must be seen as percentages of average yearly incomes for tenants in specific MARHA categories. These categories and average incomes are as follows: Elderly $5,534, Non-Elderly $6,967, Welfare $4,777, and Non-Welfare $7,317.

Table 5.2
Project 2120

Units	1	1 Bedroom	2 Bedrooms	3 Bedrooms	4 Bedrooms	5 Bedrooms	Total
Vacant	11	111	445	100	11	2	680
Occupied	9	60	449	234	18	8	778
Total	20	171	894	334	29	10	1458
Paying max.	1	3	23	22	2	1	52
Avg. rent	$60	$72	$90	$130	$143	$192	$102

Source: Mid-Atlantic City Redevelopment and Housing Authority.

to the proper authority but are not. Finally, there are employed people who do not pay rent of any kind. The latter two types seem to be composed mostly of families.

It is impossible to get an accurate count of hardcore squatters. The closest I came to some sense of the numerical dimensions of hardcore squatting was during the apartment inventory and subsequent evictions. Even then accurate numbers were hard to come by, because this is a mobile group. New people come in from week to week. Of those who are documented on a given day by an eviction team, and perhaps even evicted, some will shift to other units in the same building or to other buildings. A unit classified as vacant and welded shut on one day could be occupied by squatters the next.

The second, or "tenant," group is by far the largest and is composed of people who were at one time legal tenants but who became squatters at some point and stopped paying rent. They are indicated in "Occupied" units in Tables 5.1 and 5.2. Here, too, accurate numbers are elusive, because of MARHA's spotty record keeping and because people who are officially registered by MARHA as tenants may practice doubling-up.[8] Depending on MARHA's response to their rent being in arrears, some people in the tenant group move out and thereby add to the number of vacant units that can potentially be occupied by hardcore squatters.

MARHA places delinquent tenants in its projects into one of several categories: Moveout, Warrant, Newsuit, and Lockout (Table 5.3). In a sample range of rents that are overdue for at least three months in one project of 778 legally occupied units ("Occupied" in Table 5.2), 372 (roughly 48 percent) have tenants in the over-90-day category who are, therefore, squatting. The figures for this type of squatter are larger when the 0–30-, 30–60-, and 60–90-day categories are included. The over-90 category is most significant because it illustrates the substantial amount of money represented by the unpaid rent. The sums are considerable. For example, the annual rents billed for this entire project total $369,359.24, which, minus the $55,728.07 in collected receipts, leaves $313,631.17 rent outstanding. The outstanding rent for the over-90-day category totals $233,585.32. At another project of similar size and condition, a woman achieved notoriety because she owed in excess

Table 5.3
Delinquency Report: Project 2120

Apt. #	Amount Billed	Total Due	0–30	30–60	60–90	Over 90	Tenant Code
1D	126.00	126.0				126.00	Moveout
2A	611.90	611.90				611.90	Warrent
3E	836.05	836.05	79.00	79.00	79.00	599.05	Newsuit
6C	2569.00	2569.00			224.00	2345.00	Warrent
3D	2984.90	2984.90				2984.90	Warrent Moveout
4A	2531.50	2531.50				2531.50	Lockout Moveout

Source: Mid-Atlantic City Redevelopment and Housing Authority.

of $10,000. This amount had accumulated during a rent strike that lasted five years.

What becomes of this money? How do squatters in this category—and possibly also the hardcore employed squatters—decide to use their money? Many tenants (not all) attempt to save as much as possible. For people with meager incomes, the purchase of necessities like food and clothing are immediate concerns. However, in talking with tenants at projects throughout Mid-Atlantic City, I learned of a commonly used strategy. Many tenants decide that they want to leave public housing for something better. Their goal is a single-family house located in a nearby city. They purposefully withhold and save rent for a down payment on a house.

Eviction of Squatters

A typical eviction took between one-half and three-quarters of an hour. The policemen's behavior was perhaps the most disturbing aspect of the entire event. The police routinely ransacked an apartment. They would steal any belongings of value, such as televisions, stereo systems, or radios. This was most common if the squatter had a police record or an outstanding arrest warrant. Another pattern in police officers' behavior was looking under mattresses for drugs or drug-related paraphernalia. At times, evictees were threatened with violence, especially when the police encountered a felon. He or she was arrested on the spot, often with a spouse and children witnessing the event. The treatment of squatters was insensitive at best; at worst it was a display of institutionalized coercion that bordered at times on brutality.

The official position was that squatters forfeited their individual rights as citizens because they apparently violated property rights. In the end, squatters left with only the belongings they could carry. Some were philosophical; they assumed that in squatting they had risked eventual eviction. With a shrug of her shoulders one woman said simply, "What can you do?" This was a common response as well for those who knew that they would return to collect their possessions. Within the space of several hours, at most a day, the welded apartments were broken into by the previous occupants. Some would gather up their things and move on, often in search of another vacant apartment, while others installed new locks and once again set up housekeeping in the same apartment.

Squatters' responses usually varied according to how much time and money they had spent on fixing up their apartments. All of them went to the expense of installing their own locks. Many apartments were very neat and comfortable. They sparkled with fresh paint, carpets, draperies, modest but solid furniture, and electrical appliances. People with this sort of investment became very agitated, some to the point of crying. They often had to be physically removed. Those who offered the least resistance were destitute men who typically squatted in groups of three or four. They usually had short-term objectives—for example, finding a place to sleep for the night or getting out of the cold in the winter. Still others were incredulous. One man who typified this category of squatters could not understand why he was being evicted. Proffering a "receipt," he declared that he had been paying rent. In fact, he had been paying money, but he was the victim of a common ruse. The person to whom he had given his money was another tenant who had passed himself off as the building manager.

SUMMARY AND RECOMMENDATIONS

Like their counterparts in developing Third World states, MARHA and HUD officials see squatters as people who flout the law and the sanctity of property. Property rights take precedence over human rights in this view; the only appropriate bureaucratic responses involve eviction, locking someone out of his or her apartment, or arrest and presumably imprisonment.

In fact, however, findings show that, although motivated by a common need for shelter, squatters are—like other overlapping groups and categories, such as "the poor" or "the underclass"—not a monolithic group. Squatter behavior tends to vary with the amount of financial resources that squatters are able to garner. The same is true for MARHA public housing tenants in general. Tenants typically engage in a process of self-selection and floor-by-floor segregation. They move about within buildings, without MARHA authorization, to apartments on floors with people of comparable means and similar value orientations. One floor will be clean and occupied by families, including squatters; another will be dirty and largely vacant; and yet another, populated by drug users. Viable policy would acknowledge variations in squatter behavior and reflect these patterns.

The priority should be changing federal and local policy that fosters squatting in the first place. HUD's method of allocating public housing subsidies involves paying local authorities on a per-unit basis. It does not matter whether an apartment unit is occupied. HUD pays each authority a portion of the rent for each of its units; the balance of the rent is paid by the tenant. Taken together, these amounts make up the bulk of an authority's operating budget.

From MARHA's standpoint, therefore, it is profitable to leave units vacant: the agency realizes a "profit" in the sense that a vacant unit does not require expenditures for maintenance. MARHA management typically engages in protracted contract negotiations with unionized labor in an attempt to control, and ideally reduce, maintenance labor costs. Because materials can be used more easily in the patronage network, top management is more flexible in that respect and continues the time-honored custom of purchasing under a system of public bids and contracts. While I was employed by MARHA, HUD contracted with a major accounting firm to conduct an audit of the agency's materials inventory. The MARHA inventories of appliances, paint, plumbing fixtures, and other materials in its main warehouse ran into the millions of dollars, yet tenants in projects were going without these items for years on end. Also, the structural incentive for top management to leave units vacant had been fueled much earlier by inflationary trends in the U.S. economy, for example, the increases in fuel costs after the Middle East oil embargo in 1973. MARHA realized a profit through a reduction in energy costs when there were vacant units.

So, although not a formal policy, it was common practice for MARHA deliberately to maintain a high vacancy rate and thereby encourage squatting by people without shelter. MARHA's policies and maintenance practices also fostered rent delinquency and squatting by tenants who otherwise would have been willing to honor their contractual obligations. Political patronage and the appointment of individuals who were disdainful of tenants and who knew little or nothing about housing to key management posts made the situation much worse during the 1980s and resulted in the conditions described in this chapter.

Recommendation #1. Based on the previous analysis, my first recommendation is that HUD stop its practice of allocating subsidies on a per-unit basis and instead subsidize only occupied units. This change would require strict federal monitoring and enforcement procedures. For MARHA and other housing authorities, a change of this sort would discourage vacancies; there would be no monetary advantage in them. A policy change of this kind would be an incentive to rent apartments to people on waiting lists.

Recommendation #2. A second, related recommendation is for HUD to urge local authorities not to evict squatters automatically. For example, when hardcore squatters pay "rent" to other tenants who pose as managers, they should not be evicted immediately. Instead, local officials should investigate each case to determine whether a person has financial resources sufficient to pay rent, and if not, whether the person qualifies for some other type of shelter subsidy.

Recommendation #3. A third recommendation is for federal policy makers to develop guidelines that require greater flexibility at the local level, especially in instances when indigenous tenant organizations are in place, and in instances that do not involve intentional illegalities—that is, when people are behaving out of necessity in obtaining a basic requirement like shelter. Local agencies would be better able to fulfill the basic HUD requirement of providing "decent, safe, and sanitary" shelter if they were forced by federal guidelines to develop creative solutions to the squatters' very real need for shelter.

Recommendation #4. A final recommendation is for HUD to urge local authorities to avoid expensive, time-consuming, and humiliating eviction and collection tactics. This recommendation concerns the majority of squatters, in various delinquent statuses, and is consistent with the idea of supporting local forms of tenant organization. Federal legislators should consider a policy more in keeping with the spirit of the first Housing Act of 1934. The 1934 Act provided the basis for building public housing and stimulating construction and creating jobs. Public housing was initially envisioned as temporary, inexpensive housing for people who would eventually move into private dwellings. In a post-industrial economy, public housing has become permanent, especially for members of minority groups. A HUD policy predicated on a program that ensures jobs for tenants would facilitate a tenant's transition to the private market and to home purchase. This would be achieved by redirecting the federal government's involvement in the secondary mortgage market to providing support for public housing tenants who are potential home buyers. It should be noted that recommendation #4 is not in line with the provisions of the 1990 Housing Act, which undergird the HOPE (Home-ownership and Opportunities for People Everywhere) Program. With its emphasis on tenant ownership of apartment units, HOPE amounts to a wholesale retreat by the federal government from support of public housing.

CONCLUSION

A change in HUD policy so that subsidies pay only for occupied units appears to be underway at the federal level. However, in 1993 a federal court in Mid-Atlantic City did not support an attempt by the Coalition for Low-Income Housing to make such a change. The regional HUD office was not inclined to make the change either. It allowed MARHA to continue receiving subsidies for vacant units.

Although beyond the scope of this chapter, further analysis of the Mid-Atlantic City case could reveal the ways in which housing agencies affect metropolitan residential patterns, especially with respect to the process of class and ethnic succession in areas beyond the inner city. The case presented here suggests other lines of inquiry that could serve to elaborate a middle-range model of policy development and implementation with respect to housing authorities and their impact on local economies.

NOTES

1. See Dehavenon in this volume for a discussion of U.S. economic trends over the last two decades, including deindustrialization and recession, and how these macroeconomic processes precipitated the crisis in affordable housing and homelessness.

2. Borgos also notes that, in response to vacancies, an ACORN group temporarily squatted in a public housing project in Jacksonville, Florida (1986:439). This is the only reference to squatting in public housing that I have found.

3. Regrettably, the pernicious term "pathology" is too often used uncritically by social scientists and policy makers alike in discussions of poverty. The term invokes a fallacious use of the biological analogy, reifies a supposedly dysfunctional segment of society, and thus reinforces the belief that poor people and squatters are separated from the rest of society and therefore solely responsible for their state.

4. As used here, "key informant" refers to an individual who is trained by an anthropologist "to conceptualize cultural data in the frame of reference employed by the anthropologist" (Pelto 1970:95).

5. The total number of units is somewhat lower now as a result of the demolition of four buildings at one project site. These buildings contained 816 apartments. Following the example of the infamous Pruitt-Igoe housing complex in St. Louis, MARHA officials planned to demolish five thousand units, but they were stopped by tenant protests.

6. The rent figures in Table 5.1, of course, pertain only to occupied units, and they are averages. If these amounts seem very low, they must be understood as relating to 1983–1984, the years in which the statistics were compiled. More important for perspective is the point that rents must be understood as percentages of average incomes for tenants in specific MARHA categories. These categories and average incomes are as follows: Elderly, $5,534; Non-Elderly, $6,967; Welfare, $4,777; and Non-Welfare, $7,317.

7. Petty criminals tend to congregate in the project closest to another large city. In fact, they live in one building. I became aware of this on a visit to the project when the manager invited me to accompany him while he looked into a problem in the building. As we entered the building the manager drew a pistol from his hip pocket. In response to my question about the pistol he explained to me, in a very matter-of-fact manner, that it was common knowledge that thieves lived in the building.

8. See Dehavenon's and Bolger's articles in this volume for discussions of doubling-up.

6

Huts for the Homeless: A Low-Technology Approach for Squatters in Atlanta, Georgia

Amy Phillips and Susan Hamilton

Phillips and Hamilton write about the success of a low-cost housing program in Atlanta, Georgia. The Mad Housers and the homeless collaborated in a type of covert activity to build low-cost homes—"huts"—which challenged existing property laws. The ingenuity of both the volunteers and the hut dwellers is seen in their choice of concealed sites, their use of low-technology solutions, and their effective manipulation of the press. Recommendations are for more federal funding for single room occupancy and transitional housing.

INTRODUCTION

Early in 1987, two architecture students from the Georgia Institute of Technology were researching the shelter options of Atlanta's homeless. They found many people living in cardboard boxes and makeshift plastic tents in isolated pockets of the city's industrial areas, which they chose in preference to the crowded night shelters that many homeless consider unsafe. After discussions with these people, the architecture students realized that they could improve on the boxes and tents by building low-cost, sturdy, plywood huts. A few friends were recruited, and on Saturdays the group began to prefabricate huts of their own design, using mostly scrap materials. Under cover of darkness, they moved the huts to sites chosen by their new owners and erected them quickly. Within an hour or so, the occupants had moved in, and the "guerrilla carpenters" were celebrating their latest construction project and planning the next week's work. These volunteers, all of whom had middle-class jobs, began calling themselves the "Mad Housers," a name reflecting their anger at the plight of the homeless, their willingness to use radical means to address the problem, and a pun on the "Mad Hatter" in Lewis Carroll's *Alice in Wonderland.*

One of the authors of this chapter, Amy Phillips, is a charter member of the Mad Housers. Her initial involvement began at the first organizational meeting in early

Table 6.1
Time Spent by Core Volunteer on Mad Houser Activities, per Week

Activity	Time Spent (in hours)
Meetings	3
Low-income meetings	3
Building sessions	8
Aftercare	3
Scrap material retrieval	4
Media contacts	4
Purchase and/or pickup of new materials	2
TOTAL	27

1987 and continued on a full-time basis through June 1992. Since then, employment as a contract archaeologist in other locations has changed Amy's schedule so that she contributes to the Mad Housers on a more sporadic basis. She is involved full-time when she is in Atlanta and keeps in close contact with the current members. In addition to being a Mad Houser volunteer, Amy has served as an officer of the Mad Housers (corporate secretary 1988–1990, executive director 1991) and a member of the board of directors (1988–1992). See Table 6.1 for the time spent weekly on various Mad Houser activities.

Susan Hamilton, the other author, was limited in her ability to work directly with the Mad Housers by her residence in Syracuse and fieldwork in Argentina. However, during visits to Atlanta, her former home, in 1988, 1989, 1990, and 1994, she has participated in hut-building sessions, organizational meetings, aftercare visits, and site-selection trips. Phillips and Hamilton have collaborated on Mad Houser research and writing since 1988.

Atlanta's Homeless

Atlanta, a metropolis whose 1990 population approached a million and a half, has about fifteen thousand people who lack housing, according to the Atlanta Task Force for the Homeless, a nonprofit organization of advocates and service providers. This figure represents an estimate of homeless individuals in the shelter system and outside it, and of the proportion who have family members with them. In the metropolitan area there are eighty sheltering facilities, almost a third of which charge a fee (Atlanta Task Force for the Homeless 1990). During winter 1989–1990, more than 3,200 beds were available nightly.

Since the incidence of homelessness increased in the 1980s and 1990s, a variety of nonprofit organizations—e.g., the National Coalition for the Homeless, the Atlanta Task Force for the Homeless, Cafe 458—have attempted to alleviate the causes and conditions of homelessness. The Mad Housers were incorporated as a non-profit, tax-exempt 501(c)3 organization in April 1988 and recently received foundation status with the Internal Revenue Service. Three features of the Mad Housers program make it unusual: (1) the application of "low technology" solutions to the lack of housing; (2) the fact that it has remained a volunteer effort; and (3) the organization's informal, participatory nature, which fosters the development of cooperating communities among its clients living in the huts and of social networks among clients and Mad Houser volunteers.

The shelter system in Atlanta gives priority to homeless families with children, although the men are often lodged separately. The few single-room occupancy (SRO) hotels primarily serve adult homeless without children; 90 percent of the SRO units that existed in Atlanta in 1960 are now gone (Georgia Residential Finance Authority 1990:26), lost to the development of office buildings and parking lots. In September 1988 the waiting list for public housing in the metro area was over 5,800 families; the Atlanta Housing Authority estimates that if waiting lists were opened to all who qualify, they would exceed ten thousand applicants (City of Atlanta 1989). A 1990 study by the Federal Home Loan Bank Board found more than fourteen thousand empty apartments in Atlanta—with thousands in housing complexes but in default on loans. The Atlanta Task Force for the Homeless (1988) found that fair market rent for a two-bedroom apartment almost equals the monthly earnings of a person working full-time at the minimum wage.

During the Depression of the 1930s, shantytowns such as Hoover City in Brooklyn sprang up, housing as many as six hundred people in one place (Crouse 1986:100–101). The willingness and ability of squatters to live in areas that initially lack a basic urban infrastructure (running water, electricity, sewage disposal) does not signify that these people are indifferent to such amenities or that their real or presumed rural background makes them prefer spartan living. In fact, the evolution of many squatter communities in Latin America has shown that their residents continue to lobby public officials for the extension of urban services and transportation links to their neighborhoods, while individual families make improvements to their houses as resources allow (Mangin 1967a; Lobo 1982; Burns 1987).

Since Atlanta's social service agencies give priority to finding emergency housing for homeless families with children, the clients who come to the Mad Housers are frequently single men and women who have been on the streets for a long time. Mad Houser clients have been consistently and evenly distributed among three categories of homeless people defined by the Atlanta Task Force for the Homeless: (1) the chronic homeless, who have been on the streets for at least thirty consecutive days; (2) the situational homeless, who are temporarily without shelter due to a life crisis; and (3) the episodic homeless, alternating between short periods of homelessness and regular housing.

Relatively few of the squatters are natives of Atlanta. Many homeless come to Atlanta from other areas, drawn by the availability of social services for the homeless, the city's location at the hub of transportation systems, and a climate that is warm for seven or eight months of the year. In the 1970s, when the economy was stronger, Sunbelt cities drew many people seeking work.

Substantive Issues and Theoretical Focus

This chapter describes the Mad Houser program and focuses on one community of people living in a cluster of huts. Three principal issues are addressed. First, we address squatting in prefabricated huts as a response to the housing shortage. With the addition of simple stoves, this program has been replicated in Chicago, New York City, and Cincinnati, among other cities. Second, we address the development of communities and social networks among people living in the huts. Third, we describe the participatory nature of the project and its role in enhancing self-esteem. It becomes apparent that the definitions of "homelessness" are highly variable. The Mad Houser clients may lack conventional housing, but they effectively control their privacy through ownership of a hut, and this affects both their self-image and their public presentation. Some hut dwellers play important roles in the volunteer organization, especially in identifying and recruiting new clients. The Mad Housers accord all of the homeless a respect that they do not invariably receive from society at large.

Our theoretical approach in the Mad Housers research primarily calls on models of the social use of space (Buttimer and Seamon 1980; Duncan 1976) and of the meanings assigned to the constructed environment (Rapoport 1982; Pellow 1981). Homelessness is much more than the simple absence of shelter from the elements; it involves a fundamental lack of privacy, a curtailed capacity for expressing one's self-image and social relations, and a loss of self-sufficiency. Likewise, the process of taking possession of one's own shelter, even rudimentary shelter, signifies a new set of relationships with society, the natural landscape, and the built environment.

The literature on social networks among U.S. homeless is contradictory. Giamo (1989) describes interactions among homeless men in the Bowery district, and Rivlin and Imbimbo (1989) emphasize the extensive social interactions within a small self-help squatter community in New York City, and also between it and nonresidents. Rowe (1989) and Rowe and Wolch (1990) have done research on homeless networks in Los Angeles. However, most other writing on homelessness pays scant attention to the topic. In a book section titled "Resources of the Homeless," Wright compares a group of homeless men in Chicago with a sample of very poor General Assistance clients and concludes, "Kin and friendship networks provide the most important line of defense against literal homelessness for the extremely poor; the homeless are those among the extremely poor for whom this defense has failed" (Wright 1989:86). He apparently regards social ties and other resources as coming only from outside, from those who are not homeless.

Management and Cost Effectiveness of Mad Houser Activities

The Mad Housers have constituted a volunteer organization that from the beginning had a shoestring budget. Most of the dozen core members did not know one another before they started building huts. Although they have developed a strong sense of camaraderie that extends to other facets of their lives, they continue to hold divergent social and political opinions. One Mad Houser commented, "The only thing we agree on is building huts." Meetings, held biweekly at a tavern, are open to anyone interested in helping out. Committees are in charge of lining up new clients, finding building materials, identifying sites for the huts, handling publicity, and providing aftercare for the hut dwellers.

The Aftercare Committee attempts to follow through with services to clients. Its members visit the huts on Sundays, sometimes bringing donated food, clothes, or reading materials, and check on the condition of the structures. Although Mad Housers are not professional social workers, they try to refer their clients to appropriate agencies and assist them in obtaining services. For example, on one occasion the organization certified that it had built a hut on a specific lot, thus giving its owner an official address and clearing the way for him to receive food stamps.

Building sessions are held in donated warehouse space. By using scavenged lumber, the Mad Housers can make a hut for $40. The hut is given free to the client. The organization has received no government funding so far, but private and business donors occasionally supply cash, building materials, portable latrines, legal advice, and other contributions. The program is quite cost-effective in providing basic shelter. Building a hut with all new materials costs about $150, and a hut's average life span is three years. Using the conservative figure of $150 per hut (many are built partially or entirely of scavenged materials), the 125 huts constructed so far represent a total materials cost of just $18,750, or $59.90 per person for the 313 clients who had lived in Mad Houser huts by 1992.

The Mad Housers organization has formed an offshoot called "Shelter, Inc.," which plans to construct two modest bungalows with shared kitchen and bath facilities on a donated lot. These structures, to be built with volunteer labor, are envisioned as an intermediate step for some hut residents before they move into regular housing. Shelter, Inc., was awarded Community Development Block Grant (CDBG) funds in 1989 to purchase materials for the bungalows, but the City of Atlanta still has not released the funds—or those awarded to other organizations. While the bungalow project awaits resolution, the Mad Housers have moved forward on another program for transitional housing for the homeless. In cooperation with an architect from the Atlanta Project, they are transforming old boxcars donated by a railroad into housing units.

Role of the Media

When the Mad Housers first began their activities, they avoided all publicity for fear of jeopardizing their clients' privacy. This strategy has been modified during the history of the organization, and media attention has proved advantageous. Nevertheless, privacy is still strictly guarded. Reporters cannot record meetings or reveal where huts are placed. Permission must be granted by the individuals involved before photos are taken.

After a year of clandestine hut-building and a February 1988 rally in Atlanta organized by the National Coalition for the Homeless, the core group of Mad Housers decided to allow the news media to publicize its activities. The media quickly seized upon the story of young, middle-class idealists flying in the face of property law for a cause. The Mad Housers were featured in TV programs, magazines, and newspapers nationwide. Homeless advocates in several other cities asked for hut designs and organizational information to begin their own programs. The publicity proved beneficial for the Mad Housers' clients. Before the July 1988 Democratic National Convention in Atlanta, several homeless men were evicted from beneath viaducts near the downtown convention hall but were referred to the Mad Housers, who provided them with huts elsewhere. A red, white, and blue hut was erected outside the convention hall and was used as a booth to hand out Mad Housers literature. After the convention, the hut was moved beneath the viaduct, where it remained inhabited and in full view of passing motorists, still painted in its patriotic colors.

Land, Law, and Property

Locations for the huts are chosen primarily according to the criterion of concealment; heavily wooded or overgrown areas are preferable. They should be difficult to reach by car or truck, although this presents a challenge when delivering the prefabricated hut sections to the site. If possible, they should be near public transportation, employment opportunities, and social services. Light industrial areas have met the criteria best, in that they provide jobs, access to public transport, and people with a tolerant view of the hut communities. Several hut sites are located near churches whose members have "adopted" the residents, and some of the hut dwellers, in turn, attend the church services regularly. As of November 1994, 160 huts had been built on thirty-four different sites in Atlanta, and the Atlanta Mad Housers had constructed seven huts in other cities.

As with any type of squatter situation, the question of land ownership and enforcement of property rights is delicate. The Mad Housers have learned from experience that the generally tolerant attitude taken by police can be adversely affected by pressure from homeowners if a hut is located too near residences. Site-selection criteria have accordingly been developed, and most huts are erected in industrial areas or on undeveloped public land. Technically, hut dwellers are trespassing, but they have gained public sympathy through media coverage and have avoided confrontations with the authorities.

Homeless encampments and squatter settlements are always vulnerable. Although no lawsuits have been brought against the Mad Housers in defense of rights to property on which the huts are built, such legal action remains a possibility.

Hut Structure, Design, and Utilities

The Mad Housers recognize that six-foot by eight-foot plywood huts, big enough only for a bed and a few belongings, are inadequate housing, and their goal is to see their clients move into permanent homes. The huts are meant to be temporary, a minimal protection from the weather and the dangers of the streets. Nevertheless, as the program has evolved, new low-technology facilities have been developed to meet the residents' basic needs. Whereas the first structures were merely plywood boxes with a door and a window, huts now come in several architectural styles, including one with a sleeping loft and gable roof. Bed platforms are built-in, and the walls are insulated with scrap carpeting. Windows are screened for summer and covered with clear plastic in the winter.

A wood-burning stove was designed and fabricated from metal buckets; it is now included as standard equipment in each new hut. The stove is lit outdoors, where it can be used for cooking. When the coals burn down sufficiently, it is brought inside and attached to an exhaust pipe so it can safely heat the interior of the hut. Also, water-collection systems are being tested. They currently channel runoff water from the roof into a plastic drum behind the hut, and a faucet connection is being devised so that the water supply could be tapped both inside and outside the hut. A filtering system may also be necessary to screen out vegetable matter. The residents are cautioned to boil the water before drinking. As population density increased at several of the sites, sewage disposal became a concern, and this has been met by the use of donated portable toilets. In some areas, these can be placed directly over sewer manholes.

Some hut residents were already using car batteries and jumper cables to provide electricity, and the Mad Housers have developed a generator run by a lawnmower engine to recharge those batteries. Now the generator is being modified so that its exhaust can be used to heat water for bathing.

Technology Transfer

New technologies are being developed by volunteers with the Mad Housers organization in response to requests from the clients. However, the hut dwellers must often be instructed in the use of the new devices. For example, we found that 75–80 percent of the Mad Houser clients did not initially understand how to build and maintain fires in the stoves. However, once the residents of an existing community learn these skills, they pass them on to newcomers. Many hut dwellers ask to have an additional room or porch built onto their hut, but the Mad Housers decline to provide the labor, arguing that the need to build more huts for homeless people is of greater urgency. They do provide some scrap lumber, and, with the experience in basic carpentry gained from hut-building, many residents are making their own additions to their homes.

METHODOLOGY

The Ethnographic Lens

Our research used classical ethnographic methods of formal and informal interviewing, mapping, census taking, social network analysis (see Boissevain and Mitchell 1973), surveys, event analysis, and especially participant observation. The Mad Housers also used applied tactics reminiscent of community organizing. However, the Mad Housers do not explicitly differentiate types of social groups (Brager et al. 1987:102–112). Most studies of the U.S. homeless have relied on contacts at shelters, soup kitchens, and other public places rather than on visiting individuals at their hidden campsites and entering the social territories inhabited by the homeless themselves. (For a partial exception, see Rivlin and Imbimbo 1989.) Many of the homeless individuals who request a hut from the Mad Housers are reluctant to cooperate with "controlling" institutions like night shelter programs and hence are not likely to be included in more traditional studies of the homeless. We believe that our research covers a somewhat different population of homeless people, some of whom were heretofore "invisible."

The Mad Housers help create the structures—i.e., the huts— that their clients live in, and they influence the choice of sites for those structures. However, hut communities belong to the residents, and the volunteers are visitors there. As Pelto and Pelto (1978:183) point out, the extent to which fieldworkers become privy to information is enhanced by their status as outsiders who are nevertheless identified as insiders. Participant observation is not really a method as such, but a strategy that facilitates data collection (Bernard 1988:150).

Information about clients' lives emerged during a variety of activities, especially hut-building sessions and aftercare visits. Sometimes clients phone the Mad Housers at their homes, attend planning meetings, or help with scrap retrieval. Personal revelations might be made to the Mad Housers at any such time. For example, on one occasion we were helping residents of the Gardens Site clean up accumulated trash; the Mad Housers bought some large garbage bags, and hut residents had filled them. Unfortunately, it had been raining steadily, and the bags had become ripped and their contents waterlogged. A group of volunteers showed up early on a Saturday to rebag the contents and then haul the trash off. One of the hut residents who accompanied us in the smelly truck talked about his personal life and incidents that led to his loss of a job and housing.

Systematic fieldnotes were kept on all Mad Houser activities and clients from the organization's inception in 1987 until Amy left Atlanta in 1992, including the time she spent weekly on the various tasks (Table 6.1), the number of volunteers involved in the primary activities of building and aftercare, and the average time

Table 6.2
Hut Building and Aftercare Statistics, 1987–1992

Year	Number of Volunteers	Building Sessions		Aftercare Visits	
		Days	Hours	Days	Hours
1987	6	18	144	23	92
1988	15	24	192	22	88
1989	20	20	160	22	88
1990	22	21	168	15	60
1991	25	24	192	22	88
1992	25	24	192	24	96

Note: Building sessions average eight hours in duration; aftercare visits average four hours a day.

spent for each by year (Table 6.2). Building sessions were held on alternate Saturdays, and aftercare visits usually took place on Sundays. Planning meetings are held on weeknights. Other contacts with the clients occur on an *ad hoc* basis, when a crisis arises, or members of the news media arrange for interviews. Which clients were observed and informally interviewed varied over time, as new ones were recruited to build huts and others moved on to conventional housing. Some hut residents proved to be more "natural" informants, and they became the subjects of longer case studies, in some cases participating in interviews that lasted more than two hours.

Choice of Informants

Informants for our study were largely self-selected. The Mad Houser organization has recorded for over six years its clients' names, the date on which they moved into a hut, and the hut locations. (See Table 6.3 for residence histories of a sample of clients.) However, more personal information has been revealed only by those individuals who wish to share it in the course of informal conversations. Many people who have been living on the streets are understandably wary and weary of surveys, and they resent intrusions into what remains of their privacy. We have avoided direct questioning about clients' lives, preferring to let informants divulge information as they wish to. This most often occurs in the course of hut-building sessions and especially during follow-up visits. Fieldnotes on such confidential information and on observed client interactions have been kept throughout the program's history, and they form the basis for our analyses.

The Fieldwork Setting

The following description, drawn from fieldnotes, is of a fairly typical hut-build-

Table 6.3
Residence Histories of a Representative Sample of Mad Houser Clients

Period of Residence	Reason for Leaving Hut
Jan. 1988–July 1989	Received disability money; moved into apartment with girlfriend
Feb. 1988–June 1988	Found job that included housing
Feb. 1988–Feb. 1992	Moved in with sister
Feb. 1988–Feb. 1993	Still living in hut
Oct. 1990–May 1992	Found good job; purchased mobile home
Jan. 1990–Nov. 1991	Moved into public housing
June 1988–June 1992	Relocated into apartment by Safe House program
July 1989–June 1992	Relocated into apartment by Safe House program
May 1989–Jan. 1990	Found job; moved into apartment
Dec. 1988–Jan. 1989	Got job with company near hut site; moved into apartment
Feb. 1991–Jan. 1993	Relocated into apartment because of utility construction
June 1991–Oct. 1991	Moved in with family
Nov. 1991–Jan. 1993	Relocated into apartment because of utility construction
Jan. 1988–June 1992	Moved into public housing
Aug. 1988–Sept. 1988	Moved into personal care home
Oct. 1988–Dec. 1988	Moved into public housing with family
Oct. 1988–Feb. 1989	Found job and moved into apartment
Apr. 1988–Aug. 1988	Found job and moved into apartment
Apr. 1989–July 1989	Hut destroyed; moved to another hut
Oct. 1989–Feb. 1991	Found job and moved into apartment
Oct. 1989–Apr. 1991	Hut destroyed; relocated to new hut
May 1991–Feb. 1993	Found job and moved to apartment with former hut neighbor

ing session in which both authors participated in October 1989. The names, of course, are pseudonyms.

By 10 o'clock on a Saturday morning, five volunteers have gathered in the donated warehouse space in an old railyard. The building is somewhat decrepit, with leaks in a section of the roof. However, the weather is warm, and we can work outside in a paved area. One hut was already prefabbed last week, and we begin nailing together 2 x 4 supports for the second hut's floor. At 11 o'clock three of us leave to pick up the clients for these two huts, young men named Maurice and George, who have been told to meet us at the Auburn Cafe. The cafe is run by a religious organization and provides free meals in a restaurant atmosphere for homeless persons who are referred by other agencies. It makes a convenient meeting place for Mad Houser clients, and while we wait for George and Maurice to finish their lunch, several other people approach us to ask to be put on the waiting list for a hut. On the trip back to the warehouse, we squeeze six people into the small car, including Solomon, a longtime hut dweller who is very active in the Mad Housers organization. Maurice is a plump, overtly gay man who is in a cheerful mood, chatting with everyone. George is small and intense. He tells about a pending court case that he hopes will provide him money to get off the streets soon.

Five other people have joined in the building effort by the time we return to the warehouse. Two of them are the former architecture students who started the Mad Housers, two are new volunteers, and one is a client who is a veteran of the building process. He and Solomon patiently show George and Maurice how to measure the wood, drive nails, and other tasks, and it is apparent that neither of the new clients has previous experience with construction. A reporter from an out-of-town newspaper has been allowed to observe the building session and interview the participants; she remarks that she cannot distinguish which ones are Mad Houser volunteers and which live in the huts. There is also no gender distinction in the work party; three of the middle-class volunteers are women, and they participate equally in the sawing, nailing, and heavy labor. The weather is getting hot, and we make frequent visits to the large cooler of water, but we work through lunchtime without noticing it or the heat.

Several of the dozen workers are experienced, and no major problems come up in customizing a door frame for a scavenged door. By 3 o'clock in the afternoon, well ahead of the usual schedule, we have built the floor panel, four walls, and the roof trusses for a hut. No one has a truck available to carry these materials to the site, so money is withdrawn from the donation fund to rent a large pickup. We load the sections of one hut into it, tie them down with ropes, and set off in a caravan of cars behind the truck, headed for the new hut site some five miles away. It was recently discovered by one of the volunteers.

A short driveway opens off the major street, and although gates block the end of it, a path leads into dense woods. We park the cars on adjoining streets and race to the truck, which has pulled into the driveway. There is a sense of urgency about getting the hut sections unloaded and out of sight. At one point, a van pulls in behind the rented pickup, and we fear that the police are onto us, but the driver eventually leaves. While the pickup returns to the warehouse for a second load, the rest of us haul the hut pieces deeper into the woods. The sections, especially the floor, are very heavy, and only the more experienced Mad Housers can carry one end by themselves. The rest of us manage with three or four persons to a section. Our progress is hampered by a lack of secure footing. The woods slope steeply down from the street and have been used as an illegal dump, so we are tripping over old tires, broken and whole bottles, other trash, and vines. At the bottom of the hill is a level space where we deposit our loads, gasping and sweating.

The more experienced Mad Housers take over, placing four cinder blocks on the ground as a foundation for each of the huts, settling the floor on those, and nailing in the wall sections. Homemade ladders are used for climbing up to position the roof trusses, attach the plywood panels, and to tack down the rolled asphalt roofing. Each hut is erected in about fifteen minutes, and someone takes a photograph of George and Maurice standing in their respective doorways. All twenty of us are tired, grimy, and grinning. The group then splits up, and the new clients are given a ride downtown to collect the belongings they will move into their new homes. One veteran Mad Houser returns to his hut community, but the rest of us meet at a local tavern for beer, where we are joined by the wife and baby of a volunteer. The merits and drawbacks of the new site are discussed, and we make plans for the next building session in two weeks.

Opportunities for Structured Data Collection

Mad Housers check regularly with residents of hut communities to ask whether they like the hut, what improvements could be made to it, how the neighbors are getting along, whether the person has a job, and if she or he knows how to contact social service agencies that can assist with food stamps and other benefits. The Mad Housers' biweekly meetings are also attended by some clients, who may bring up issues that stimulate further research. For example, when complaints about the use of stoves surfaced, we did an informal poll to determine the extent to which hut dwellers had experience in lighting and maintaining fires.

The most structured means of collecting data is through aftercare visits, usually done on Sunday afternoons when clients are most likely to be at their huts. Aftercare visits are the primary source of life-history information on the clients. In-depth interviews using questionnaires were conducted with eight clients whom we knew well. The following description from our fieldnotes illustrates a typical round of aftercare visits that the two of us made in January 1989.

One of Susan's friends has donated some clothing, books, and canned goods that we take with us to distribute. At the first site, containing three huts, we find two residents and one of their friends, Kenny, who is planning to pitch a tent near the huts. He has just returned from California, where he ran into T-Bone, another former hut resident.

Our next stop is at the Gardens Site. Paula and her husband meet us at the car and look through the donated clothing. She is very upset because someone stole the propane heater from her hut. She had no lock on the door but had a stick propped against it. Almost at the point of tears, Paula bemoans her misfortune, complaining, "What use is it having a man, if he doesn't do anything for you?" She adds that only the Mad Housers care about her. (Later we learned from other hut residents that Paula had sold the donated heater so she could buy cocaine.) While we are talking, Buddy and his girlfriend come home to their hut. Unmoved by Paula's complaints of thievery, he remarks that a padlock was the first thing he bought after getting a hut.

Next we stop at two nearby sites. Nobody is home at the first one, but at the second we find Tommy. He is excited to tell us about a potential janitorial job that a police officer told him about. The officer stops by periodically to check on Tommy's hut and brings him clothes and shoes; he even wants to get Tommy into school. Tommy asks us for a ride to the hut-building session on Saturday so he can help out.

We simply drive by the next two sites, located downtown in fairly open areas. They are more independent of Mad Houser involvement and do not call for as much aftercare. The sites have a reputation for violence. Several huts have been burned by enemies of the residents. The site is under the viaduct and now surrounded by a plywood fence on which is written "keep out."

At the next site we find a gay couple, Oliver and Rufus, at home. They have made a number of additions to their hut, including carpeting the inside of the hut for insulation, and decorating the outside with pictures and ornaments. They have assembled lots of castoff furniture that is grouped in the yard around the hut. The couple has even built a miniature hut for their cat and three dogs, which all appear to be well-fed and healthy.

We check two other sites but find no one at home. We leave notes tacked to the doors of all unoccupied huts, letting the residents know that we stopped by to see them and urging them to call the Mad Housers if they have any problems.

FINDINGS

Why Does Atlanta Have Squatters?

Squatting is usually associated with cities of the developing world, where a common solution to the dilemma of expensive private housing and few public subsidies is for people to occupy vacant urban land and to build homes in these pioneering communities. However, deindustrialization in Western Europe and North America in recent decades has altered urban land values, leading to gentrification and abandonment of buildings (Hopper et al. 1985), which in turn contribute to homelessness and squatting. Now, "some of the most affluent cities of the world contain homeless people who are desperate enough to break the law by seizing empty housing and then to resist eviction by legal authorities" (Adams 1986:528). Although most squatting in the developed world today involves invasion of existing buildings rather than land, the Mad Houser program constitutes an exception.

Mad Houser clients, like their counterparts in Latin American squatter settlements, are concerned about the security of their huts' ownership. Before they receive their huts, Mad Houser clients are told that they are officially trespassing on public or private property where the hut is to be placed. They are given the volunteers' phone numbers so they can contact them in case of trouble. If a landowner confronts hut residents, they are instructed to tell her or him that the hut can be moved, and then to contact the Mad Housers. However, this situation seldom occurs, because the Mad Housers take pains to choose sites that are secluded and not in use. Hut residents have less fear of displacement when they move into a hut community that has existed for some time; when the police or members of the surrounding neighborhood acknowledge their presence in a friendly way; and when their developing social networks assure them that they will receive early warning of impending trouble. Once they perceive that they will not be physically displaced, they often invest in improvements. Other similarities to Latin American squatter settlements include recourse to communally based infrastructure, such as latrines, and a strategic use of the news media to gain political support.

There are some significant differences between homeless squatters in Atlanta and squatters in developing countries. Rather than undertake massive invasions of a large tract of land on the outskirts of the city, the Mad Housers assist their clients to occupy small parcels that are generally hidden from view in industrial areas or on the edge of transportation facilities. The largest Mad Houser community contains only twenty-one huts. In Latin American countries, squatters forming new communities usually come from rural areas and are composed overwhelmingly of families (Mangin 1967b). Most Mad Houser clients are unattached men and women or couples without children, and most were raised in a city. Residents of squatter settlements in Latin America often possess the skills needed for construction of their own shelters. Their migration to the city is likely to have been planned and supported by a network of relatives or hometown friends who help them find employment (Doughty 1970; Butterworth 1980; Kemper 1980). In contrast, Atlanta's homeless, if they did not originate there, are likely to arrive with few contacts and few home-building skills, drawn by hopes of warm weather and a growing Sunbelt economy.

Roughly one in six of the Mad Houser clients is female, and the racial makeup is 50 percent African American, 47 percent white, and three percent other. As of April 1992, 125 huts have been built in Atlanta, and 313 individuals have lived in them. Some of the structures are relinquished by persons who move into other housing. See Table 6.4 for the reasons that fourteen clients have lived in more than one hut. It is important to note that over 95 percent of the Mad Houser clients have occupied a single hut rather than move around. This is a remarkably stable population in that respect. It is difficult to estimate with much reliability the percentage of the homeless that are disabled or receive unemployment insurance, because of the size and turnover of the population and because a relatively small proportion of them are interviewed by service providers. Similarly, it is difficult to assess precisely the representativeness of Mad Houser clients. However, it should be noted that it is rare for families with children or for physically disabled persons to live in Mad Houser huts, because they can get a higher priority than individuals in the shelter system and public housing projects.

A representative array of Mad Houser clients and some of their reasons for being homeless are given here.

Table 6.4
Reasons for Moving to Other Huts, February 1987 to April 1992

Reasons for Move to Another Hut	Number of Clients
Problems with neighbors at original site	1
Moved in with another person at same site	1
Homeless again after moving out of hut	2
Site destroyed or hut destroyed	10
Stayed in same hut	299
TOTAL	313

- Buddy worked as a truck driver until he was involved in a chemical spill that burned him over 50 percent of his body. The resulting disability made it very difficult to find work, and he became homeless.

- Dana suffered a mental breakdown at her job and was hospitalized for two months. As a consequence, she lost her apartment and her job.

- Oliver was on his way to California on a bus that made a stopover in Atlanta, and he simply stayed. He went to college. Later he decided to experiment with an "alternative life-style." After a decade or so, he wanted to move back into the mainstream but lacked money for rent.

- Leo came from Florida with his wife and children. After a divorce, he began to drink and decided he had nothing to live for, and he lost his home. As a child, Leo had been rebellious, and his parents had institutionalized him from age nine to nineteen. Leo lived in a hut from April to July 1988. In August, he called several of the Mad Houser volunteers to say he had been staying with friends near downtown. In a few days he would be moving into a boarding house that rents for $65 per week.

- Wendall received his hut in February 1988, but after a few months he disappeared. His hut was given to a homeless man, and when Wendall showed up again in June he moved in with another hut resident. During an aftercare visit, a Mad Houser asked Wendall where he had gone. He replied that he had been using crack cocaine and felt that he could not be around the volunteers when he was like that. But he had gotten himself straightened out and was to get an apartment in a few weeks; he had found a job caring for a handicapped person. Wendall helped build huts for others on a regular basis. Several Mad Houser volunteers visited his new apartment in July 1988, and he said that he missed his hut friends.

- Darryl was employed by a long-distance bus company for eighteen years, but after he began to experience health problems—back trouble, colon cancer, and a nervous condition—he was fired. The company was being taken over, and he lost his pension and health benefits. Darryl's medical condition kept him from working steadily, and he wound up on the streets. When he came to the Mad Housers for a hut in August 1988, Darryl's family did not know he was homeless. He was unaware that it is necessary to apply three months in advance for Social Security checks, so it took him four months to receive the first check. In September 1988, Darryl was able to move into a personal care home.

Where Are the Atlanta Squatters Located?

Low-cost services for the indigent in U.S. cities used to be concentrated in "skid-row" neighborhoods that provided employment contacts. Now, homeless shelters and soup kitchens are usually grouped in downtown areas, whereas unskilled jobs have mostly moved to the suburbs. In Atlanta, the homeless are dispersed fairly widely, taking advantage of the topography and historical development of the city's infrastructure, which have left numerous small pockets of underused land. Mad Houser huts are located on both private and public land. Out of a total of thirty-four sites, twenty-three are privately owned, four are on public

Table 6.5
Reasons for Removal of Mad Houser Huts, 1987–1993

Reason for Removal	Number of Huts
Land redeveloped by city	
For new sports stadium	18
For city park	2
Land redeveloped by State Department of Transportation	
For freeway widening	3
For new highways	14
Huts too close to railroad tracks	3
Land redeveloped by utility company	9
Private land development	26
Hut too close to residential neighborhood	1
Huts destroyed by vandals	9
Huts destroyed in domestic disturbances by residents	10
Hut worn out	1
Huts combined into large structure by unknown persons	4
TOTAL	100

land, and seven are on private land that has been converted for public use as in, for example, highway construction. The longevity of a given site for Mad Houser purposes does not appear to depend greatly on its type of ownership. In a sample of three sites built on public land, one was occupied by hut residents for six years, another for five years, and a third for just two months. A privately owned site was occupied for four years, while another site on private land had huts on it for only four months. Table 6.5 details the fate of one hundred huts that have been destroyed or removed from their original sites; eight of these were moved to other sites and reoccupied by clients.

Mad Houser clients have asked to have their huts erected in sites scattered in an arc to the east and north of downtown Atlanta—precisely the sectors in which most commercial and residential development has occurred over the past forty years. This dispersed pattern may take homeless individuals farther from social service agencies, soup kitchens, and friends, but travel can be managed. For example, sympathetic railroad employees allow the hut dwellers to hop rides on their trains for a quick trip across town. Residents of three hut communities use the railroad as regular transportation. (When Phillips was visiting a hut built along railroad tracks by a Mad Housers chapter in Chicago, food was tossed from a train to the person living in the hut.)

Social Networks and Community Development

A homeless man or woman can obtain a hut by requesting it from the Mad Housers, who maintain an informal network of referrals through its clients and volunteers. Some hut dwellers play important roles in the volunteer organization, especially in identifying and recruiting new clients. The Mad Housers accord all of the homeless a respect that they do not invariably receive from society at large. At times, there is a waiting list of up to five or six people, and the average wait is two to four weeks. The clients are strongly encouraged to help build their own huts, and several are themselves regular volunteers in constructing huts for other homeless persons. Individual choices for hut sites are honored if deemed feasible according to Mad Houser criteria.

Through their experiences with the Mad Housers, clients become familiar with the various hut sites and their residents, and their social networks thereby expand. Several hut sites are located near one another, which fosters interaction. Adjacent communities on the west side of Atlanta take turns holding cookouts and parties attended by residents of other sites. At a Mad Housers meeting, people from one community offered advice on conflict resolution to a client from a different site. Residents of the Gardens Site have volunteered to frame-in new, prefabricated huts for the homeless on the Mad Housers' waiting list.

Some hut sites have proven more secure and convenient than others, and they have gradually grown. In April 1992, one contained nine huts and another, twenty-one. Low-technology sanitation and the need for concealment impose limits on the size of hut communities, but the advantages of increased population include a greater sense of identity and social organization. After a newspaper published a feature on one of the larger sites (dubbed "Hutville") and referred to one resident as its "mayor," residents of other hut communities chose names for their sites as well. Pride in their homes, humble though they be, is evident in the efforts some residents have made to landscape their surroundings, build porches, paint, plant gardens, erect fences, acquire furniture, or even build a miniature hut for their pets. Of course, conflicts do arise between neighbors, but in most cases these are resolved by one party requesting a hut in a different location.

The following study of "the Gardens Site" (a pseudonym) illustrates aspects of community development and network formation as experienced by many clients of the Mad Housers. It is followed by the case study of Buddy, the "mayor" of the Gardens Site, and by a case study of Dana, whose experiences illustrate community sanctioning.

The Gardens: A Site Study of Primordial Community Development

The history of the largest site, the Gardens, is not necessarily typical, but it illustrates the progression and regressions that a community of hut dwellers can take. The site was originally a residential street with conventional homes, as shown on the Aerial Surveyor street maps of Atlanta for the years 1959 to 1971. By 1974 the houses had been torn down, with only the foundations and sidewalks remaining, to clear the area for a new school that was never built. Though adjacent to a busy thoroughfare, the site is concealed by vegetation and bordered by railroad tracks and a commercial facility (see Figure 6.1).

In January 1988, Mad Housers began placing huts on the remnants of old foundations. The cozy neighborhood atmosphere lent by the sidewalks and yards made the site popular, and many homeless people requested huts there. By 1991, twenty-one huts with twenty-four residents were placed in the Gardens. Another five huts were lost due to damage in domestic disturbances. Four of the residents were women, a ratio that is fairly representative of Mad Houser clients. All community members received food stamps, and most were employed through labor pools. During a two-month period in 1991, six people left the Gardens to move into apartments, and their huts were reoccupied by other people needing homes. During its four-year history, the Gardens community was populated by five different groups of people, as some moved out and others were added. Mad Housers donated a picnic table where residents gathered for community meals and socializing. A nearby business allowed the Gardens residents to use its outdoor faucet to obtain drinking water. The new water-collection system was more convenient for laundry and bathing. A portable latrine provided sanitary facilities for the entire community. Residents were eager to get a generator to recharge batteries, thus allowing every hut to have limited electricity for lights and radios. (The generator was installed as a pilot project at another site.) The Mad Housers were considering the residents' request for a small community building to house a generator, hot-water showers, perhaps a donated TV, and a communal gathering place.

When a hut was left vacant or a client for a new hut asked to be located at that site, all members of the existing community had to approve the newcomer. On one occasion, members of the Gardens community unanimously evicted a resident caught stealing from the neighbors. The dynamics among residents of the site, and with the Mad Housers, were clearly revealed in an approach to a trash-disposal problem. Garbage had been left to accumulate by some former residents, and after a community meeting the leadership council requested that Mad Housers recommend that current residents clean up the area by a specific date. By displacing the cleanup request onto the Mad Housers, community leaders wanted to avoid being seen as authoritarian. The Mad Housers agreed to supply garbage bags and remove the trash once the Gardens' residents had bagged it. Later on, city officials agreed to provide regular curbside trash pickup for the site.

In 1992, the land on which the Gardens Site was located was put up for sale by the industrial firm that owned it, and the residents were relocated, some by the Mad Housers to other hut communities and some on their own into regular housing.

Case Study of Buddy: Community Leadership in Its Most Basic Form

Buddy, in his thirties, became homeless after a work-related accident. In 1988, he became the first resident of the Gardens Site. He lived there for two and a half years, receiving food stamps and waiting for his disability payments to be approved. Buddy was the informal "mayor" of the Gardens, acting as the primary contact with the Mad Housers. Buddy was

Figure 6.1
Mad Housers Gardens Site, 1992

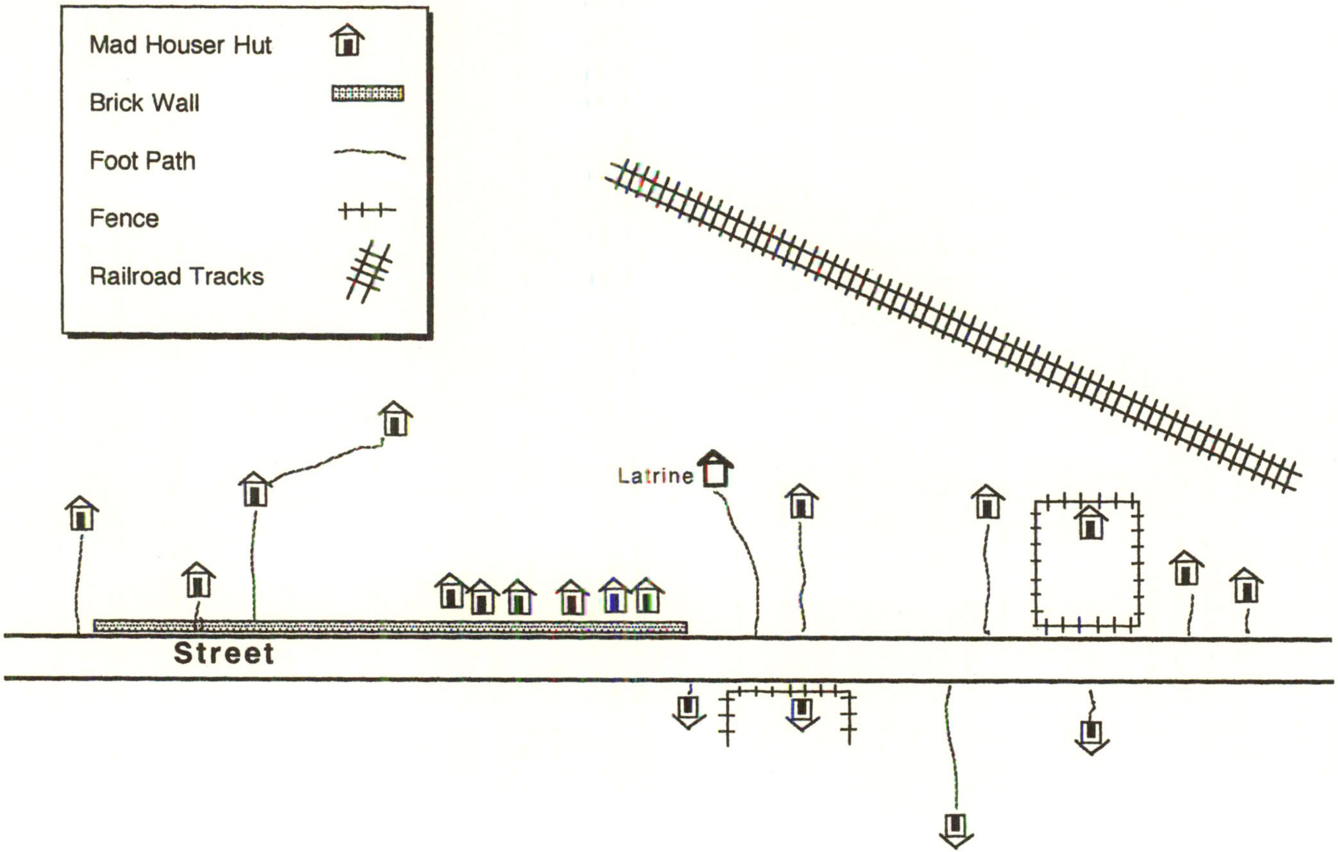

Mad Houser Hut

Brick Wall

Foot Path

Fence

Railroad Tracks

Latrine

Street

concerned about the trash around the Gardens Site and tried to clean it up himself and to get other residents to do so as well. The area has been used in the past as an illegal dump. Occasionally, other hut residents complained that Buddy was interfering in their lives a bit too much and asked that the volunteers intervene. However, the Mad Housers reminded them that each person owns his or her hut and no one has complete authority over the site, so they would have to work out their problems as a group. In July 1989, Buddy moved into an apartment with his girlfriend, and shortly thereafter his empty hut burned. Other residents of the Gardens said that Buddy had committed the arson to keep his girlfriend from moving back to the hut.

Case Study of Dana: Community Sanctioning

The following description of Dana illustrates important mechanisms of social sanctioning.

Dana, a woman in her thirties, had been chronically homeless. She lost her job and apartment after a mental breakdown, and she contacted the Mad Housers through the Auburn Cafe. She was given a hut in the Gardens Site in March 1989 and lived there for nine months. She had problems with certain members of that community because they found out that she had been stealing their clothes and burning them to stay warm. The Mad Housers had to deliver firewood to her and teach Dana how to build a campfire. Eventually she moved into a transitional program sponsored by the city and received Social Security and food stamps.

In April 1990, Dana again contacted the Mad Housers. She had quit the transitional program because of "too many rules and people telling me what to do." So a group of volunteers moved Dana's possessions out of the women's shelter. They entirely filled a pickup truck. Dana had boxes of books and files and said she was writing a book. Since she had quit the transitional program, she had been staying at the shelter and friends' apartments. Dana's new hut was located away from downtown, along a railroad. Because it was too close to the track, railroad employees demolished it after four months. Dana wanted to move anyway, saying the site was too isolated and she wanted to be "mayor" of her own site. In late September 1990, the Mad Housers built her a new hut closer to downtown, and placed a hut for her friend next to it. The friend's Social Security funds came through, and she moved to an apartment. Another person moved into the second hut. Police questioned him about an alleged offense, and the landowner was contacted. Mad Housers were then obliged to move the two huts and Dana to another community. She lived there for about a year and a half, having no problems with her neighbors. Dana painted her hut, and her art work was creative enough to be featured with a Mad Housers exhibit at a gallery in 1992. Recently she has moved into an apartment and is dating one of the Mad Houser volunteers.

SUMMARY AND RECOMMENDATIONS

Mad Houser huts are designed as temporary refuges, providing a minimal protection from the weather and the dangers of the street. The Mad Houser program is cost-effective, supplying basic shelter at an average cost of less than $60 per client served. Low-technology facilities have been added to improve their comfort, including built-in beds, stoves for cooking and heating, water collection systems, and portable toilets. Choosing an appropriate site for the hut is important. It must usually be concealed; most huts are erected away from residences, in industrial areas or on unused public land. Low-technology sanitation and the need for concealment put an upper limit on the size of hut communities. However, siting huts in clusters enables their residents to develop a greater sense of identity and social organization.

Members of the larger hut communities have a higher rate of relocation into conventional housing than do individuals from more scattered huts or those who move around frequently. Over half (56.5 percent) of Mad Houser clients have moved to conventional housing. Clients who reintegrate themselves into mainstream society and move into standard housing possess or acquire basic survival skills reminiscent of rural Americans in earlier times. About a third of the Mad Houser clients have had an experience with rural living at some time. However, urban homeless who lack a cultural repertoire for coping with "rural life" on the city streets can learn simple techniques of carpentry, fire-building, and cooking. Much of the instruction comes from more experienced clients who live nearby.

Funding continues to be a problem. The city of Atlanta has failed to release 1989 CDBG funds awarded to Shelter, Inc., an offshoot of the Mad Housers. This has prevented the purchase of materials to construct bungalows as transitional housing. In 1991, the city had to return $16 million to the U.S. Department of Housing and Urban Development because the funds had not been spent during the allotted five-year period.

Federal-Level Recommendations

Recommendation #1. Federal programs should emphasize the creation of specialized housing in cities, especially SRO and transitional units that are currently in very short supply. Where local nonprofit groups have experience in managing such programs, they should be given the opportunity to develop them with federal funds.

Recommendation #2. The federal government should reexamine its housing code standards for federally funded housing units. They may be unnecessarily stringent if they prevent or make prohibitively expensive the legal reuse of abandoned buildings or the construction of minimal homes. Stringent standards make little sense when many people are sleeping on the streets in cardboard boxes.

Recommendation #3. The federal government should take a bold step by permitting squatters on vacant federal land, as do other countries. A firm commitment must be made to provide secure tenure and sanitary services to those who build their own homes there.

State, County, and Local-Level Recommendations

Recommendation #4. Atlanta and other municipalities should set a high priority on developing plans and timetables for using federal housing funds. Citizen advisory boards overseeing the allocation and timely disbursement of CDBG funds should include representatives from nonprofit, religious, and business organizations.

Recommendation #5. Local public housing authorities should apply for federal funding to repair and renovate their vacant apartments, which then could be rented to homeless persons and especially families.

Recommendation #6. Application processing for the various social services for the homeless should be centralized, and enough social workers should be employed to allow social service offices to be set up in some of the large shelters.

Recommendation #7. Cities should formulate plans for quickly expropriating tax-delinquent vacant buildings that could be made available to nonprofit housing providers for renovation and rental or sale.

Recommendation #8. Developers should be required to replace housing that is converted into condominiums or torn down for new commercial construction.

CONCLUSION

We have described the Mad Housers organization during its first five years, as it pioneered the strategy of using volunteers to help homeless people build simple shelters of their own. It is a project that goes beyond mere construction, by providing a program for problem-solving aftercare visits and encouragement of mutually supportive communities among the clients living in the huts. We do not regard the homeless as isolated individuals. Instead, we look at their social networks and low-technology survival skills as assets that can be recombined, adapted, and used again to fit the always uncertain environment of the streets.

Since April 1992, several major changes have occurred. The Gardens Site, as noted above, was put up for sale by owners of the land, and its residents were relocated. Most of the huts were torn down by the landowner, although nothing else has yet been built there. The Hutville Site in the heart of downtown Atlanta stood in the path of construction of a new domed stadium. The Mad Housers assisted in negotiations with the city to relocate the hut residents to permanent housing. In July 1992, the Georgia Dome Authority financed a $105,000 program supporting the moves of seventy-eight hut dwellers into an apartment complex, with their rent and utilities paid for the first six months. The residents insisted during negotiations that they be relocated together rather than scattered among different apartment buildings. At the end of the six-month period, forty-nine of the seventy-eight residents remained in the apartments, paying their own expenses. Some who left moved in with their families, while others are enrolled in long-term alcohol and drug-rehabilitation programs.

Residents of another site were forced to move when the land was taken for a highway. The Mad Housers relocated some of them to other hut communities, and other clients moved into permanent forms of housing. A utility company redeveloped yet another hut site in 1993, but in negotiations with the Mad Housers it agreed to pay $4,000 to move ten residents into apartments, with rent and utilities paid for three months. These individuals were given employment counseling and assistance in finding work. The relocation of hut residents into permanent housing has gone so well that the city of Atlanta plans to implement a similar program in the future. The city's Housing Commissioner was quoted in the *Atlanta Journal* (February 27, 1993) as saying, "To be honest with you, it was far more successful than I anticipated."

A major focus of our future research will be on the longer-term results of the various relocations. It is significant that former hut residents have been resettled as a group, because U.S. relocation policy and practice have typically been based on individual compensation and "choice" of new housing locations. In fact, the people in most communities that are displaced by urban development or natural disaster are scattered, because it is difficult to find housing together. Social networks are disrupted or lost. The fact that in one instance Mad Houser clients negotiated the right to relocate as a group makes their community unusual and testifies to the strength and utility of the bonds they have forged. The literature on resettlement (Cernea 1990; Hansen and Oliver-Smith 1982; Partridge 1989) suggests that when people are moved together, the social, psychological, and physical stresses are lessened. We plan to follow up on the experiences of former hut residents in their new homes and to observe the ways in which their social networks are affected by the relocation. We will continue research among the residents of remaining hut communities and among the clients living in the new forms of transitional housing—the renovated boxcars and the bungalows.

7

Piety and Poverty: The Religious Response to the Homeless in Albuquerque, New Mexico

Michael Robertson

Robertson writes about two contrasting charitable groups with very different views of the homeless. Fundamentalist religious groups value self-reliance, rehabilitation, and salvation through Jesus Christ as the means of combatting homelessness, so they seek to help the "most worthy" of the homeless. Mainstream church groups, on the other hand, value the experience of charitable work as an enriching experience for the church members. They obtain government help, which comes with some restrictions but allows them to assist the very poorest of the poor, including the mentally ill and the addicted. Both groups have a place in the system of agencies and programs assisting Albuquerque's homeless. Robertson recommends that the federal government simplify its grants process by reducing the paperwork demands and complex regulations that hinder small, poor agencies from applying for public funding to help the homeless, and that a greater proportions of these funds be allocated locally through Community Development Block Grants.

INTRODUCTION

Since the early 1980s, public policies have encouraged the private, nonprofit sector to respond to the social service needs of America's poorest citizens. In fact, direct assistance to the homeless has arisen primarily from the philanthropic efforts of private, nonprofit agencies, particularly from the nation's religious organizations.

In Albuquerque and throughout the state of New Mexico, religious groups have been the backbone of, and major force behind provision of, basic services to the area's homeless. The effectiveness of this arrangement for direct assistance to homeless people may have serious implications for public policy formulation and fulfillment. Where service provision has become the province of religious organizations, and where there is a gap between public sector arrangements and religious organizations as central service providers, it is possible for goods and services to become disconnected from the intended target population.[1]

This chapter describes how religion-based nonprofit agencies in Albuquerque respond to the basic needs of homeless people, and it identifies public policy implications of their involvement in service delivery. If the call for increased private response is acknowledged, and the existing challenge is taken up by religious organizations, then public policy must become more receptive to this state of affairs. This chapter suggests that a more socially progressive response by religion-based groups to public involvement in support of the homeless needs to take place. Further, the chapter suggests that public involvement should help to coordinate the response of religious groups so that all segments of the homeless population are addressed equitably.

Government policy needs to be sensitive to the concerns and limitations of private religious relief agencies—if government is to utilize their involvement in meeting the basic needs of the homeless, and if goals of establishing partnerships are to be realized. Public/private partnerships are not only advantageous in meeting the needs of homeless people but are unavoidable in the present economic and political climate. For public/private partnerships to work, progressive forces in both sectors must be willing to work together on policy development and implementation.

It should not come as any surprise that religious groups play a principal role in emergency assistance to the homeless, especially in medium-sized and smaller cities (Glasser 1988:21; Cooper 1987). Historically, social welfare activities have been heavily sectarian. Religious and charitable groups have been in the forefront of dealing with America's poor (Axinn and Levine 1982; Reid 1977; Tropman 1989:104). Religious groups and religiously based organizations figure so prominently in emergency assistance that if they ceased offering services direct aid in most cities would be seriously diminished. In spite of their importance, the role of religious groups with regard to the nation's homeless has barely been explored.

The literature on homelessness in the past dozen years centers on: (1) its etiology and extent (Ropers 1988; Rossi 1989; Wright 1989); (2) demographic analysis of homeless populations and subpopulations, in order to identify their particular vulnerabilities (Rousseau 1981; Crystal 1982, 1984; Robbins 1984; Stoner 1983); and (3) medical and psychological factors, where so much of homeless research funding is directed (Lamb 1984; Brickner 1985; Fisher and Breakey 1986). In contrast, there is little information on the sociocultural context surrounding the homeless, that is, on the community that interacts directly with homeless individuals and provides them with services. Consequently, there is little knowledge of the distribution of services among the homeless—who is getting what, and how they are getting it. As I will show, the views and objectives of provider organizations influence the kind of services received by different types of homeless individuals.

Albuquerque's Homeless Services

This study is based on ethnographic research conducted in Albuquerque, New Mexico. A city of nearly one-half million residents in the sparsely populated Southwest, Albuquerque has harbored at least three thousand homeless persons each year since 1990, a minimum of 1,400 individuals on any given night.[2] The city's homeless population is largely transient. Most (about 60 percent) are homeless when they arrive in the city, and slightly more than half have lived in the city for less than one year. Nearly two-thirds are from New Mexico and contiguous states.

Feeding, sheltering, and clothing these persons falls upon fourteen agencies or service sites.[3] Over thirty organizations directly assist Albuquerque's homeless, but these fourteen are the only ones serving them exclusively, and they are the focus of this report.[4] Most of the city's direct homeless services are located in the downtown area in old, modestly rehabilitated buildings. Only three of the fourteen sites are not in this district. The city's main family shelter is located inconveniently outside the city limits; it is a daycare center for homeless children and one of the largest meal programs, serving dinners Monday through Friday. All but one of the fourteen agencies have a Christian religious affiliation. A similar configuration holds true for the agencies that provide basic care assistance only to the homeless throughout New Mexico.

The religious connection of these agencies is of two general types: (1) Christian fundamentalist, or (2) mainstream Protestant and Catholic. Nearly all of my service-provider informants, particularly those in the fundamentalist group, labeled these agencies with one or the other of these designations. Of the thirteen religiously based agencies, eight are Christian fundamentalist and five are Christian mainstream in outlook and practice.[5]

All thirteen agencies rely primarily on private, charitable donations for funding—largely from their affiliated denominations.[6] Six of the eight fundamentalist-affiliated agencies do not receive any public monies, according to a city human services planner, because they do not seek public funds, at any level of government. Albuquerque does not provide funds for emergency shelters because of church-state authority disagreements. Informants from the emergency overnight shelters say that they do not seek public monies because of misgivings over conditions imposed on them by accepting funds. Also, small, poorly staffed agencies feel ill-equipped to pursue state and federal funding, which is a complex and demanding undertaking. Therefore, even those with an interest usually opt to forego such attempts.

The shelters are the only agencies offering anything beyond basic or emergency services to the local homeless. All shelters offer some types of advocacy and personal assistance. However, fundamentalist-based shelters tend to eschew entitlement, housing, and legal advocacy, asserting that values of personal responsibility rather than government assistance should motivate homeless people. Of the mainstream shelters, none is adverse to such efforts, although only one actively plays an advocacy role on behalf of homeless clients. The paucity of advocacy efforts is linked partially to the lack of specialized personnel in these agencies (Robertson 1991).

METHODOLOGY

Participant Observation

My research is grounded in data derived from informant interviews and first-hand ethnographic observations of real-life behavior. It is not merely a gathering of socially related statistics, although these are also used. I have been a participant observer from two standpoints: (1) as a fellow service-provider, worker, and staff member, and (2) as a homeless person using services.

In 1989 and 1990, I conducted one-hour taped, formal interviews of thirty-three individuals at thirteen of the fourteen religion-based homeless agencies. I interviewed three members of each of the seven largest shelter agencies, which offer the most services. I interviewed two members at each of the six smaller agencies, which included four meal programs and two clothing and goods centers. All but one of the thirteen agency directors (seven fundamentalist, five mainstream), and twenty other staff individuals (twelve fundamentalist, eight mainstream) were interviewed. Of the entire sample, eighteen were men and fourteen were women. Except for one woman, every agency director was male; among other staff, thirteen of the twenty were women. One man and two women among the general staff were Hispanic; all other interviewees were Anglo.

The interviews were conducted at the sites where staff members worked. I questioned them specifically about their daily work, individual roles in providing service for the homeless, and their understanding of their respective agency's missions toward the homeless. I inquired about the characteristics of particular parts of the population that they dealt with most or were most familiar to them. I asked about their understanding of homelessness in general.

The knowledge of agency staff seemed very "in house" and job-connected. For example, few staff members from either the fundamentalist or mainstream group seemed to know much about the daily lives of the homeless they interacted with. On the other hand, they could deftly describe at length the array of needs and strategies presented by homeless persons at their agencies. Curiously, their overall knowledge of the causes and consequences of homelessness seemed to accrue more from media and popular accounts than from their own experience. I asked questions about their individual concerns for the homeless, about who should be helped and what criteria should be applied, and how services should be conveyed to the homeless. I asked particularly about their perceptions of the role of the religious community in providing help. Knowing that virtually all of the direct basic-services agencies were religiously affiliated, such questions steered my inquiry.

My selection of informants was built largely on multiple contacts made while playing three different participant observation roles: administrator, volunteer, and homeless person. As the director of a homeless mental health program, I became an "insider" among administrators of other homeless service agencies. In this capacity I had occasion to interact with most of the service agency directors and to initiate interviews.[7]

To observe daily operations at service sites and establish contacts with the staff, I also volunteered as a client check-in and monitor worker at three shelters (two men's shelters and one day shelter) and served food at two free meal sites. These episodes of participant observation occurred during evenings, weekends, and lunch hours over a period of about fourteen months and involved a minimum of ten hours at each meal site and forty hours at each shelter. These experiences helped me not only to meet potential staff informants but also to discover their attitudes, concerns, and work procedures with each other and with homeless clients.

From 1985 to 1992, I periodically posed as a homeless man.[8] In the spring of 1986 I spent my first extended period, nine days, on the street. Since then I have lived as a homeless person on three separate occasions, with the final episode in July 1992. The longest period of time amounted to twenty-seven days. Altogether, I spent almost three months living on the streets as a homeless person. Virtually all of this fieldwork occurred in spring and summer months, with one brief stint in the autumn.[9] I used all service utilization sites and services available to the homeless of the city, excluding entitlement and employment agencies. With the exception of the two women's and children's shelters, I used all of the service sites in this study many times.

A Grassroots Perspective

This "view from the bottom" is quite sobering and permits one to obtain an entirely new perspective on the needs of the homeless and their access to services. For example, the competition for scarce resources, the drudgery of waiting in long lines, the daily dealing with crowded conditions, and the aching boredom and surrender to despair about a limited future, are all profoundly unnerving. The variation in service availability, quality, and accommodations are revealed to the street ethnographer who "goes native" in such a way. One quickly learns the qualifications of specific services (for example, I.D. requirements at shelters) and the limitations on the number of nights per month that a person can stay. Service responses to subpopulations vary, but women and children are always first, and the mentally ill and intoxicated are shunted to the side. Attitudes to homelessness vary by the religious orientation of providers. Fundamentalists focus on redeeming souls, mainstreamers, on ministering to the poor. All of these factors can be examined directly and intimately using these participant methods. This "bottom up" perspective (Hannerz 1992:4) is necessary for establishing a holistic view from which to construct policy.

FINDINGS

Evangelism or Ministry

When I asked Reverend Bob, an administrator with one of the older gospel missions in the city, what he thought about the homeless, he had this to say:[10]

People who have fallen to this level of society are much in need of religious guidance, of Christ's touch. They are lost souls, distant from God, and desperately in need of the kind of values that can get their lives together, and get them back on their feet so they can become productive citizens once again. Our work is to bring the healing word of Christ into their lives so that they can begin this process.

Brother Gerald, the head of a recently established shelter, responded to the same question:

Homeless people normally cannot make it back into the mainstream by themselves; they need help. But the help they need is more than simply a meal and a bed to sleep on at night. No, they need inner nourishment and the rest that comes from knowing you're heading in the right direction. Spiritual food is the answer. Unless a person suffering from a life on the street is willing to reject the weaknesses that brought them to their predicament and accept his or her responsibilities as a committed Christian, there is little chance for them to return to the mainstream.

Both men used the terms "evangelical Christian" and "Christian fundamentalist" to describe themselves.[11] These self-descriptors are frequently heard in the majority of shelters and service sites ("fundamentalist" more often and "evangelical" less often), and they reflect the religious orientation of the agencies. Fundamentalist groups manage most of the basic, or emergency, services for the homeless. The remainder are administered by mainstream Protestant denominations and Catholic charities. The local increase in the numbers of Christian fundamentalists compared to other Protestant denominations partially explains their more extensive involvement in basic services. Of greater significance is that fundamentalists choose to cultivate missionary activities among the less fortunate. Brother Ben of the Salvation Mission told me, "The homeless are ripe for hearing the call to Jesus. What better place to spread the gospel than on the streets where the poor and the lame live?"

Most of these agencies consider themselves nondenominational and as representing diverse groups. To insiders they are diverse. Conversely, to outsiders, these service-provision agencies are all alike. Nevertheless, the general base of support for each agency stems either from fundamentalist or Christian mainstream–affiliated congregations or parishes. The difference between the two categories in this respect centers on evangelism and its linkage with service provision to homeless individuals. Agencies of the religious mainstream provide services while professing to ask nothing of homeless persons in return; their religious purpose is expressed in the idea of a "ministry," an offering of themselves as resources to help the homeless. Instead of actively recruiting new followers, the religious mainstream encourages church members to view service as an opportunity to be personally involved in a ministry to the poor and the homeless. Fundamentalist and mainstream congregations maintain different functions at service sites, resulting in divergent environments and tactics for service delivery.

The Fundamentalists

At the New Hope Gospel Center, lunch is served daily Monday through Friday. Prior to the actual serving, however, a prayer service is conducted for about fifteen or twenty minutes, sometimes up to a half an hour. Brother Ralph and Brother Tom take turns speaking, each calling on members of the audience to cleanse themselves by seeking God's grace; to give up the "evilness of drinking and drug use"; to raise a hand if they need Jesus in their lives; and finally, to come forward if they desire to change themselves. Those that do come forward usually end up first in line for lunch, so numerous people answer the call. At "Christ's Soup Kitchen," Sister Darlene leads a similar daily prayer meeting before lunch, although it is usually shorter and there is no call to come forward. Prior to evening meals at Jubilation House, homeless individuals are given handouts containing prayers and devotional songs so they may follow along with the meal director's presentation.

Although such religious activities are common, only a few sites require participation in order to receive food. One prayer-service leader, a soft-spoken man in his early thirties, believed obligatory participation was necessary to reach people who otherwise would not listen; "Sometimes people who are suffering don't hear what might be of some good for them. How else can you get them to hear the message?" Brother Ralph of the New Hope expressed the view that "people need to feel that they are a part of the process, not just simply receivers of some service. . . . It builds a sense of community that's good for all of us."

Attendance at prayer services and Bible study classes, and other religious activities as well are also required of residents to varying degrees at fundamentalist overnight shelters. One family shelter demands that "guests" attend two Bible study groups per day, with the exception of those out looking for work. The exemption is understandable, since those who are job-hunting must submit four job applications per day in order to remain at the shelter. At two shelters, long-term stays are available for those willing to commit themselves to several weeks of nightly religious study classes and instruction in literacy, job-finding skills, and other subjects deemed essential for getting one's life together. At all of these agencies, volunteers from affiliated churches work as program leaders or teachers.

Common themes running through the programs of fundamentalist agencies are a desire to change people's lives and a strong belief in their need for rehabilitation.

As one program director expressed it, "We are not much good to our people [the homeless] unless we are honestly helping them to rehabilitate themselves into a better life, and they are not much good to themselves unless they are committed to doing that."

Almost every staff member I encountered spoke of "rehabilitation" many times in referring to their work with the homeless. The term most often meant restoration of the homeless person to his or her former status as a housed, working, and family-oriented person. "Each person must get back to a settled, proper life," Reverend Bob told me, "even if they should choose not to walk with the Lord." The belief that homeless persons have fallen from a presumed higher social status is pervasive. It echoes the theme of Man's Fall from Grace. However, it also characterizes homeless persons as sinking to the lower depths of human living and morality. Inherent in this view is a concern for replacing the debased motivations connected to homelessness with values of the American Christian working class.

While persons such as Reverend Bob are not oblivious to the numerous circumstances that lead to homelessness, they are not inclined to examine causes. Instead, they prefer "action plans" aimed at reconnecting clients with what they presume were their previous, more stable lives. Clients with long histories of street life and "deviant behavior" do not readily adhere to such rehabilitation regimens and, therefore, frustrate agency staff. This leads most agencies to invest their efforts selectively.

Fundamentalist agencies unequivocally broadcast that Christian religious beliefs and values are, or should be, important to the people they serve. Homeless persons are enjoined to respond positively to the evangelical call and to renounce their personal sins and create their lives anew. The service providers believe that unless the homeless person does so, escape from a homeless state is virtually impossible. This belief suggests that homelessness carries an innate, negative moral quality that clearly reflects on the individual. On the other hand, I rarely heard overt expressions of blame directed at homeless persons. The moral failing attached to homelessness seemed to be considered an affliction to which humanity was all too prone.

Fundamentalist agencies rely solely on charitable contributions from individuals and churches to finance their operations. They resolutely reject government funding from city, state, or federal sources. Their decision largely stems from the rules and regulations attached to the funds. Brother Gerald pointed out that "government funding always has strings that become ropes," which constrain the evangelical mission and limit independence of action. One shelter established itself outside the city limits partly as a precaution against potential municipal rulings that might affect operation of the facility.

The agencies are not obliged to account to any external authority, so they can devote themselves entirely to the mission of rehabilitating the homeless. By confining themselves to persuading individuals to adopt certain beliefs and behaviors, these providers tend to ignore the larger socioeconomic context of homelessness.

Some analysts suggest that the involvement of religious groups in direct assistance to the homeless shows a growing propensity to see poverty issues in concrete terms of food and shelter, thereby avoiding the larger underlying issues of social and economic inequality (Stern 1984).

This approach does not mean that fundamentalist providers are politically passive. The overwhelming majority (over 80 percent) of interviewees who were associated with fundamentalist agencies overtly supported a politically conservative national agenda. Nearly all accept the contemporary conservative doctrine that government should "get off our backs," that government should not be expected to resolve such problems as homelessness, but that local community relief, grounded in "traditional American values," is the proper source of remedial action. Many fundamentalist providers were antagonistic toward welfare and other entitlements. Some believed that public assistance—"liberal handouts" as one gentleman called them—were detrimental to the rehabilitation of homeless persons. Arnold, a program director at Reach Out Ministries, expressed the view that entitlements only fostered dependence and encouraged individuals to make demands for services they had no right to claim. The overall thrust of the fundamentalist effort was to cultivate self-reliance and to enhance self-esteem through biblical study and the acknowledgment of Jesus as the source of their personal salvation.

The Religious Mainstream

Agencies affiliated with mainstream Protestant denominations and the Roman Catholic Church are less concerned with the religious careers of homeless persons and concentrate instead on their basic, immediate needs. The services of these agencies are directed more to chronic street people rather than the episodically homeless—the "higher functioning" and "able-bodied"—whom the fundamentalists target. Mainstream providers are much less selective than fundamentalist agencies and commonly see their mission as helping those who have nowhere else to go. Typically, they do not enlist people into extended religious instruction but prefer to concentrate on the daily provision of basic resources to their clientele.

Mainstream agencies are more willing to accept public monies and may seek government grants to develop or enhance their services. Most staff from these agencies are willing to work with local officials and community leaders. They regularly participate in task forces, coalitions, and town meetings on homelessness. "We have to seek a united front," one shelter administrator stated, "or we'll never end the problem."

While these agencies do hold some religious observances, participation is never required as a condition of service delivery. Evangelism is generally eschewed. "We're not in the business of selling religion," the director of a free meal program asserted. "We're summoned to help as many people as we can in as many ways as we can." The objective of a service site is simply to be open and available to the homeless. As Sister Mary Rose says, "We try to be there for someone who has no one else, to bring as much love as we can to these people, because that is how we serve God. That is what we are called to do."

The sense of being personally called to serve is a distinguishing characteristic of mainstream providers. Many of them express the belief that it is not their place to tell others how to live their lives. "That would be too judgmental," asserts Sister Mary Rose. Instead, the goal is to share oneself with those who need help, particularly the poorest of the community. The agencies provide environments where members of the congregation may experience personal religious growth in the service of God. They are places where staff and volunteers may practice a Christian ministry. Marie, a staff member of a day shelter stated, "My job is not just to help meet the needs of the homeless, but to help provide an experience for volunteers who want to serve God. We [the staff] want to help the community make contact with the homeless so they can have a chance to experience true ministry."

Homeless relief agencies thus represent an opportunity for mainstream religious organizations to volunteer community service. One of the day shelters alone has volunteers representing over twenty denominations. Meeting the needs of the volunteers is a major concern of these agencies. Service to others is thought to be psychologically therapeutic, as well as morally uplifting. As Marie put it: "our volunteers have as critical a problem as the clients. This is really a challenge—I mean our volunteers, like 20–30 percent, are in recovery programs of one kind or other. What better place to help work on your problems than helping others work on theirs?" In contrast to the fundamentalist agencies, then, the goal of mainstream providers is less to change the homeless than to change themselves.

SUMMARY AND RECOMMENDATIONS

Because there is a gap between public, governmental supports and private, religion-based organizations, partnerships between the public and private sectors should be encouraged. Coordination of services is a frequent suggestion, one given so continually that it has become a cliché. In fact, little has been done to bring public and private agencies together.

In the city of Albuquerque, no one has yet asked how religious agencies might be willing to forge alliances with the public sector. Some mainstream providers and contacts in city government have expressed a willingness to begin a dialogue over the matter. Even some fundamentalists would consider working with government agencies in certain defined roles. Some Albuquerque city officials in the Community Services Department believe that there are ways to get around the inherent difficulties in church/state coordination, in order to forge alliances. For example, religious agencies would have to agree that religious practice will not be a requirement for service. On the other hand, federal regulations may make participation by some religious organizations difficult. Regardless, all levels of government should reexamine their requirements in the area of church/state partnerships to see if adjustments can be made that would foster greater interaction and enhance services for the homeless. Further recommendations based on my work in Albuquerque include the following.

Recommendation #1. The federal government should simplify the grants process by reducing paperwork demands and the complex regulations that hinder small, poor agencies from applying for public monies. Federal agencies should also furnish more direct assistance at the local level, for example, in local HUD offices. At present, it is often necessary to contact regional or even national offices in order to acquire the proper forms or obtain assistance in filling them out.

Smaller agencies provide more personal care and attention than large, bureaucratic agencies. Homeless people require more than standardized resources at large "one-stop shopping centers," whatever their efficiency in delivering services. Homeless persons long for individualized, direct, human caring. Federal or state funds could be channeled to the local level via provider "cooperatives" or coalition groups. Smaller agencies could then thrive by dealing with a sole-source, local entity rather than immense and separate federal bureaucracies.

Recommendation #2. A greater proportion of federal homeless assistance funds should be allocated locally through community development block grants. Local needs are better known at the local level, and changing needs can be targeted more rapidly and efficiently. A policy of this type could become an incentive for cooperation and organization among local agencies, public authorities, and resource organizations. It would decrease the involvement of federal bureaucracy and its time-consuming, top-heavy grants process. Federal bureaucrats could put their energies into monitoring the use of funds rather than administering the inefficient, program by program, process of assisting local populations. A more sensible approach may be decentralizing resource authority—where the use of funds is best determined—and centralizing monitoring and accountability in federal agencies.

Recommendation #3. Action steps leading to the creation and protection of existing SRO (single room occupancy) housing must be taken by the federal government immediately. The federal government's action in this area has been weak and ineffectual to date. In fact, there is little to be protected in Albuquerque, since nearly all SRO housing was destroyed by the 1960s urban renewal programs. Federal assistance in developing SRO housing would help the homeless in every city. If anyone on the street hopes to hold down any kind of job—even simple part-time work—it is absolutely necessary for them to have stable, medium to long-term housing. Shelters will not allow individuals to remain for weeks at a time, trying to save money for an apartment, when so many others need immediate shelter. Providing rooms to let on a weekly basis would do much to assist employable individuals.

Recommendation #4. Federal jobs programs should clearly be created and stabilized over the long term. Temporary and part-time work that pays a living wage must also be seriously considered, because many of the homeless simply cannot hold down full-time employment, for a variety of reasons. In Albuquerque, community recycling programs have provided both, although they are small efforts.

The Department of Labor's Manpower programs provide a helpful model, but they also present many difficulties for the homeless. For example, most jobs require one's own transportation, and individuals are not paid often enough to meet their immediate needs.

Recommendation #5. Federal agencies should provide better support for family-preservation programs, which may include case management, counseling, jobs assistance, advocacy, day care, and training in parenting skills. These programs would not simply create more demonstration projects but would provide long-term, consistent assistance. Demonstration programs waste too much money on unneeded research, and they subordinate direct services to formalized studies that pay the wrong people to produce research results that are barely noticed. We already know what the most promising approaches are.

CONCLUSION

The city of Albuquerque's dual-affiliation, religion-based relief agencies, organized by fundamentalists and mainstreamers, are the primary providers of basic services to the homeless. Yet the effectiveness of their service delivery varies, because of the two blocs' differing assumptions and intentions in determining how and for whom services will be delivered. For example, fundamentalists tend to select homeless people who are the "most promising" for rehabilitation and to concentrate their energies on highly motivated, well functioning individuals. This forecloses services to the disabled and least successful among the homeless, leaving them for mainstream agencies to assist. Single women with children, and especially intact families, are their priority. Furthermore, they are antagonistic toward most public social services—e.g., welfare and secular counseling programs, especially if nonreligious family planning counseling is involved. Fundamentalists insist that individual bootstrap efforts and modified behavior are required.

Mainstream agencies are far more open to the most ill and disabled among the homeless, but they are less likely to work with them over the long haul. The exceptions are programs for the mentally ill, which exist to provide help over many months. Therefore, while the fundamentalist agencies are more selective in their efforts, they often work with the homeless for longer periods—if the motivation for rehabilitation is there. Mainstream agencies, by contrast, commonly provide short-term assistance.

Fundamentalist providers focus largely on client pathology and moral weakness. This approach removes homeless individuals from the contemporary urban socioeconomic context, internalizes their circumstances and transforms them into personal failings. Such a view ignores the broader, causal antecedents of their homelessness.

Religious groups structure the delivery of basic assistance to the homeless in such a way that analysis of homeless services cannot be undertaken without reference to the groups. Nationally, it appears that there is an increasing trend toward reliance on the private sector to respond to the homeless people we see around us. With a prolonged economic downturn and fewer public dollars available for homeless services, demands on the private sector will become greater. This trend will have an impact on the homeless and on religious communities in every municipality. If conservative religious groups—the Christian fundamentalists—sponsor most agencies, then local communities may welcome the decline in government involvement. Delivery of basic services would then survive in an environment less interested in causes and solutions than in the immediacy of saving selected souls.

In Albuquerque, the majority of provider agencies are managed by Christian fundamentalists. These groups appear to be expanding both their role and their influence on homeless services. If this trend continues, then the range of alternative responses to the homeless would become increasingly limited, and service delivery would become more restricted to those individuals most amenable to evangelical calls for rehabilitation and "right living." Mainstream religious agencies, concerned with benefiting their own membership, appear oblivious to this movement. They are not alert to the fact that a significant downturn in public funding would jeopardize their efforts and diminish the scope of services they wish to promote. Fundamentalists, by avoiding public scrutiny, push for a bootstrap approach that classifies homeless persons according to their capacity to cooperate with a particular rehabilitation plan. They deal with those who are judged worthy of assistance and rationalize their rejection and abandonment of others. Moreover, the fundamentalists' lack of interest in deeper causes and broader solutions may doom community response to homelessness to simplistic reactions and discourage measures that promise to halt the rise in numbers of homeless persons.

NOTES

1. By "public sector" involvement I mean primarily government participation, whether local, state, or federal. The "private sector" commonly connotes business involvement in community or national life, but here it refers to what is called the "nonprofit sector," or "independent sector," specifically with reference to religious organizations (cf. Hall 1992).

2. Demographic information is extrapolated from three separate provider-agency surveys of the local homeless population conducted in 1991, and an earlier city-funded enumeration and demographic study (Robertson 1987). These surveys provide the most reliable data on the area's homeless population. However, they are skewed toward the service-using portion of the population.

3. As of 1993, there were fifteen direct, exclusively homeless-assisting agencies in Albuquerque providing basic services—shelter, food, and clothing. At the time research was conducted, there were only fourteen such agencies. (One additional agency was providing health care service to the homeless.) However, I do not wish to discount additional basic services for homeless persons from local friends, family, or other sources in the community, from time to time. My focus here is on service providers and agencies, not local alternative resources, which have been examined elsewhere (Robertson 1987).

4. These agencies' only reason for being is to provide services for homeless people.

The fourteen agencies include three men's shelters (one also accepts a small number of women and children); two family shelters (one accepts only women and children, and no men, regardless of family affiliation); two day shelters; one daycare center for homeless children; four independent meal sites (serving either lunch or dinner, but each shelter providing at least two meals per day, open to all homeless persons); and two free clothing and personal goods centers (a few shelters also supply some these as well). Shelters are open every night, but on weekends there is a dearth of other services. For example, both day shelters are closed, as are the four independent meal sites. However, the overnight shelters serve breakfasts and dinners. While there is much duplication of services—in many ways, a positive situation for local homeless persons—several agencies (particularly meal programs) have made efforts to operate at times when similar services are scarce or unavailable. This variable scheduling among agencies has made daily life for many homeless individuals confusing and troublesome.

5. All the shelters, including day shelters, have a religious affiliation. Three of the five overnight shelters and one of the two day shelters are run by Christian fundamentalists. All meal sites have a religious affiliation, as well, two fundamentalist and two mainstream. Both of the clothing and goods centers have a fundamentalist affiliation.

6. Five of the thirteen receive some public money, although only one receives substantial amounts. Two are fundamentalist shelters, and each receives small awards (under $15,000) from city government to operate modest programs ancillary to basic services. (A "rescue van" operation, in one case, picks up street people during winter months and takes them to shelters; the other is a program of short-term housing for families, using a motel voucher plan.) The other three are religious mainstream agencies. One, a meals program, receives about $10,000 for operating costs; the other, a day shelter, receives about $100,000 in city money for shelter operations, a homeless jobs program, and a motel voucher program for homeless mentally ill persons. The day shelter also obtains considerable funding—over $250,000—from the federal government, via state agencies, for a mental health service and housing program for the homeless mentally ill. Finally, a women and children's shelter receives general operations money from city government of about $35,000.

7. One of the fundamentalist shelter directors refused to meet with me, stating, "People who call themselves researchers are nothing but reporters and government investigators out to make us look bad." After some negotiating over many weeks, he did finally permit me to interview two selected staff members of his organization. Research interviews did not include the lone holdout from my sample of agency administrators—a fundamentalist director who rarely interacted with other agency heads, and even then only occasionally dealt with other fundamentalist-affiliated programs. To establish interviews with other directors and allay suspicions concerning my dual role as administrator and researcher, I used the cover of being separately engaged as a consultant to do research on mental health issues and the use of services by the homeless—which was in fact true.

8. In spite of my varying levels of involvement and visibility with homelessness locally since 1985, I have, surprisingly, never once been recognized or identified, by providers or by other homeless persons, during any of the periods I spent passing as a homeless individual. This was due largely, I believe, to a frequent turnover of homeless people in the city and a significant turnover among "line staff" at service sites, as well as my skills in altering my appearance (e.g., removing my beard and cutting my hair extremely short) and my maintaining a low profile on the street and within the population.

9. I took little advantage of shelters during the winter, because of the high demand for

beds by homeless persons during these months, when temperatures drop below freezing nearly every night.

10. All names of individuals and agencies are pseudonyms.

11. The religious historian George Marsden says that American Protestant fundamentalists are exemplified by their strict millenarianism and insistence on biblical inerrancy (Marsden 1980). Another religious scholar, Bruce Lawrence, asserts that "the presentness of the future for all Fundamentalists looms as a cataclysmic judgement" that requires soul-saving actions or activities in the daily lives of believers (Lawrence 1989:26). This is done through the reconstruction or rehabilitation of individual lives that have fallen away from or remained ignorant of "right living," and it must embrace traditional mores expressed in the Bible. He points out that inherent to fundamentalist belief is the rejection of modernity, "above all . . . increasing bureaucratization and rationalization" of human life (1989:26). Those I call fundamentalists in this study commonly expressed these characteristics.

8

Suburban Homelessness and Social Space: Strategies of Authority and Local Resistance in Orange County, California

Talmadge Wright and Anita Vermund

Wright and Vermund capture the perspective of suburban homeless park dwellers in their analysis of resistance to the authoritative strategies of the government bureaucracy in Orange County, California. From the authors' research, park dwellers struggle with local police and the degradations of applying for welfare, in an attempt to maintain their dignity in a desperate situation. In opposition to the humiliation experienced at the hands of police and punitive eligibility technicians, the park dwellers create extensive social networks and redistribution systems with rigorous rules of fairness. The park dwellers deploy tactics to evade local rules which are often used to force them from the park they occupy. The authors explore fully the deep divisions and confrontations that ensue and recommend that the federal government renew its commitment to the provision of low-cost housing, raising the minimum wage, and creating a national health care system.

"Everyday life invents itself by poaching in countless ways on the property of others."

> Michel de Certeau, *The Practice of Everyday Life*.

"To live on the streets is to be a criminal!"
> Lester, Garden Grove Park, Garden Grove, California.

INTRODUCTION

Lester, a fifty-four-year-old white male, lives in a small suburban park, Garden Grove Park, in Orange County, California.[1] His forced street living is accompanied by degradation at the hands of local authorities, who perceive him as "out of place" and therefore "out of control." He is a subject to be surveyed and monitored. In living on the streets, he is taking the risk of "poaching" on the property of others in ways that allow him to construct an everyday life at odds with authoritative definitions of spatial comportment.

This study examines the ways in which the members of a marginalized population resist institutional power and challenge the mainstream definitions of the "proper" use of space. The issues explored in this study are: (1) the inequality and polarization of social and physical space, (2) the impact of empowering the homeless, and (3) the struggle over the definition and use of city and suburban resources. We will examine four dominant, authoritative strategies used by local governments in Orange County, California, and the corresponding homeless resistance of a small community of city park dwellers.

During the course of our investigation we were parties in the formation of a group designed to empower the homeless population with which we worked. The Homeless Action Project (HAP) was composed of homeless persons and community activists equally represented in both the lines of authority and the decision-making process of HAP. The tactics of HAP and their impact are incorporated into our analysis.

Debates on the causes of homelessness, whether in the popular press or in the academic literature, often focus on the complexities of entitlement, displacement, and redevelopment (Bassuk 1984; Hoch and Slayton 1989; Kozol 1988; Mair 1986); on capitalist economics (Marcuse 1988) and the transition to postindustrial society (Adams 1986); on economic dislocation (Belcher and DiBlasio 1990); lack of affordable housing (Friedrichs 1988; Hopper and Hamberg 1986; Watson and Austerberry 1986; Fallis and Murray 1990); and the deinstitutionalization of the mentally ill and their subsequent confinement in service "ghettos" (Dear and Wolch 1987; Lang 1989; Wolch, Dear, and Akita 1988). In less generous writings, homelessness is attributed to individual pathologies to be rectified by a stiffer application of disciplinary policing combined with voluntary charity.

Still other studies maintain a strict empirical focus and attempt to define quantitatively a "homeless population" (Bingham, Green, and White 1987; Burt 1992; Robertson, Roper, and Boyer 1985; Rossi 1989). Cohen and Sokolovsky (1989), and Rosenthal (1989) conduct ethnographic research within homeless communities to determine who the people are, how they operate, and what their relationships are with mainstream society. However, rarely are the utterances of homeless persons given weight within a larger consideration of the surveillance and spatial domination of homeless populations. Notable exceptions include Cohen and Sokolovsky (1989), Kozol (1988), Paschke and Volpendesta (1991), Wallis (1991), Wright and Vermund (1990) and Rosenthal (1989). Theoretically, our research is guided by an integration of (1) neo-Marxian theories of social space (Lefebvre 1976, 1979, 1991; Gottdiener 1984, 1985; Mair 1986; Marcuse 1988; Mingione 1983); and (2) postmodern theories on localized strategies, tactics, and actions within a larger system of generalized power relations (De Certeau 1984; Foucault 1979, 1984; Ruddick 1990; Soja 1989).

A Theory of Power and Urban Space

We propose that the development of contemporary market economies leads to the differentiation of urban and suburban areas into marginalized and pleasurable spaces. In both the process and the physical spaces themselves, the poorer segments of society confront dominant, authoritative strategies with local resistance tactics. By "strategies" we mean the larger, overarching, more complex sets of decisions and actions by powerful social groups; by "tactics" we mean the more immediate, reactive, less planned decisions and actions by less powerful social groups, like the homeless. Strategies are associated with the authority to identify a place as "proper." Strategies of the powerful that are designed to maintain mainstream, functional definitions of space meet resistance by the homeless, who contest established definitions by engaging in "tactics." Tactics are a vehicle of the powerless. They are defined by such temporal features as "seizing the moment." The homeless lack control over place, so they exercise tactical power through time.[2]

Large-scale resistance to authoritative strategies of dominant social groups often makes its initial appearance in small actions at the local level. Rosenthal (1989) demonstrates the ways that homeless populations affiliate with mainstream society and resist authoritative strategies designed to marginalize them. Snow, Baker, and Anderson (1989) show that socially defined "criminal behaviors" are an adaptive strategy for those who have to live on the streets. The construction of novel street identities provides another form of resistance to the stigmatization of homeless individuals (Snow and Anderson 1987). Public theatrical performances (Burnham 1987) and poetry readings by the homeless, the organizing of homeless unions (Cress 1990), cultural productions (Paschke and Volpendesta 1991; Wallis 1991), and the occupation of boarded-up houses and public squares all demonstrate significant levels of cultural and political resistance.

Park dwellers inhabit a border between the pleasurable spaces of city parks and the marginalized spaces of the outcaste. They exist on the definitional edge of the "correct use of space." This contested territory comprises a multiplicity of physical sites for local resistance. Park dwellers tactically manipulate their terrain, creating "backspaces" out of "frontspaces," after Goffman (1959, 1963, 1961, 1971). They are able to confront and confound the authorities by creating what Ruddick (alluding to Foucault) calls a "heterotopia," or "spaces of deviance," or a space to contain "fragmentary possible worlds" (1990:188).

Contesting the "proper" use of space and the degree that different physical and social spaces are to be concentrated, separated, and arranged, lies in the domain of strategy and tactics. Indeed, following de Certeau (1984:36), powerful strategies are associated with the authority that can establish a place as "proper." This control over place is not a given. It is not a systemic oppression, but rather a strategic oppression that depends, according to Lefebvre (1976:28), on the actions of individuals acting on behalf of institutional interests within well defined spatial and temporal boundaries. Strategies can be contested, negotiated, disrupted, or abolished at all levels of society through what de Certeau (1984:34–38) calls "tactics" or what we term "local resistance."

Places, Spaces, Authoritative Strategies, and Local Resistance Tactics

City and suburban life is increasingly characterized by polarized social and physical spaces: palaces for some, cardboard boxes for others. There are "pleasure" spaces (Zukin 1988, 1991; Harvey 1989a; Gottdiener 1986; Shields 1991, 1990), and "lost" or "derelict" spaces (Trancik 1986; Jakle and Wilson 1992; Greenberg, Popper, and West 1990; Winchester and White 1988). These polarized spaces are a product of increasing social and economic inequality, corporate restructuring, urban redevelopment, and a declining "social wage." Pleasurable and derelict spaces result from complex social dynamics based on gender, race, and class. They are arranged in a far more complex manner than simply as "rich" and "poor" spaces— as in the "dual city hypothesis" (cf. Mollenkopf and Castells 1991; Sassen-Koob 1987).

Geographic sites within urban and suburban areas become contested in the struggle over the definition and use of resources. In this disputed landscape, the imposition of definitions of "proper" use of space involves seemingly reasonable arguments that promise to improve the lives of all. However, these arguments obscure the impact of the definitions for some segments of the population, and also their implications for policy. The "reasonable" arguments conceal both dominant strategies of authority and local resistance to that authority. For example, in Columbus, Ohio, so-called "rational" organization of downtown areas via corporate redevelopment required the expulsion or marginalization of the homeless (Mair 1986).

If social space is for the reproduction of the "relations of production" (as opposed to the "means of production"), and if social space represents a productive force that shapes and is shaped by the participants inhabiting that space, then increasingly polarized social spaces present a real problem. (For definitions of neo-Marxian terms and processes, cf. Lefebvre 1976, 1979; see also, Gottdiener 1984, 1985; Martins 1982.) As social spaces become more polarized, it becomes more difficult to reproduce the "relations of production." Instead, polarized spaces produce violence and confrontation; increasing levels of violence are countered by increasing control and surveillance strategically engineered by government and the private sector. The strategy of maintaining authority through expanded systems of control and surveillance operating within, and as, a "disciplinary space" (Foucault 1984, 1979) enforces the dominant, functional interpretation of social space.[3]

People in marginalized spaces witness city inspections, warrant checks, and extensive police patrols, but often little community interaction. For people in pleasurable spaces, surveillance takes on a less obtrusive form in marketing surveys, credit screenings, zoning regulations, and local homeowners associations. Dear and Wolch (1987) demonstrate the extension of surveillance into inner-city service ghettos by applying Foucault's concept of "micro-powers." In the last instance, the homeless occupy the most extreme form of marginal residential space (Winchester and White 1988:44).

To understand how this process operates, we will first give a brief description of the people we studied and of our methods. Second, we will describe authoritative strategies and local resistance tactics in relationship to space and place in Garden Grove Park. Third, we will analyze how these strategies and types of resistance tactics operated. The impact of HAP on the park population will be included as one aspect of local resistance. We conclude with a number of policy recommendations for federal policy makers.

METHODOLOGY

The Place and People

Orange County, California, is a suburban extension of Los Angeles, with a population of over 2.2 million people, a relatively high median income of over $44,000 a year, an official homeless population of six to ten thousand individuals, and a high poverty rate of 13.7 percent. Close to the center of Orange County, and within the city of Garden Grove, is a small park with the same name: Garden Grove Park is bordered by a freeway to the north, a high school to the east, a boulevard to the south, and residential suburban homes to the west. Next to the park's western entrance is the central branch of the county social service office. We located our study within Garden Grove Park and the immediately surrounding area.

In 1987–1988, Garden Grove Park was considered "home" by a small core group of four homeless families and seventeen single men and women. The majority had previously lived for five years or longer as "housed" residents of Orange County. In a county-wide survey of homeless persons seeking services in 1990, the three most important reasons for becoming homeless were losing one's job, not being able to afford housing, and being evicted.[4]

For the purposes of this study, park residents were defined as those who appeared there on an observably regular basis, from weekly to several times a month. However, the aggregate park population varied widely from week to week, on occasion swelling to forty or more and at other times dropping to zero. The racial and ethnic composition was predominantly Anglo, with a few Hispanics.[5] Blacks, who represent only 1.3 percent of Orange County's population according to the 1980 census, and Asians, 4.5 percent, did not appear. Age varied from mid-twenties to mid-sixties. The families all owned cars or campers. Single men and women without cars caught rides with others who did. A survey of the Orange County homeless in 1990 revealed that 25 percent of the respondents had spent the previous night in a car, van, or truck; 20 percent had been "on the street"; 16 percent had been in shelters; 15 percent had been in a motel or hotel; 13 percent with family or friends; 7 percent in their own homes; 5 percent in a park or on a beach; and 1 percent had been in a campground (Orange County Homeless Issues Task Force 1990:11).

Garden Grove Park was a convenient location for park dwellers. There was ready access to a local freeway. The park's central location made traveling to dispersed services easier. The topography of the park, the layout of bushes, tables, parking areas, and rest rooms facilitated interaction among the park dwellers. Many services were located quite close—for example, a local food bank and the central social service office—which was an important feature for people without cars. Social networks were an important factor. One resident had relatives "living over the fence." Another had her child in the nearby school. Still others were former residents of the area. The social ties they established with each other were important in maintaining the park as a central location to which all returned.

During the six months between May and November of 1987, we made weekly visits to the park to interact with and observe the people living within its perimeter, in vehicles, or on the street nearby. We would also accompany them on visits to the social service office next to the park. Our involvement had been first catalyzed by an overt display of police power at 4:00 A.M. one morning. Officers dispersed four families living in their cars from a suburban parking lot, whose owner had given them permission to stay there. The police expelled them on the grounds that sleeping in their cars was a "health hazard."

Access, Participant Observation, and Interviewing

At the time of this study, the authors were involved in work that led both directly and indirectly to contact with the local homeless population. One of us was employed at the Fair Housing Council of Orange County, a nonprofit housing agency that addressed issues of affordable housing and housing discrimination. This work led to numerous meetings with shelter providers, city and county agencies, and segments of the local homeless population who would often call to ask for assistance. The other author was employed by a county health care agency as a mental health outreach worker. Her position brought her into daily contact with street people throughout Orange County. We came to know each other's work through our attendance at local meetings of county shelter providers.

The project was initiated when we received a call one day from the leader of a local shelter who informed us of the police action mentioned above and asked if we could help. The shelter leader took us down to the park to meet some of the people who had been dispersed, people he had been assisting for several months. It was at this point that we met Paul, a formerly homeless member of the park population, who offered us a cup of coffee from the back of his van and became a key informant for our project. Paul, Glenn, Lester, and others in the park became key informants. However, to us they were not just informants in a study, but, more importantly, active participants who stood up for their rights to the best of their ability. During the course of the study we were joined by community activists and park residents in a collaboration to develop a nonprofit organization dedicated to empowering displaced people and to serving those living in the streets by combating police abuses. Homeless participants named the group the Homeless Action Project. This group, in addition to our work roles, legitimized our access to the park population and helped to provide them with additional resources.

Paul, Lester, Glenn, and other homeless people had their own agendas, which had to be nurtured and respected. Both of our agencies granted us time to work with these populations as part of our employment, and, in the case of the housing agency, the space to conduct the initial meetings. In all meetings, the park population would have equal say in decisions about what would be done. A dual power arrangement was established, with one homeless representative and one housed representative for each position: President, Co-President, Vice President, and Co-Vice President. Paul, Donna, Lester, and Glenn became more than subjects—they became friends and fellow researchers and advocates.

Ethnographic methods included direct participant observation, regular weekly meetings and informal interviews with park residents, and occasional meetings with local social service workers and city and county employees. Meetings with the park population took place every Thursday at noon, which was when the largest number of people appeared, for a free lunch served by a local church group. This gave us an opportunity to catch up on park activities, new arrivals, and needed services. For the park residents, it was an opportunity to eat, exchange information, swap stories, and talk with church workers and community activists. We also stopped by on a less regular basis, at different times of day between early morning and sunset. Paul, who had been homeless for eighteen months prior to securing a position as a local shelter manager, assisted us in making contact with other park members. His intimate knowledge of the local park population enabled us to gain access to their world.

Data were gathered through on-site, qualitative observations of park dynamics and through participation in many of HAP's actions. In retrospect, we were using a variation of Rosenthal's method of "hanging out" (1991a), by involving ourselves in activities related to homeless life in the park. This took the form of eating and drinking with the homeless, exchanging stories, taking them places, and attempting to mediate for them with the authorities. Near the end of our involvement with the park population, oral histories were gathered using field recordings. The purpose of taking the histories was to examine the difficulties park residents had with the welfare system. Analysis of these data involved looking closely at linguistic strategies, both verbal and nonverbal, that were used by homeless people and social workers.

Notes were taken at HAP meetings and upon returning from the field. Quarterly reports detailing group accomplishments and observations about the park population were prepared for the local housing agency that employed one of us. Observations were made on the speech patterns and comportment of park residents and non-homeless institutional personnel (police, social workers, and community activists), and how the park population and social workers dealt with the frustrations of not being understood. Observations of HAP activities, group decision-making processes, and park resident interactions both among themselves and with authority figures were recorded.

FINDINGS

We will explore four dominant authoritative strategies in this chapter: exclusion, repression, displacement of conflict, and assimilation of the population and its leaders. "Exclusion" is defined as those actions that exclude populations from particular areas and means of communication. "Repression" is defined as forcible removal, punishment, or harassment for occupying space or communicating in ways not sanctioned by authority. "Displacement" is defined as those social actions that displace the causes of conflict from one source to another that is less threatening. "Assimilation" is defined as the absorption of protests or the redefinition of space in a way that favors elite interests; it can involve the use of police informants to spy on park residents or the granting of privileges to a few park residents rather than to all. All of these strategies and resistance to them can be viewed within the physical spaces of Garden Grove Park. Authoritative strategies are designed to control the use of public and private resources, to maintain the boundaries of what is considered by the authorities to be "public" and "private," and of the "proper" use of space. Strategies take the form of close regulation and monitoring of the behavior of park residents by police and city park personnel, often on an hourly basis.

Exclusion

In Garden Grove Park an exclusionary strategy of periodically cutting off electrical power to a section of the park was followed. One couple practiced "electrical poaching," by attaching electric lines to the local power lines, thus enabling them to receive electricity illegally, in order to keep their camper refrigerator going. Others saw their personal possessions confiscated and discarded by highway and park cleanup crews.[6] Public rest rooms would be periodically closed, and watering schedules would be changed to discourage sleeping in the bushes.[7] Exclusion from the immediate surrounding community was manifested by the separation of local residents from park residents. Glenn, one of the park residents, said that his former house was just over the fence on the western side of the park. He said, "My house is right over there. You could throw a rock at the house I used to own. I got three kids. Do you think they'd ever come out here and even talk to me in the park? Right here, I lay in this park and had a heart attack."

Students from the neighboring high school stayed along the eastern access road, close to the school. Rarely would they mingle in the central parking area when this area was occupied by the homeless.

Repression

Repressive strategies were more direct. Park residents complained of continual police harassment and surveillance.[8] While they acknowledged that some police officers were sympathetic to their situation, they reported daily and occasionally hourly checks for identification and vehicle registration. Park residents also noted being awakened in the middle of the night by the police and being subjected to verbal threats. Several families informed us of an incident in May 1987, when ten families were awakened by the local police at three in the morning in a nearby supermarket parking area and given notices warning against further sleeping in parked cars, because it violated a city health ordinance. They had received the consent of the owner to park on his property. Verbal threats about the real possibility of having their children taken from them were directed at the families.[9]

Another police tactic consisted of "picking up a transient" and driving him to Santa Ana, about five miles away, on the pretext of "taking him in." He would then be "released," having to walk back to Garden Grove Park, with no record of the event having been kept. Several park residents corroborated this strategy. One park resident described what happens when an officer "picks you up":

Lester: Oh, yeah. He's going to take you down, he's going to take you. . . . He used to take you down to Garden Grove, turn you loose there, and then you had to walk back. But then he started taking you down to Orange County [jail], all the way down to Santa Ana, 'cause he thought that walk wasn't far enough, so he'd take you down.

Q: They take you and drop you off.

Lester: No, they take you in the jail, in the front door, an' let you out the back door.

Q: They just take you in the jail and let you out the back door?

Lester: Right! That's exactly what they do. And then you got to walk back. And from Santa Ana, from the main Orange County jail in Santa Ana, to the Garden Grove Park is an all-night walk. Believe me, I know. 'Cause, see, by the time they roust you out, it's usually two or three o'clock in the morning, between one and three o'clock in the morning. And when they finally take you down there, and then they ask you a bunch of questions, an' they sit out there in the park and everything, and they go through their routine, you know, checking for wanted warrants, and they go through all that routine, by the time you get down to the jail and they turn you loose it's after, it's maybe two or three o'clock in the morning, an' then you walk the rest of the night.

Resistance to Authoritative Strategies: Forming New Social Networks

Resistance against the strategies of exclusion and repression was acted out through four tactics: (1) forming new social networks for support, (2) maintaining and expanding contact with sympathetic institutions, (3) violating established boundaries for use of public and private facilities, and (4) increasing mobility.[10]

Exclusion and separation of park residents from surrounding communities appeared to be the norm. However, park residents often resisted these attempts by forming their own social networks and their own communities that were independent of surrounding neighborhoods. Security is one of many benefits that comes with the constructed social network of a housed person. A homeless person's main social network is supplanted by a new network, however unstable (Cohen and Sokolovsky 1981, 1989; Lovell 1984; Mitchell 1987; Rosenthal 1989; Rowe and Wolch 1990). In the following example, local resistance was manifested in socializing and the sharing activities among park residents.

At 7:00 A.M., campers and automobiles filled with mounds of clothes and miscellaneous possessions would arrive, driving down the access road, and parking at the northwestern end of Garden Grove Park. Near the parking area was a "pavilion," a large structure with barbecue grills and picnic tables beneath a canopy, under which park residents occasionally gathered. With automobiles and campers lined up, camper doors were opened and small groups of park residents gathered near the pavilion, telling stories and eating whatever they had been able to save or find. Single men, both young and old, emerged from the surrounding bushes and took up places near the families. Several of the tables were occupied by clusters of single men, while families remained around their campers, often cooking inside. On occasion, families also used the picnic tables, sharing them with lone individuals. "Swapping" of food and sharing of personal items occurred at this point.[11] They told us that if one person was in a position to secure a number of items, such as razors, then he or she would distribute as many as possible to those who needed them within the park.

Park residents clustered in groups, rarely remaining alone. One person might wander off a short distance, perhaps fifty feet, but would still be in calling range of the group. When asked why they clustered together, residents responded that they needed mutual protection. It was this mutual support provided by the network that constituted one form of local resistance to the authoritative attempt to exclude and separate the homeless. Informal social networks, developed out of survival needs, provided a means of socializing and passing the time for park residents, in a manner similar to patterns documented by Whyte (1955), Liebow (1967), Cohen and Sokolovsky (1989), and Stack (1974).

Resistance to Authoritative Strategies: Contact with Sympathetic Institutions

Like Rosenthal's (1989) sample of Santa Barbara homeless, our sample of homeless people interacted on a frequent basis with schools, church organizations (who offered free lunches in the park), social services, nonprofit organizations, shelter groups, an advocacy group (HAP), Federal agencies (the Veterans Administration), and legal service organizations (Legal Aid of Orange County and the American Civil Liberties Union, or ACLU).

Most of the children of park residents attended the local high school, but they suffered from the stigma of "homelessness." Attendance was sometimes discouraged by school employees, who requested a permanent address before admitting a student. In one incident, the teenage son of Alex, a single woman living in her car, was turned away from the high school next to the park. This action was contested by Paul, a co-president of HAP, who convinced the school principal to admit the student.

The most visible religious organization was the Redeemer Church. Every Thursday at noon a free lunch was set up in the pavilion to feed the homeless. Another church group set up a dinner on two other days of the week. Many of the park residents expressed thanks for the hospitality; however, they were resentful that the churches were unwilling to involve themselves further in their problems. The park residents' ambivalence toward the lunch program was expressed in a mixture of sympathy to the church workers and a feeling that they were doing this just to make themselves feel good. This attitude became painfully obvious when the Redeemer Church suspended its operations within the park, explaining that, "God's work was finished here." In an aside, one worker mentioned that the church had decided to suspend the program because the members felt that people were taking advantage of the free lunches without taking steps to improve their condition.

The role of the local nonprofit housing agency, in which one of us was employed, was more circumscribed. The agency provided the first meeting place for the development of HAP, plus the time for one of its staff to initiate weekly contact with the park population. The agency was able to provide support services in the areas of housing and housing discrimination. However, its main impact was through staff time and in providing an initial meeting area for the homeless.

Before HAP entered Garden Grove Park, another local nonprofit shelter group distributed food to park residents; of those residents, Paul became the cofounder of HAP. The shelter group furnished a long-term meeting place down the street for HAP and other interested park residents. They also operated a local food distribution program, which some park residents used. Park residents often came to the distribution center to "hang out" and, occasionally, help. The shelter group was helpful in finding spaces within their shelters for park residents.

The Veterans Administration became interested in the park population as a result of personal contact with homeless activists and social workers. It sent a representative to the park and was able to assist one male, "Pops," a disabled veteran fifty-eight years of age, to receive emergency medical care after he contracted pneumonia in the park. HAP provided transportation for medical appointments and many other necessary activities. Tragically, Pops returned to the park, where he died of exposure. He said prior to his hospitalization that he wanted to die in the park, where his close friend had died.

Dominant authoritative strategies and resistance to them can be seen more clearly within the local social service office, which was adjacent to the park. Some park families received Aid for Families with Dependent Children (AFDC) or State

Disability Insurance (SDI), but many single persons received few if any benefits. Several individuals received General Assistance, SDI, and Supplemental Security Income (SSI), but the majority were either penalized with "sanctions" or did not want to go through the application process. They depended upon the families and individuals receiving assistance for much of their support, even though many of them were only working at odd jobs. Benefits were insufficient to allow either families or individuals to rent a living space. A 1985 study of Orange County homeless persons showed that 87 percent of those who were homeless and eligible for General Assistance did not receive any aid (Lovell 1985).

Boundaries in the Use of Public and Private Facilities

Authoritative strategies are diffused within open public areas, and the enforcement of authority in open public areas can be sporadic but intense. On the other hand, institutional public areas, such as in the social service office, provide a setting for systematic intensification of control and discipline. Enforcement in institutional public areas may be continuous, if less intense.

Exclusionary strategies appeared to be most common in the social service (welfare) office, followed by displacement of conflict, repression, and assimilation. Control over the poor is reinforced by the panoptic (cf. note 3) architecture of the local social service office, by its organization of authority and language, and by the use of lower-skilled eligibility technicians instead of skilled case workers. All these factors increase the exclusion of the homeless from access to needed benefits. The main reasons for exclusion from social services that park residents defined were (1) attitude problems generated by waiting, (2) perceived arbitrary exercise of authority, and (3) constantly varying amounts of benefits.

Time became a crucial factor in forming the attitudes of the eligibility technicians and the homeless. Being obliged to wait to fill out numerous forms—"red tape"— was perceived by the homeless as an arbitrary use of power. In the words of one park resident:

Lester: Well, first of all you got to realize, when you go in there, you fill out your form and you turn it in at the window. And then they give you two more forms to fill out. And then you have to wait for a social worker to call you, and you wait, and you wait, and you wait. The first day I was in there six hours.

Q: So how long is it before you get to talk with a case worker?

Lester: I talked to my case worker, let's see, after five and a half hours.

Social service workers exercised arbitrary power by identifying "attitude problems," which in turn manifested themselves further as "communication problems" with the park population. For the eligibility technician (ET) the long waiting process was perceived as a necessary precursor to the interview process:

Q: Why is there such a wait?

ET: Basically, because there's just, it takes so long to do an interview. It might take an hour and a half or so to do an interview.

While waiting for benefits can be singularly degrading to a homeless person, when it is a perceived arbitrary exercise of authority, the social space created is experienced as an overt disciplinary measure. The homeless can contest decisions made against them. However, often these decisions are reinforced by the immediate supervisor.

Lester: The whole thing is . . . the whole decision depends on that case worker. If they don't like the color shirt you got on or they don't like you personally, something doesn't strike them right, they flat turn you down. And the other thing you can do is you can talk to the supervisor, you have that right. But . . . the supervisor is a "polly parrot." She comes right out and says almost verbatim exactly what the case worker said.

ET: Usually the supervisor will back 'em up. And if that's the case they can always file for a fair hearing. The directions are on the back, and that's an 800 number they can call, and it's completely different from the Social Services Department. So they can always call there and make a complaint. . . . They have that right. It says so right on the back of the notices.

Waiting, combined with a perceived arbitrary exercise of authority, is rendered even more difficult by the knowledge that waiting may not produce consistent results. The constantly changing amounts of benefits awarded, as a result of a complicated set of regulations restricting what can and cannot be counted as income, made waiting a painful experience.

Lester: You feel angry as hell, and you want to walk out. But, you know, the last time I got only $17 worth of food stamps I didn't know what I was going to get. . . . I haven't got the same amount twice yet.

Q: They never tell you up front?

Lester: They don't know. They take down what your income was for the month and then they somehow or another arrive at a figure. They counted my SDI as income. This month I got $527 from SDI. The maximum you can make without any food stamps at all is $597. So I'll get another $10 this month and that's it. . . . A lot of people I know have no income and only get $81 a month in food stamps. That's for a single person.

Repressive strategies included warrant checks, the presence of a police officer on the premises, and sanctions that were perceived as arbitrary by the homeless.

The withholding of aid because one did not follow agency regulations to the letter appeared to be quite common. Most of the individuals who had received General Assistance within our park sample had received a sanction at one time or another that rendered them ineligible for aid for thirty days. We were told by the park residents that if one appeared dirty or disheveled in applying for General Assistance, he or she was immediately referred to a local official for checks on outstanding warrants, even before seeing an eligibility technician. Since to live on the streets means that one invariably breaks a particular law of some kind, warrant checks acted to discourage those who would benefit the most from securing General Assistance.

Displacement

A social displacement strategy allows the eligibility technician to distinguish among the homeless between the "undeserving poor" and the "deserving poor." "Blaming the victim" is accompanied by technician "burn-out." The organizational position of eligibility technicians ensures their isolation from the homeless. Their looking down on the homeless is perceived by the homeless as a lack of understanding of the real conditions of living on the street. Glenn gives a good example of this.

Glenn: Before you started all this you didn't know anything about it did you? You couldn't relate to somebody sleeping out in the rain. You didn't even know if anybody is sleeping out there. A guy walks in there and he's cold and hungry. They've never done it [case workers]. They never had to be out in the cold or be without.

Q: On General Relief, what was it she said, that she wanted you to do some running around or something?

Glenn: Yeah, she wanted me to go look for a job. Like, how in the hell are you going to look for a job when you ain't got any money? When you're sick? Ain't nobody going to relate to anybody out here unless they been here before!

This lack of understanding is compounded by attitudes of the eligibility technician, who may have stereotypical views of the homeless as lazy, irresponsible, and alcoholic. These views are conveyed by both verbal and body language that compounds the sense of inferiority of the homeless:

ET: I think that the people you interviewed, because we have park people right across from our office, and the people that are in the park have an axe to grind with the agency because they can't get any benefits, because most of them are sanctioned. . . . They kind of have that feeling, so they're antigovernment. That's why they're there. We get a lot of them, 'cause when we go for walks they'll come up and ask for money. We'll say, we tell them to go right across the street—"They'll be happy to give you something," and they say, "Well we can't,

I'm sanctioned," with their alcoholic breath as they fall down. . . . So that's it.

Personal attitudes and lack of cooperation with the program were attributed to the people on the streets. When eligibility technicians were asked why people applying for benefits often fail to show up or do not have the proper documentation for verification, the following comments were given:

Q: What do you see as the obstacles to completing an application?

ET: I think, basically, the main ones would be they have to attend a group orientation of their rights and responsibilities. A lot of them fail to show up for appointments. And a lot of them—we ask them to bring verification for certain things and they fail to come back with them. They just don't show up. They make appointments and don't come back.

Q: Why do you think that is?

ET: I don't know, . . . unless they don't have the verification, or they're just too lazy, or— I have no idea. It's a small thing to do for free money. It's a characteristic of a welfare recipient, because that's what causes them to be where they are, a lack of responsibility and a dependency on other people.

Displacement of the structural dimensions of homelessness onto moral choices and individual responsibility provides a way of avoiding larger social issues of wealth and power and thereby gives the eligibility technician a means of feeling in control. The ideology of choice serves to mask quite real limitations. When an eligibility technician was asked why there were so many families living in the county parks, he commented:

ET: A lot of them I think, I don't know, it's just a misuse of funds. The rents are high in Orange County. I tell them to get an apartment in Riverside or San Bernardino where the rents are lower. Orange County is an expensive area. But there's other areas of the county and the grants are the same all over. But a lot of them, I think, misuse their money and a lot of them have credit cards and things like that. And they've just charged up and they got bills, and so they're living there by choice. So I don't know. . . . A lot of them have little trailers and they seem to think it's okay.

These attitudes breed resentment between eligibility technicians and park residents. This hostility often expresses itself among the park residents through displacement onto bureaucratic and racial resentment.

Glenn: Okay. You're broke, no money. And you're settin' here in the park, and you go up to apply. Okay. They put you in one of those little rooms, and they go on their break and they walk up and down here for an hour—while you're sitting in the room up there waiting. And especially, if you're sick like I was. Then they accuse you of fraud and all this mess, accuse you of trying to get something for nothing. Then you blow your stack and you say, "the hell with it," and make it the best way you can.

Q: You think they really believe that, that you're trying to get something for nothing?

Glenn: Sure.

Jack: But, if you're a Vietnamese or a goddamn Japanese or something they'll help you right out. They do! You could be next in line. . . . Some of them come over here and get social security and never worked a day in their life. That's wrong! . . . We didn't ask them to come over here. Come over here by the boatloads. They're takin' the country over. And you're going to wake up one day and you're going to have no country, . . . 'cause they're going to have it. You don't see none of them on the streets. . . . You don't see none of those Vietnamese in the streets.

Displacement also operated among park residents through their self-concepts. Their self-identification as "respectable" derived from particular moral positions learned from the larger society. According to park residents, this was expressed in the form of a clear status hierarchy, descending from those who owned campers, through families, to single persons with transportation, to single male drinkers. Large campers parked on the access road were followed in status by families in the center parking area, who were followed in turn by groups of single males gathered around a small picnic area, perhaps accompanied by an occasional lone female. Resistance against displacement from the larger society was facilitated by a well developed social network that acted to bind people together through rigidly enforced rules of fairness and sharing. To act against the group was to risk exclusion from the park residents themselves.

Assimilation of the Population and Its Leaders

Assimilation included attempts by local authorities to recruit members of "the opposition" to help neutralize the impact of asking for benefits. When several of the park residents began to contest successfully the practices of the local social service office, the leaders were asked to "control the members of their group." Park leaders were therefore subject to "push" from the social service offices and "pull" from the park residents. Leaders were offered other possibilities for assistance from county and state officials, which helped to reduce the volatility of the situation. Several of the community activists whose livelihoods depended upon city and county funds were also told to reduce their hours of working with the park population, and they complied.

The social service workers' monopoly on the regulation of information, the organization of waiting, the arbitrary use of power, the ability to vary the amount of benefits, and the use of sanctions to discipline recipients all communicate a fundamental shift of institutional strategy from "charity"—the displacement of systemic social problems into individual salvations—to "disciplining the lazy" and the exclusion and repression of the "undeserving poor." Idleness replaces the "global charitable socialization of the poor." It affixes poverty and homelessness to the apparatus and requirements of production. These "micro-physics of power" are strategic in attempting to discipline the body, thereby increasing productivity (Foucault 1977; Lemert 1982:74). In the words of Foucault, "The problem is to set the 'able-bodied' poor to work and transform them into a useful labor force, but it is also to assure the self-financing by the poor themselves of the cost of their sickness and temporary incapacitation" (1980:169).

Work is "make-work"—disciplinary work for being poor. Social service carefully monitors its clients through interactions with other agencies. Whether it is the police (through the use of warrants checks), hospitals (through medical exams), or such other agencies as the District Attorney's office, surveillance is all perceived by the homeless as pervasive. This surveillance, through extensive record-keeping of applicants, increases the power of figuratively panoptic space.

Resistance to Authoritative Strategies: Use of Advocacy Groups

Resistance to this panoptic space of surveillance and discipline was difficult at best, but not impossible.[12] Many park residents believed that it was better to do without than to degrade oneself by entering into such a program. However, they would join if they felt that arbitrary sanctions could be contested. Of the four types of local resistance mentioned previously, the most effective was working with an advocacy group and reaching out to other organizations. If a park resident could demonstrate that he or she was part of a larger, well organized group with ties to the community, or had an advocate present during the intake interview, exclusionary strategies of authority could be blunted. Mobility and violating established boundaries were ineffective without community support. A community legal organization distributed a chart that mapped the bureaucratic levels of power for individuals within social services. The chart made it easier for park residents to appeal a case, since they could ask for a case worker's supervisor by name. This form of knowledge was so effective that HAP received calls from the local welfare office to please "lay off." It was a very effective form of resistance.[13]

Intervention often required direct action, sometimes just a phone call. The following cases of Lester and Eddy, in which we were involved, illustrate what was required. Both men had been denied benefits. Lester had been denied four times, even with his back injury. Eddy had been denied benefits because of a minor infraction of the social service regulations. Their cases were successfully contested by the direct action of community advocates, who sat with them during their intake interviews. As a result of this action, Lester began to work with both HAP and a neighboring shelter group.

Direct-action advocacy was used numerous times with other members of the park population until all those eligible for benefits had received them. HAP attempted to train some of the more vocal park residents in how to confront the welfare system. This had mixed results. One person left the office during the intake interview uttering profanities; another did not show up to accompany one of the other park residents. However, according to one park resident, organizing for benefits was a very good way of empowering the homeless:

Q: So what do you think we can do to change it? What's the top priority?

Lester: What I'd suggest, if you find somebody like myself, like I was at that point, just go down and throw your card at them and represent them—I think that if they get enough exposure, these case workers. . . . I really don't think a person has to have a Ph.D. after his name or something like that. All he's got to have is a card with the Homeless Action Project, and go in there. And when they ask, "Who are you?", you say, "I'm here to assist this gentleman; that's our function. He's homeless and we're here to assist him, to see that he gets his legal rights." And I'll tell you right now, I don't care who you are or what it says on the card, they're going to start backing down. Because they're running scared. They don't know, they aren't well versed enough to know how much damage you can cause them. . . .

. . . If an organization, but I'll use HAP as an example, if HAP wanted to rattle some cages they could take and compose a letter and put the names right on it of the people, how long the individual had to wait there to be interviewed, and I don't know where you would send it to. . . . But it would have to go to some office, you'd definitely rattle some cages. There's no excuse for this [the mistreatment]. No reason for it whatsoever.

In the above examples what appeared as significant was the association between the park resident and someone whom the social service office perceived as a figure of authority in the community. The use of formal business cards extended and anchored that authority by indicating a telephone number which could be called for verification.

Legal Aid of Orange County became involved with the park residents through HAP. They explained their legal rights to park residents and encouraged them to come to the office to contest any unfair actions by either the local police or welfare institutions.[14] Legal Aid services were utilized by some of the park members to contest AFDC sanctions and amounts. However, the location of Legal Aid in Santa Ana, about five miles distant, made it difficult for most park residents to use its services. This was particularly true for the park residents on foot. Furthermore, for any official action to occur, park residents would have to identify themselves in a formal complaint. Park residents were fearful of such identification, inasmuch as they could then be singled out for attention by authorities.

Having proof of affiliation with an organized group worked as a form of resistance to exclusionary strategies. This was demonstrated when Lester was stopped by police for sleeping in an abandoned building. He was able to avoid arrest by presenting a HAP card with a telephone number. By connecting with HAP, park residents were able to have a telephone and an address where mail could be delivered, making them eligible for welfare benefits. HAP's connection with local job banks and detoxification centers provided employment openings and places for park residents who were trying to "dry out."

Resistance to Authoritative Strategies: Mobility and Violating Established Boundaries

Mobility as a form of resistance was crucial in evading attempts by local authorities to control public space. During the evenings the park would appear empty, as vehicles moved to local residential streets or county parks to spend the night. During the day they moved back to the park, usually just after seven A.M. Most of the park residents left the park for short periods of time—days or weeks—but invariably returned to make contact with other park residents. During the day, park residents would come and go at will. If park residents were harassed, they generally moved to surrounding city and county parks, drifting back to Garden Grove Park when the "heat" died down.

The novel use of public space for private ends is a necessary survival response and a form of local resistance to established definitions of social space. This can be illustrated in drinking alcoholic beverages and taking showers. Picnic tables were gathering points for both eating and drinking alcohol. A large number of the single males, varying in ages from approximately mid-twenties to their late fifties, would spend their time in the park drinking. Occasionally, families would join in. Drinking served as a way of passing time, according to the residents. They explained that drinking was the way they managed boredom and the frustration of dealing with public officials.

Resistance to exclusion was manifested by "sneaking" into areas reserved for specific functions such as local tennis court shower rooms—if residents could comport themselves in a "respectable" manner. Park residents would carry duffel bags to appear as if they were going to play tennis, and then sneak into the showers.

Lester: What we used to do, somebody would come up there with a car, one of the guys had the car, and we'd load the car up, four, five, six of us, as many as we could get in, and we'd go up to Mile Square Park. In Mile Square Park they had a shower room, and everything in there, for the people out there playing tennis and handball, and things like that. And we would go in there and take a shower and shave and change clothes, and get a change of clothes, if we had clean clothes, and get all cleaned up. But [emphasis], if this facility knew, of course, we pulled a phoney deal, we carried duffel bags like we were playing tennis and everything like that, but, if they knew we were coming in there doing it, they would probably put a guard on that door. You know, we weren't breaking the law or anything, it's for the use of the public. But if they knew street people were coming in and using those facilities, they'd put a lock on it. They'd block it off. You see, we've been doing that for months. But you got to be careful the way you do it. You don't go over there with no thirty guys and take over the place, you go four or five at a time.

Q: It's almost sneaky.

Lester: Well, it is sneaky. It's perfectly legal. It's for the public. But you have to sneak around, otherwise they're going to cut it off on you.

Q: So even though it's for the public, it's almost like people who are on the streets are not the public.

Lester: That's true. That's it exactly. You have no rights! Public facilities are not available to you. Like in the parks, for instance. Alright, the park closes at eleven o'clock. If you're caught in the park after eleven o'clock, what happens? You're either going to get hassled out or you're gonna be taken down [to the police station]. One of the two. It depends on who the officer is and what his attitude is at that particular time.

SUMMARY AND RECOMMENDATIONS

It is our contention that local resistance to dominant authoritative strategies based on an inequality in power arises as a means of survival required by particular situations. The adaptations necessary for surviving on the street and securing basic necessities conflict with the life-styles of "housed" persons, and hence, with those state institutions developed to protect and regulate property. Government and private business attempt to mute this conflict by strategically managing specific definitions of space and behavior. Dominant authoritative strategies include but are not limited to exclusions, displacement of conflicts, assimilation of populations and leaders, and repression. Exclusions and repressions appear to be the most common strategies for coping with the homeless, followed by displacement and assimilation.

We have illustrated the main tactics of resistance that the homeless use against authoritative strategies, including forming and using new social networks; maintaining and expanding contact with sympathetic institutions, including advocacy groups; violating established boundaries for use of public and private facilities; and maintaining a high degree of mobility.

The appropriation of public space for private ends is a result of social and economic inequality generated by large disparities in wealth and power. There are many Garden Grove Parks around the country, and federal policy should increase the supply of low-cost housing. However, the provision of housing alone is insufficient for solving all the problems of homelessness. As this chapter illustrates, income and health care should also be addressed. Many members of the study population were on public assistance or working at irregular low-wage jobs, usually without health coverage.

Federal policy should address growing economic and political polarization. The notion that economic growth can, by itself, solve the problems of homelessness is based on the assumption that the effects of growth will "trickle down" to lower-income individuals. However, rarely do the benefits of economic growth reach the lower classes. Industrial policy does not directly address the degree of inequality between classes, so economic growth is an incomplete solution. Furthermore, when the politics of growth fail, the politics of repression dominate, in an effort to avoid redistribution (Wolfe 1981; Gross 1980). The result is that the benefits of economic growth become increasingly concentrated among the rich.

Recommendation #1. The federal government should develop a comprehensive and progressive housing policy, and it should coordinate fully with state and local governments. Almost all other industrialized nations have coherent housing policies. The United States has at best only a patchwork of federal programs (Gilderbloom and Appelbaum 1988; Lang 1989; Appelbaum and Dreier 1990; van Vliet and van Weesep 1990).

Recommendation #2. The federal government should renew its commitment to the funding of public or "social" housing programs, which provide such auxiliary services as empowerment training and skills development in community organization among poor residents.

Recommendation #3. The federal government should encourage zoning policies and urban redevelopment programs that address low and moderate-income housing needs through subsidized single-room-occupancy hotel construction and provision of auxiliary social services (Hoch and Slayton 1989).

Recommendation #4. The federal government should raise the minimum wage and institute a system of national health care to help improve the well-being of the homeless and poor.

Recommendation #5. The federal government should encourage the indexing of welfare benefits to the Consumer Price Index, just as Social Security is indexed.

Recommendation #6. The federal government should take the lead in improving the process of setting welfare standards and implementing them appropriately, so that everyone who is legally eligible properly receives the payments.

Recommendation #7. The federal government should adopt a more progressive tax policy that reduces deductions and increases taxes for corporate income, stock ownership and transfers, inheritance over $90,000, and the incomes of the top 5 percent of wage earners.

The social benefits from an increase in housing and collective empowerment programs sponsored by the federal government should be shared by both middle class and the working poor segments of society.

CONCLUSION

Park residents were able to multiply their resistance tactics to dominant authoritative strategies with outside resources and the assistance of community activists. Contesting authoritative strategies in open public areas produced a significant curtailment of repressive police practices. The integration of outside advocates into the activities of park residents reduced (but did not stop) their marginalization. Park residents moved from a simple geographic power base that relied on concentration and dispersion, to one of strategic institutional power that could contest other institutions, however briefly. Contesting power led to higher levels of activity and self-esteem among both park residents and activists, and to higher levels of empowerment on an individual level.

Broad-scale empowerment of the homeless, which envisioned a developing political power, was considerably more diffuse and problematic among residents of Garden Grove Park, partly because it was dependent upon political actions at the state and federal level. However, one should not be quick to dismiss the micro-level resistance tactics of the displaced. While their difficulties may be problematic for a political theory of resistance, this in no way negates the role that local micro-level resistance tactics play in grounding larger political movements. Resistance is often important to the homeless themselves, even if conditions are not sufficient to sustain a resistance movement beyond the local level. Resistance tactics require a high degree of risk that may not be immediately acceptable to particular homeless populations.

NOTES

We are indebted to Jennifer Wolch, Michael Dear, Mark Gottdiener, Michael Rotkin, Sue Ruddick, and Roger Keil for their critique and helpful comments on earlier drafts of this paper. A preliminary version of this paper was presented at the 1990 Annual American Sociological Association conference, Washington, D.C.

1. All names of interviewed persons have been altered to protect their anonymity.

2. Giddens's notion of time-space continuity and discontinuity (1981:150, 1984:110–145) can be used to understand the relationship between larger forces of institutional control and surveillance, and one's physical body and self-image.

3. As de Certeau notes, "The 'proper' is a triumph of place over time" (1984:36). He further writes that it is the control over and the division of space which "makes possible a panoptic practice proceeding from a place whence the eye can transform foreign forces into objects that can be observed and measured, and thus control and 'include' them within its scope of vision" (1984:36).

4. This study was conducted by the Orange County Homeless Issues Task Force (1990) and covered 1,974 persons, 36 percent of whom were children. While the study does not focus on a strictly random sample, it does profile the types of homeless persons who asked for assistance. We know that there are many who do not ask for assistance.

5. According to the 1980 census, Hispanics represent 14.8 percent of Orange County's population.

6. In 1988 the city of Santa Ana, California, used local park employees to follow-up a police sweep of the civic center plaza by confiscating bedrolls, blankets, and other belongings stored by the local homeless in the bushes. These possessions were then thrown away. This action by the city produced a large public outcry and legal suits, forcing the city to modify its policy by providing limited storage for homeless belongings. On April 25, 1990, fifteen local homeless people received a settlement from the city of $50,000, or $3,308 per person.

7. Public rest rooms used by park residents were locked several times by park officials

in response to vandalism. The park residents, who were blamed for these actions, contended that the damage was caused by local teenagers from the nearby high school.

8. Systematic police sweeps occurred within the park. One park resident who was active in resisting these practices asserted that cities will often conduct police sweeps to rid the parks of homeless people on the eve of a study or count, which then results in no homeless people being found in the cities.

9. This threat appeared to originate with one police officer. The residents said that he would bully the residents and threaten them after they arrived in the park at 7:00 A.M. When asked why they did not report him, they said that it would not do any good and would just increase the pressure on them to move. However, this activity was curtailed when homeless advocates and several park residents called the local police commander. Assurances were given that the officer would be reassigned.

10. The disruption of daily routines (for example, not sleeping in a stable location) serves to maintain authority over park use. Rowe and Walsh (1990) note that these discontinuities adversely affect a person's sense of identity and self-esteem but that they can be resisted through the development of social networks. These networks, with their intimate social bonds, were extensive among homeless people in our park sample.

11. See Stack (1974) for a discussion of swapping in poor communities.

12. Perrot, in Foucault's *Power/Knowledge* (1984), presents the notion of "revolt against the gaze," a revolt that refuses the inspection of authority—a revolt observed in workers not turning up for work (Lemert and Gillan 1982). One can observe similar rebellious behavior of the poor against the disciplinary nature of "make-work" programs. Sanctions are used extensively to punish violators. The punishments can be leveled for something as petty as being fifteen minutes late for work.

13. In the first three months of 1988, HAP assisted over a thousand people with food, clothing, shelter, jobs, vouchers for gasoline, bars of soap, and tubes of toothpaste, in addition to assistance in qualifying for financial benefits.

14. The ACLU, like Legal Aid, was interested in the plight of the park residents but was constrained by inadequate funding and staff. However, they did gather records of complaints against local police and treatment of park residents by the police.

9

"There Goes the Neighborhood": Gentrification, Displacement, and Homelessness in Washington, D.C.

Brett Williams

Washington, D.C., city officials value gentrification, according to Williams, because it reverses urban decay and boosts the tax base. Banking and real estate interests value it for the profit generated from speculation. However, gentrification destroys traditional, largely African-American communities, because rising house costs force them to move. Family structure becomes more nucleated; single men move to public shelters; people split up, double-up, improvise; and some move into the street. Williams recommends firmer regulation of land use, speculation, access to credit, tenant protection, and tax reform.

INTRODUCTION

This chapter explores gentrification, displacement, and homelessness in Washington, D.C.[1] In the neighborhood of Mount Pleasant, the African-American population has plummeted in the last twenty years, from 75 percent of the residents in 1970, to 29 percent in 1990. Over two thousand African Americans have apparently been "vaporized," and they continue to go. Despite the "feel" of science fiction, real social relations are at work here. Tracking where these residents go clarifies two processes: (1) the ways people cope with displacement, as they split up, double-up, improvise, find precarious housing, and move into shelters or onto the street; and (2) the linkages between gentrification and other real estate activities, such as speculation, abandonment, and fraud. In this chapter, I examine the interaction between gentrification and other forces that make low-income housing more besieged.

Explanations of Gentrification

Gentrification refers to the process whereby new residents—disproportionately young, white, well-educated, salaried, and professional—move into urban neighborhoods that are often populated by people of color who are older and poorer. A small but growing literature on this process features different explanations of gentrification. Some scholars draw on cultural explanations and a frontier analogy to hail the urban pioneers who reject the "white-bread suburbs" of their parents to seek diversity and excitement in the city. These explanations stress the values of the new homeowners as agents in spearheading gentrification (Gale 1984). Other writers argue that banks, real estate companies, speculators, and even the government preceded these "hardy pioneers." They feel that the nationalist, conservative, do-it-yourself ideology of urban homesteading masks these more fundamental processes. They believe that the only frontier involved is a profitability frontier that divides disinvestment from reinvestment, as early developers work on the extreme edge, where traditional lenders are reluctant to invest.

Smith (1981) writes that gentrification is best understood in terms of a "rent gap" that occurs when the actual ground rent is much lower than the potential value of the land. He argues, along with similar writers, for a historical perspective that looks at land use over long periods of time. Often a predictable "devalorization cycle"—including initial use, transfer to landlord control, blockbusting, redlining, and abandonment—prepares a neighborhood for reinvestment and gentrification. Capital must first move out of a neighborhood and then back in. These writers argue for a global perspective that examines the movement of capital in and out of different areas of investment, including stocks and bonds, money markets, and property.

Devalorization Cycle

A rent gap began with the movement of capital into the suburbs after World War II. A loose coalition of financial institutions and business leaders deliberately developed many urban areas as slums by refusing to lend money for mass transportation, affordable housing, or productive investment—except for the freeways that liberated suburban workers from the city's grasp. Later, urban property became attractive again, with the shift in urban economies from industries to services and the need for highly technical workers at the urban core. The spread of businesses globally and the increased use of sophisticated communications technologies centralized a new elite and simultaneously decentralized many clerical staffs into back-office "paper factories" in the suburbs.

Gentrification reflects large-scale economic and political forces, and conscious decisions by people with money and power to reinvest in an urban environment that they once let decay. It reflects and propels the extraordinary polarization of America's cities in terms of both housing and work. From this perspective, the members of the baby-boom generation, with their pluralistic values, are consumers, not agents, responding to the political economy of urban growth (Cordova 1991; Palen and London 1984; Smith and Williams 1986). The value of this interpretation is that it helps place gentrification, gentrifying neighborhoods, and the populations they displace in a larger and more dynamic context.

Consequences of Gentrification

The debate over the consequences of gentrification is reflected in writers' wildly different notions of how to name it. "Gentrification" is the most neutral term, but some writers argue that it gives prominence to individual agency and is more appropriate to the British experience. Others, including many city officials, *celebrate* gentrification for reversing urban decay and boosting the tax base. They often refer to it as "revitalization," drawing on the metaphors of disease, deterioration, death, and rebirth to talk about urban history (cf. Conquergood 1992). Palen and London (1984) suggest that the term "invasion" would better capture the processes of assault on the community, loss of affordable housing stock, displacement, resegregation, ghettoization of crime, and the development of health hazards and homelessness that inevitably result (see also Nyden and Wiewel 1991). In fact, they suggest that "reinvasion" would be preferable, since deteriorated neighborhoods are likely to be the same ones that whites fled in the 1950s and 1960s. With the demise of the restrictive convenants prohibiting the sale of houses or the extension of FHA mortgages to those who would alter the racial composition of a neighborhood, whites left neighborhoods rather than live with blacks (Palen and London 1984; see also, Hartman, Keating, and LeGates 1981).

Displacement

Another debate focuses on the relationship between gentrification and displacement. Some writers argue that the two processes are not connected, especially in light of more prominent urban forces, such as job loss or the lack of accessible public transportation (Cameron 1992; Gale n.d.). Others argue that all roads lead to displacement, although the routes are hard to define and tricky to measure. In fact, Hartman, Keating, and Legates (1981) suggest that official statistics deliberately undercount displacement in order to warp public policy on behalf of the gentrifiers. Writers disagree on how to define displacement, though most agree it is a process whereby a household unwillingly relocates.

In gentrifying neighborhoods, displacement can be "direct," that is, economically motivated, in that rents or taxes are raised; or it can be "physical," for example, when the heat is turned off in buildings being readied for conversion; or it might be exclusionary, if a household that could have previously afforded to live there can no longer move in. It might simply reflect the pressure to sell because of high prices for housing. "Last resident displacement" refers to those who leave because all their friends and neighbors have gone (Marcuse 1985). All of these processes are hard to measure and interpret, in part because families may be displaced more than once as gentrification spreads, and in part because displacement studies overmeasure the better-off, more traceable people.

Finally, who has to leave, where do they go, and are they better off when they do? Several researchers have tried to address these questions quantitatively. Again, there is little consensus. Some argue that the elderly are disproportionately displaced, but others argue that female-headed households are the most likely to be forced out. Most writers agree that the lower the income, the more vulnerable the residents, and that previously mobile residents are the most likely to have to move again. Some writers insist that displacement causes no measurable hardship, and that many people report being better off. Others connect displacement to various difficulties, including repeated displacement if they settle nearby; increased transportation costs and loss of community if they move far away; crowding and illegal conversions if they double-up; increasing segregation if they resettle in single-race or -ethnicity ghettos; and a serious financial squeeze if they must pay more for shelter. For the elderly, displacement can mean severe depression and even death (see especially Hartman, Keating, and Legates 1981; Lee and Hodge 1984; Marcuse 1985; Schill and Nathan 1983; Singelakis 1990).

Ethnography in a Context of Political Economy

This literature is provocative but incomplete. I am persuaded by those writers who argue that gentrification must be seen in a fuller political, economic, and historical context. At the same time, I believe that this overwhelmingly macro-scale and quantitative literature can profit from ethnographic research grounded in one place and in real people's lives. I know of very little such research, except for Conquergood's work in Chicago (1992), which reveals dramatically and persuasively that groups and institutions propelling gentrification mobilized against a multiethnic tenement community and effectively destroyed it. In my earlier work in Washington (1988), I suggested that newer residents should work to prevent displacement, but I did not see at the time the brutality of dislocation for a very large number of poor African-American residents. I hope here to redress that oversight and to contribute to the debates over gentrification by looking inward and outward at the same time, seeking the ghosts of a vaporized community, yet placing that community within larger urban processes.

One must examine Mount Pleasant in 1993 within the larger picture of Washington, D.C., and its changing real estate patterns. I hope that this political economic context will set the stage for understanding the circumstances of the displaced.

Social Ecology of Washington, D.C.

I begin with Washington's subway map (Figure 9.1), the most widespread and best-known icon of the city. Though largely stylized, it reveals alternative constructions of five different residential zones, which both reflect and influence real estate activity. Zone 1, west of Rock Creek Park (marked by subway stops with bucolic nineteenth-century names such as Woodley Park, Cleveland Park, and Tenleytown), houses mostly white and affluent residents. Government officials, lobbyists, professors, and international workers come and go. The area has wit-

Figure 9.1
Subway Map

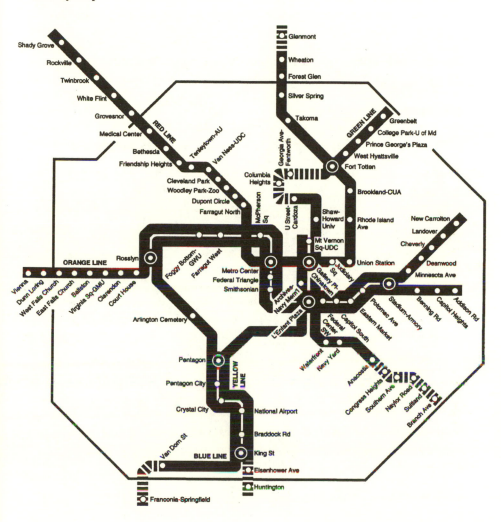

nessed a good deal of speculation, investment, and rehabilitation of single-family homes in the last twenty years. Housing prices are the highest in the city.

In Zone 2, just east of Rock Creek Park, there are pockets of integrated neighborhoods that were settled at the turn of the century as streetcar suburbs. They were the first to experience gentrification, in the 1970s. They include Dupont Circle (on the subway map in Figure 9.1) and Mount Pleasant and Adams Morgan (on the neighborhood map in Figure 9.2), and, after some stalling of gentrification in the

Figure 9.2
Neighborhood Map

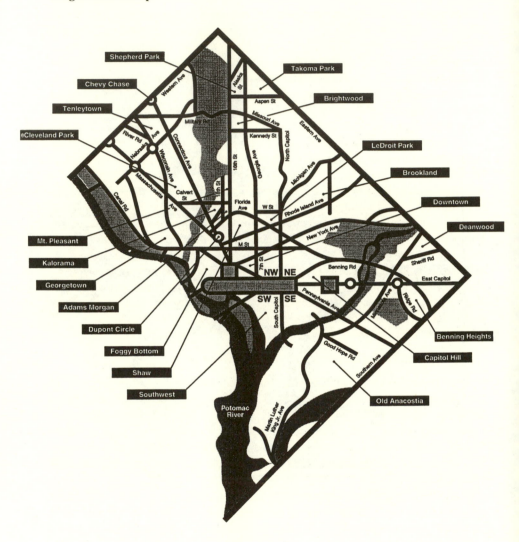

1980s, other neighborhoods to the east, such as Columbia Heights, Petworth, and Shaw (Figure 9.1) and Brightwood (Figure 9.2), which are all in Zone 3. One mark of gentrification (in addition to barred windows) is lobbying by residents to have their local station renamed in "west of the park" fashion: thus Georgia Avenue, for example, becomes Petworth. Several of these neighborhoods have also taken on the tasteful, valued garb of historic districts.

Zone 4 comprises Foggy Bottom and Southwest on the subway map in Figure

9.1, and Capitol Hill and Georgetown—which was gentrified long ago—on the neighborhood map in Figure 9.2. The desirability of the neighborhoods in Zone 4 contributes to the viselike squeeze experienced by residents in many eastern neighborhoods—Hillcrest, Riverview, Woodridge, Benning Heights, Ivy City, Trinidad, Fort Dupont, Fort Totten, Bradbury Heights, Valley Green, and others. The symbolism of the subway map places all these varied neighborhoods in what comprises Zone 5 but denies them names, relying instead on stops designated for institutions and avenues. Zone 5 houses many people who were displaced from other parts of the city during the last thirty years. Note that only Fort Totten among the names in Zone 5 graces a subway stop. Residents here must cope with systematic public sector neglect, underfunded schools, a dearth of jobs, and serious housing problems. This entire part of the city, which houses much of the city's labor force, is buried in political speeches and by the mass media in homogenized specters of a vast "black underclass" that was allegedly left behind to wallow in self-perpetuating pathologies when middle-class African Americans moved away. Politicians, reporters, and community organizers speak often of Washington as a city of neighborhoods, although that status may be denied communities in the eastern part of city. This turn of phrase helps to disguise the connections among Washington's neighborhoods, the vertical connections between neighborhoods and developers, and the flow of dislocated people in between neighborhoods. Looking at Washington's neighborhoods together, in the context of gentrification, abandonment, and displacement, can help to refute many misconceptions.

Segregation, Urban Renewal, and Moving On Out

I will begin this history in the 1940s, when the Committee to End Segregation in the Nation's Capital described inner city Washington as a "racial enclosure." This term reflected many residents' feelings of being trapped by residential segregation, restrictive covenants, and obsolete buildings, and choked by an overload of industrial facilities and the urban renewal process (Landis 1948). (See the map in Figure 9.3, which shows where the racial enclosure, or what was then known as the city's "Black Belt," was found.)

In the 1950s, the Redevelopment Authority developed a plan to remove all black residents to the city's far southeastern portion in order to reclaim the schools, land, parks, and recreational facilities for more affluent people who would bolster the tax base. Historian Constance Green writes: "In short, a magnificent white metropolis was to rise with the servants' quarters at the rear" (1976:279). Congress temporarily blocked this blatant scheme but collaborated with it later in the decade by approving plans to raze existing communities in Foggy Bottom and Southwest Washington and "renew" them with expensive housing, federal buildings, and new highways to transport white residents to the new federally subsidized suburbs. Thousands of residents were displaced and forced to move across the Anacostia River or within the city's Black Belt.

Figure 9.3
Map Showing 1940s Racial Enclosure

1 Washingtons over-crowded slum areas occupied by Negroes

2 Are opened to white development. The wreckers arrive and

3 New housing for whites is erected. The displaced colored people are relocated within shrinking area.

NO PLACE TO GO

The courts no longer enforce restrictive covenants but a silent conspiracy does.

Pressure groups force housing and planning boards to tighten segregation.

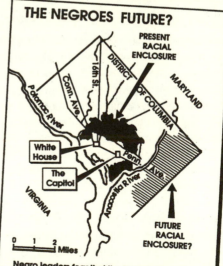

Negro leaders fear that the Park and Planning Commission intends to segregate the entire Negro population across the Anacostia River.

This reclaiming of the city's core, which has not relented, made housing for low-income black Washingtonians viselike. In my earlier research, and in later interviews conducted among public housing residents by Joseph Jordan, Theresa Trainor, and Carmen James, people spoke of feeling "bottled up" or "piled up." They talked at the same time of "moving round and round" during those years, or "just moving around." They lived on different streets and in several quadrants. They lived with relatives, then left them, rented rooms, tried with optimism the new housing projects, and at times saw their homes, blocks, and neighborhoods razed for urban renewal (Jordan 1990; Trainor 1992; Potomac Gardens interviews, n.d.)

Yet for some of the more fortunate minority residents, 1960 brought change, as more whites fled the streetcar suburbs they had settled at the turn of the century to escape the central city. The *Bolling v. Sharpe* school integration decision drove the final nail in the restrictive-covenant coffin, and many remaining whites moved to the suburbs, where schools were still largely segregated. Black residents who had been trapped in the central city's Black Belt enthusiastically moved, aided by block-busting realtors. People discuss this time in terms of greater space and freedom. Some bought houses, sponsored kin coming to Washington from the South, opened small businesses, planted gardens, boarded buses for better schools, and enjoyed the comforts of shopping more freely and using public restrooms.

For about fifteen years Mount Pleasant housed mostly black residents, and almost every business on its main commercial street was black-owned. However, by 1980, the black population had dropped to 43.6 percent, and by 1990 to 29.8 percent. Those who remain are overwhelmingly older and more prosperous homeowners, and only one black-owned business now graces Mount Pleasant Street. Today refugees from Central America vie with Anglo gentrifiers for control of commercial and public space (Blake n.d.) The disappearance of the black population has coincided so dramatically with gentrification that it would be hard to argue there is no connection. However, there are two caveats. First, Mount Pleasant was never a timeless, organic black community; it was always connected to other neighborhoods and to public policy and real estate investment decisions throughout the city (cf. Palen and Nachmias 1984). Second, the squeeze on the displaced today can only be understood in the context of real estate activities throughout the Washington area "Shatterbelt."

Several trends characterized the late 1970s and—after an economic stall induced by high interest rates—most of the 1980s. There was heady speculation that Van Dyne (1988) refers to as the "house game," in which houses became "money machines" for the more affluent. Rapid rises in house prices were accompanied by a euphemistically titled "affordability crunch" for clerical, service, and public sector workers (even if the racial divide cut house prices in half on the eastern side of the city). West of Sixteenth Street, affluent professionals bought and sold expensive houses with every expectation that prices would rise each year. The wild speculation peaked in 1989, when the Washington economy endured a serious recession, from which prices have not yet recovered. Most who bought in Mount Pleasant have seen values drop.

Larger developers, with very few exceptions, have not built low-income housing. They have gambled on middle-income apartment complexes and office buildings in the suburbs. Even Washington's far exurbs present extraordinary housing
opportunities for those willing to undertake a long commute. However, overbuilding, high vacancy rates, debt, and bankruptcy have resulted for many exurb developers. To some extent, space and height restrictions have limited overbuilding in
Washington itself. Developers still concentrate on office buildings and luxury housing downtown, along with the "hospitality industry," symbolized most recently by
plans for Washington's second convention center (Spayd 1993). Development has
also centered on areas surrounding Metro stations, making Washington's model
transportation system something akin to a land development scheme.

This combination of development efforts seems to be creating a new vise for
low-income residents—as tourist facilities, such as the convention center and its
surrounding hotel and restaurant entourage creep north from Mt. Vernon Square;
as "Legoland" threatens Ivy City further beyond to the northeast. As anonymous
partnerships buy up land near Buzzards Point near the Washington Navy Yard, a
new stadium is planned for Chinatown, and Capitol Hill's prize real estate also
expands north and east. Low-income residents are squeezed out as waterfront
projects arise adjacent to downtown office areas and as middle-income services
and residential developments grow around Metro stops, such as Minnesota Avenue. Even across the river in Anacostia, the Green Line of the Metro has sparked
a wave of rehabilitations. Land prices rose from $2 per square foot to $55 in the few
months following the court order to proceed with construction (Mariano 1989).

Recent years have been marked, and marred, by several different forms of corruption and discrimination in real estate. These include racism in granting mortgage
and home equity loans, and sham home-improvement schemes common to many
cities. Public corruption is evident in the recent disclosure that the D.C. Housing
Finance Agency, created to finance low-cost housing, cannot justify at least
$750,000, and possibly $1.2 million, in questionable spending on items like parties,
travel, gifts, flowers, and mopeds (Henderson 1993). One of the most serious examples of corruption resulted in the devastation of the Trinidad neighborhood in
the northeast (often touted as representative of stagnant underclass life) and, to a
lesser extent, North Capitol Hill, Deanwood, Congress Heights, and Anacostia (see
Figure 9.1).

In the mid-1980s a group of large developers noted gentrification creeping north
from Capitol Hill toward a neighborhood apparently oblivious to it. There were
landlords who wanted to sell, and few who wanted to buy; prices were cheap. The
"profitability pioneers" considered speculating. The problem, however, was that it
was still very risky: how could they be certain to find second-line buyers to buy the
properties from them? The result was an elaborate scheme to ensure that the government would take the risk. They bought up properties and resold them, sometimes on the same day, to fake buyers who were usually their friends. These buyers

were able to obtain FHA loans because the buildings cost less than $120,000. Fake appraisers (also friends) held the buildings to be in good condition, and the developers faked financial credentials for the buyers. (All parties looked to the FHA to be financially wise with respect to creditworthy buyers and good-risk buildings.) The buyers were able to evade a rent-control loophole, because they, in theory, owned only one four-unit building. They immediately raised rents and allowed the buildings to deteriorate, milking their value and reneging on their FHA loans. The government eventually foreclosed, but not before many tenants had to leave and the neighborhood had been skewered. Although a number of developers went to jail or paid fines, this massive real estate fraud cost Washington some two thousand buildings offering affordable housing and contributed immeasurably to the housing vise. The property values in these neighborhoods were distorted by false appraisals, which made them less attractive to real investors, to say nothing of distorting the district's tax base and thus doing long-term harm (cf. Downey 1991).

This, then, is the "shatterbelt" context in which gentrification and displacement in Mount Pleasant must be understood. Gentrification is not an isolated process. It is linked to the redevelopment of the Washington waterfront, the rise of hotel and convention complexes, disinvestment, abandonment, and decay in some low-income areas, and wild speculation in others. Gentrification is a visible spatial component of social transformation. As wealthy people try to wall themselves off in gentrified neighborhoods, the housing squeeze in the neighborhoods facing abandonment gets worse. This happens in part because the displaced move east and south, further crowding those already trapped in several directions by today's tourist and office buildings downtown. Then, as gentrification itself oozes east, more people get displaced (some for the second or third time), and developers feel pressed to invest in the gentrifying areas and abandon the neighborhoods housing low-income residents. Gentrification and abandonment feed each other in a vicious circle, and the poor are continuously threatened by the displacement that both generate (Marcuse 1985).

METHODOLOGY

Displaced residents are like ghosts: they are difficult to find and talk to. Even quantitative researchers have discussed the difficulties of doing research among them. I tried several different approaches in search of answers to the following question: Where did all the black residents of Mount Pleasant go? I had worked in a nearby neighborhood during the 1980s, and I have been active in the public schools, public humanities programming, and community events for many years. I therefore began with people I knew: the remaining black shopkeeper, a man who runs a light hauling business that relies on homeless men, a woman who had organized tenants against displacement, and several people who had been public figures in the life of the street. These key people knew me well, and I was forthright about my purpose, asking if they knew where so many of the black residents had gone. Sometimes I modified my questions when inquiring of people I suspected to have been at great risk, or when asking about others they might know. These first contacts were helpful, and they referred me to others in a snowball fashion.

I made repeated visits to Mount Pleasant, talking to black residents who were still there—a few of the remaining homeowners and the (mostly) men who came back to socialize in the mornings on the street. I sought out places where people gathered in the hope of being picked up for day work, and I lingered there to ask my questions and find out how people were doing. From there, I began to range outside the neighborhood, looking for those I'd been referred to and sometimes finding them, in places ranging from a church basement to the east to a quarantined room in Howard University Hospital, where I talked to a man dying of pneumonia related to HIV. Many were people I had known and worked with before. My questions were simple: Why did you leave Mount Pleasant? Where have you been living since?

All told, I talked to people representing about thirty households, just a tiny fraction of the displaced. However, they have much to reveal, for two reasons. First, though there are definite patterns that echo and further illuminate the findings of quantitative researchers, there is no single story. During the urban renewal projects of the 1960s, observers could describe the demolition of an entire community; gentrification-induced displacement is much more slippery and complex. Sometimes an individual's life is representative of a larger group, when, for example, an entire building is cleared for conversion. But these individuals have taken many different paths, including displacement from conversion. Secondly, because these people are still tied to the neighborhood, they include those who found it most difficult to leave. They are indeed the ghosts of gentrification: they do not want to go.

FINDINGS

The stories of displaced residents are all different, but I have clustered them into five types.

The Elderly

As several other researchers have found in their quantitative findings, the elderly seem to be at great risk. In some cities this is a problem reflected in the rise of single-room-only residences (SROs), and this is part of the context in Mount Pleasant as well. Two of the fifteen men I talked to had lived in an informal rooming house of six elderly male friends, one of whom owned it. This had been a very satisfactory arrangement, as they could come and go as they pleased, cook and eat on their own, yet find company in the living room or on the front porch when they were home. They had lived together like this since the mid-1970s. As property assessments rose, however, the owner found that to keep up with his taxes he had to charge his friends higher rent. Two had to go, one moved in with a woman friend who lived several miles to the east, and the other returned to the small North Carolina town where he had grown up.

Some of the elderly residents of Mount Pleasant have died, contributing a small amount to the population loss there. One man, when I asked what he thought had happened to all the black people, replied, "They're all in jail or dead." Some who died were renters and people well known in public life. Several owners have died, as well. In each case that I know, their heirs sold the house, again contributing to population loss, but understandably so. The modest houses that were difficult for people to maintain and pay taxes on became a prime source of equity for the next generation—too tempting not to sell. In every case they were replaced by whites, and the adult heirs moved to low-rent suburbs.

The elderly experience other patterns as well. Widowhood meant for Mrs. Billings that she could not sustain her small house; on one fixed income, the rent was too high. Her sons moved her into senior citizens' housing several blocks to the east, but she has found it grim and alienating. She feels lonely, misses her neighborhood, and has been seriously troubled by arthritis since the move. Mrs. Samson also sold her house and moved to her daughter's home in Maryland when her husband died. Most of the elderly and their heirs were able to find alternative housing. The issues for those I talked to were partly financial but more dramatically about the loss of community. They missed having friends to talk to and garden with. They felt dispersed and somewhat alone. Displacement was a major, depressing disruption that made being old very difficult.

Triage

Many families pressed for space and resources felt compelled to "triage" or ease-out difficult kin. One woman, Mrs. Harris, lived with her brother, who was mentally ill. He could not work, and he suffered from hallucinations that caused him occasionally to walk up and down the street screaming. His neighbors knew and looked after him, saving aluminum cans for him to sell and sometimes feeding his dog. After Mrs. Harris retired from domestic service at Howard University, she found it difficult to pay her escalating property taxes. Also, as her neighbors left, she found it increasingly difficult to deal with her brother. She, too, moved from her house and was forced to set her brother on his own. He now stays in a downtown shelter and seems to be chronically in an unsettled and florid state.

Another man, Eddie Jones, was similarly forced to evict his mentally troubled nephew, Sam, who had lived with Eddie for his entire adult life. Sam was not dangerous but walked down the street gesturing and talking to himself. When Eddie moved into a one-bedroom apartment he had to ask Sam to leave, and I was unable to find him. Similarly, a third family, forced to leave their apartment building after repeated fires, institutionalized their young son in a home for the mentally retarded. (Cf. Hopper 1981, for a discussion of the term "triage" in this context.)

Wanting to Buy

Six families moved because they wanted to own houses and knew they would never be able to in Mount Pleasant. Three couples moved with their children to far Northeast Washington to purchase tiny row houses. They have been content with the move, although they find the distances to work and school very cumbersome to travel by public transportation. Several of the adults miss Mount Pleasant and return often to socialize. Two women with their children have also moved to Northeast Washington; one survives by taking in boarders, the other has three grown sons who participate in both the formal and informal economy. The last woman was very fortunate in winning the housing assistance lottery, and she qualifies for government aid. Yet she has been unable to obtain any kind of bank loan at all, in spite of her twenty-three years as a civil servant and her work as a foster parent, because she carries many crippling small debts (on credit cards and to department stores) and because she co-signed several family loans that went bad. She now rents a tiny apartment with her two foster children and continues to seek a mortgage.

Conversions

A number of renters were forced out by the conversion of their buildings, but here too their experiences vary, and there is no single story. One man, among the first to be displaced, was pushed out along with all the other tenants in his building so the landlord could let it sit idle for two years in order to convert it to condominiums. The tenants unsuccessfully protested the conversion of their building—many of them had lived there since 1960. A second man left recently when his building was purchased by a Latin American advocacy organization to be remade into a co-op. Along with their families, they have moved to Prince Georges County, Maryland, but both frequently return to Mount Pleasant. A third woman with two children was forced out of her building because of a series of fires in the garbage room—a not-uncommon strategy for clearing an apartment building, although there is no evidence of arson that she knows of in this case. She lives with her mother in Northeast Washington. Finally, a fourth woman, a school secretary with a grown son, is trying to leave because of the abominable condition of her building and the impossibility of maintenance. (She spent last winter with no heat.) A longtime community leader and civic activist, she leaves with great regret. She has also found it nearly impossible to find another place to go. (Some researchers estimate that a worker must earn $14 an hour to rent a two-bedroom place in Washington without a severe financial squeeze.) Finally, a mother and her teenage son have moved to Virginia, and a grown daughter and her mother have moved to Maryland, unable to pay the progressively escalating rents.

Men on Their Own

Finally, I found that single men were at great risk in Mount Pleasant, especially renters. The thirteen men described here range in age from twenty-five to sixty-five. All have worked for most of their lives in Washington's service sector and lived in apartment buildings in Mount Pleasant. I am not sure why their experiences have been so hard. In some cases it may be because they are the already triaged, difficult members of their families, though this is not true in every case. Their problems may reflect the difficulty of surviving on one income in Washington, the lack of non-clerical jobs, and the criminalizing of young black men engaged in the informal economy.

Once again there is no one story to tell. Two of the men, both in their twenties, returned to North Carolina, but they do not stay in one place. They lived with different relatives for brief spells, seeking temporary work, and then moved on. One spent some time in jail. They also return to Washington occasionally and stay with friends, relatives, and in shelters. Two other men doubled-up more permanently with women friends, and one stays in his parents' basement in Prince Georges County. Two found places to stay in Mount Pleasant, both basements, in exchange for cleaning the buildings. Two others stay in shelters and return to Mount Pleasant for day work, usually small hauling and moving jobs. Two others have found rooms to the east, which they rent by the week and pay for by doing restaurant work. Finally, two of the displaced men recently died of complications associated with HIV. They were on public assistance and virtually alone at Howard University Hospital. Their experiences are emblematic of the problems all these men face: no medical insurance, no savings, no reliable work, almost no cushion between themselves and disaster. Displacement, I believe, made them much more vulnerable, because they no longer had the same kind of community base.

Larger Processes at Work

These stories reflect processes that have occurred in other cities: the loss of small rooming houses, the conversion of rental units, and the economic displacement of low-income renters and homeowners on fixed incomes. Crowded, squeezed families do resort to triaging their more problematic kin. Harassment of tenants through fires, turning down the heat, and failing to collect the garbage has occurred in other places. In Mount Pleasant, many people hung on as long as they could in spite of these pressures, because they had found the neighborhood an affordable and pleasant place to live. Many have suffered stages of displacement, as their housing grows increasingly precarious over time. For some it has led to homelessness. For many others it has meant a financial squeeze, a more nucleated family structure, the loss of community networks, public life, and cushions for emergencies. Thus, the Washington experience makes clear that supposedly underclass households are not isolated, but battered. Many people displaced from Mount

Pleasant are among them.

Many metaphors mask these processes, beginning with the notion of gentrifiers as urban pioneers. Washington's subway map affirms other portraits of this eastern city as more a stagnant quagmire than part of the Nintendo-like scene where land capitalists maneuver. The myth of the organic black community, past and present, masks both Washington's Black Belt past and Mount Pleasant's brief moment in history as a fairly prosperous, richly civil, black-owned and operated neighborhood. The sense among some Anglos and blacks that the problem in Mount Pleasant is that "the Spanish took over" fuels antagonism among those who will inhabit shared, multiethnic space and leaves the true villain, gentrification, unscathed. The poorly housed and the unhoused are not behavioral groups; social class is not personal behavior; and neighborhoods do not stand still.

The displaced people of Mount Pleasant are like Muley, who, when complaining of homelessness in *The Grapes of Wrath*, says, "I'm just an old graveyard ghost." Like graveyards haunted by those who do not want to die, our cities are haunted by those who must but cannot leave. If we can understand that the displaced, and the homeless in particular, are like ghosts, I believe we will have found an appropriate metaphor.

SUMMARY AND RECOMMENDATIONS

Many good ideas for preventing displacement have emerged in recent years, and the experiences of the people of Mount Pleasant help to illuminate the wisdom of most of them. Currently, both federal and local government policies are so biased in favor of both gentrification and home ownership that they probably encourage the affluent to "overconsume housing" (Schill and Nathan 1983). In many cases, policies encourage gentrification as well. Recommendations for changes that would discourage displacement cluster in five issue areas: landlords, zoning, taxes, banking, and affordable housing and social property.

Recommendation #1: Landlord Issues and Recommendations. Washington, D.C., has taken several measures to protect tenants, including rent control and tenants' right of first refusal to a landlord who wants to sell. However, there are too many loopholes in these provisions, and as we have seen in the local HUD scandal, they are not rigorously enforced. Tenants need greater security, and there are several ways to provide it.

The local government could work harder to prevent harassment, disinvestment, and the denial of proper living conditions. Evictions could be regulated, and families in trouble provided with rent assistance. Commercial rent control might help to preserve public space and the kinds of stores that poorer people need. SRO housing could be specially protected by recognizing its importance and that it is endangered. If SRO housing were registered, the city could restrict conversions until there is a normal vacancy rate, and could insist that SRO housing be replaced on a one-to-one basis. All elderly tenants should be granted lifetime tenancy regardless of the fate of their building.

Recommendation #2: Zoning Issues and Recommendations. Local governments now conspire to provide diminishing and uneven public services to changing neighborhoods. Sometimes rigorous code enforcement forces poorer homeowners to rehabilitate or sell, especially when facing historic-district designation of their neighborhood. Zoning issues are hot ones in gentrifying neighborhoods, as witnessed by continuing conflicts over liquor licenses.

Zoning regulations could be used to preserve mixed-use districts. If we remember that gentrification and abandonment, are inextricably connected, local governments would work harder to take public control of development, pouring public resources into areas of potential abandonment and developing "discouragement" and "encouragement" zones for development. Some zones could be protected from gentrification altogether, others allowed conditional reinvestment with careful safeguards against displacement. Neighborhoods should be involved in the decisions about designation. The point is that government can regulate land use through zoning laws to promote affordable housing rather than support economically discriminating zoning that keeps out the poor (Marcuse 1985).

Recommendation #3: Tax Issues and Recommendations. Government bias toward homeownership includes income tax deductions for mortgage interest and property taxes, in addition to many tax breaks for renovation expenses or weatherizing and energy-saving ventures. These tax breaks interact insidiously with inequality in public schools (Kozol 1991) and subsidize the rich, who deduct all property taxes and mortgage interest, and they cost the federal government more than four times the HUD budget for low-income housing. For example, Jay Rockefeller received a tax subsidy worth $223,000 on his $15.3 million mansion in Washington.

There are many ways to make tax policy work against displacement. One might start by capping the mortgage interest deduction for the affluent and expanding it for the rest, and by adding tax credits for poorer home owners to do repairs and maintenance on their homes in both gentrifying and abandoned neighborhoods. In conjunction with zoning, governments might discourage gentrification by expanding assessments upward or encourage it by lowering assessments. Governments might impose a luxury housing surcharge as well. Washington, D.C., has an anti-speculation tax, which is a great idea, but once again it is riddled with too many loopholes and exempt categories of buildings. A strict anti-speculation tax might penalize quick, profitable resale. Resale prices should be strictly controlled to control speculation and discourage using houses as money machines. People on fixed incomes should get fixed assessments, and possibly mortgage subsidies. To prevent the displacement of homeowners, perhaps tax "circuit breakers" should kick in automatically when assessments become too large a percentage of their income and begin to overload households of moderate means. Washington's homestead exemption to the property tax provides a valuable tax break to families and individuals who live in the houses they own. The city also has a "Clean It or Lien It" law allowing the government to seize properties for which owners or landlords owe

delinquent taxes. Again, this is rarely enforced. For example, a number of large
landlords owe the city millions of dollars in water bills (Tucker 1993). Yet tax delinquency is a conscious, capital-accumulating strategy connected with abandonment, as landlords both use and disuse property to displace the poor. When landlords begin to pay off taxes, this may mean they are preparing for gentrification.
Governments should be more vigilant in taking into public ownership those buildings that are delinquent, and also in watching for changes in tax delinquency
strategies as warning signals of gentrification.

   Recommendation #4: Banking Issues and Recommendations. Government must
do more to regulate the lenders who provide capital for gentrification but fail to
provide it in other parts of the city. We could begin by enforcing nondiscrimination
in mortgage and home equity loans. The Community Reinvestment Act, a law now
on the books, requires banks to provide low-interest loans in their communities,
and this should also be enforced, because the denial of credit to poorer people
makes it very hard for them to own housing. There are many other models for ways
that banks can help with the housing problem, including low down-payments on
conventional mortgages, government-insured mortgages, loans for cooperative
ventures, and refinancing multifamily units to decrease rents. Again, the crucial
issue is access to credit, and government should make banks meet community
credit needs.

   Recommendation #5: Decommodification of Housing. Many argue that we must
remove at least some housing from the speculative market and move it into the
social sector, which would be to "decommodify" it. Congressman Dellum's bill, the
National Comprehensive Housing Act, proposes that some housing be
reconceptualized as social property and that the enormous costs linked to
debt-financing be thereby removed. Numerous experiments around the country,
ranging from cooperatives (some built on "sweat equity") to Cincinnati's Community Land Trust, try for limited-equity, resident-controlled alternatives. Undoing
the idea that a house is more of an investment than a home might be difficult, and
many layers of players have stakes in the debt-financing that Americans take for
granted, although it has little to do any more with the cost of building or operating
a residence. Certainly government should also work to maintain and rehabilitate
existing private and public stock and to build affordable housing, which might also
help to provide jobs for people at risk.

CONCLUSIONS

   In Washington, D.C., the fact of an additional political layer becomes a problem,
as much of the City Council's initially progressive legislation tends to be watered
down for or battered by Congress. In spite of the support of President Clinton,
statehood legislation for the District of Columbia has languished in Congress, and
the prospect of immediate statehood seems unlikely. This is unfortunate, for if
Washington were to become a state, it might be able to enact many of the above

measures. The city has already pioneered in many areas of housing legislation. Americans need to decide, I think, if we want to preserve cities at all, or to build luxury cities, or polarized cities, or simply to militarize and privatize them, and abandon them to the very poor. The conservative, deficit-driven political agenda of the 1990s evades the fact that poverty is an emergency, too, consigning the children of the poor, and their children, to generations of joblessness and homelessness. Considering what the $2 trillion cost of "winning" the Cold War might have done for urban America, Los Angeles historian Mike Davis (n.d.) points out that the interest on the deficit that mounted during the 1980s is six times larger today than the annual combined budgets of America's fifty largest cities. The voters are in the suburbs, and we have every reason to fear that the same tax breaks and subsidies that have encouraged overdevelopment there will complement a continuing, savage, hollowing-out of jobs, housing, and public services in the cities. Washington's gentrified enclaves, abandoned buildings, and urban ghosts play out these processes harshly but well. We need to set aside the myths, understand the processes, and continue to organize.

NOTE

1. The title "There Goes the Neighborhood" reflects ironically on a sentiment Americans often attributed to middle-class residents facing neighborhood integration.

Conclusion

Anna Lou Dehavenon

Homelessness in the United States had been increasing for eight years when the idea for this book was suggested in 1988. That increase continues today. The previous chapters have shown how many homeless people are forced to breech the norms of U.S. culture and engage in civil disobedience in order to survive. They also show how public and private social programs fail to prevent poverty and homelessness which are largely the result of important structural changes in the U.S. sociopolitical economy since 1970.

The authors of these chapters do not consider themselves to be public policy experts. However, they agreed to try to frame recommendations on how to prevent homelessness based on the findings from their research. The summary analysis of these recommendations reveals that they fall into four principal categories—(1) temporary shelter, (2) permanent housing, (3) adequate income, and (4) adequate health—thus further substantiating Hopper and Baumohl's (1994) finding that homelessness is not an isolated phenomenon and the homeless cannot be viewed as "a discrete subclass of the poor."

Presupposing a basic human right to housing (Paul, Miller, and Paul 1992; Sachar 1994, 1995; Steiner and Alston 1996), this chapter further analyzes these recommendations in terms of the levels of government at which they would be implemented and whether they depend on long or short-term action. It concludes with a discussion of the likelihood of such action being taken in the current political climate which appears to support Draconian cuts in education and human services rather than the investments in the human capital needed for the United States to continue to compete in the global marketplace in an era of "man-made brainpower industries" (Thurow 1996).

TEMPORARY SHELTER

Immediate action to prevent homelessness is needed in all four categories, but an adequate supply of decent emergency shelter has an urgency all its own. The implementation of these recommendations depends on short-term action and pre-supposes that people who live in the world's most advanced industrial nation have a right to acceptable temporary shelter until they can move into more permanent housing. The federal government should:

- support more assistance to the homeless at the local level and reduce the paperwork and complex regulations that hinder small, low-budget private agencies from applying for federal money to help shelter the homeless;
- allocate a larger proportion of federal assistance to the homeless through the Community Development Block Grant program, because local needs are better known and more rapidly targeted at the local level; and,
- permit states and localities to make use of the emergency assistance funds now allocated for temporary shelter for the construction of permanent housing.

The three levels of government should collaborate to:

- provide an adequate supply of small-scale shelters for homeless adults; small-scale shelters and scatter-site safe-homes for lone teenagers no longer able to live with their families, and, those in flight from spousal or other domestic violence; and transitional shelter with bath and cooking facilities for individual homeless families;
- give local nonprofit groups with experience in managing these kinds of shelters opportunities to develop them;
- centralize the application process for welfare and other income-maintenance and homeless services by locating social service offices in intake shelters; and,
- offer comprehensive case management services to homeless families, including those living in the apartments of relatives and friends in unstable, overcrowded double-ups; these services should include job training and search assistance, welfare and housing advocacy, day-care, and other social services that foster family preservation.

PERMANENT HOUSING

Immediate action should be taken to work on the longer-term goal of increasing the supply of permanent low-income housing. As suggested by the findings of Phillips and Hamilton (chapter 6), when provided with stable rudimentary housing many homeless people are able to get on their feet, move into more conventional housing, and lead productive lives. This is a strong justification for aid that provides individuals and families with secure homes, not simply stopgap shelter, so they can work rather than worry about where to sleep. The long-run benefits to society will repay the immediate costs of such solutions with interest, and as the longer-term effects are felt, the original costs are likely decrease. The following recommendations are in three areas of prevention through the provision of permanent housing.

#1. Preventing Homelessness by Helping People at Risk of Homelessness Remain in Their Current Housing

These recommendations presuppose that enabling people who would otherwise become homeless to remain in their own housing prevents homelessness. To help realize this goal, which is also based on shorter-term action, the federal government should:

- ensure that the Department of Housing and Urban Development directs local administrators of public housing to support local forms of tenant organization and entrepreneurship and avoid expensive, humiliating eviction and rent collection tactics;
- ensure that HUD fulfills its mandate of providing "decent, safe, and sanitary shelter" by developing solutions to the housing needs of squatters; and,
- require federal subsidy programs for the homeless to include support for low-income people who own their homes to make needed repairs.

The three levels of government should collaborate to protect existing low-cost housing and minimize the impact of economic development that reduces the stock of low-cost rental housing by:

- ensuring that local governments have the authority and funding to enforce codes that improve the quality of the apartments and mobile homes rented to recipients of welfare and other subsidies;
- providing property tax credits to low-income owners who maintain and repair their homes in gentrifying neighborhoods;
- allocating housing rehabilitation grants and loans on a community-by-community basis;
- providing people on fixed low incomes with fixed tax assessments and mortgage subsidies, in order to discourage housing loss and displacement;
- limiting the right of people who own subsidized housing to sell it;
- enacting a tax that penalizes the quick, profitable resale of private-sector, low-income housing to discourage speculation;
- protecting vulnerable, low-income tenants from the loss of rented housing through change of property ownership, condemnation, and major rent increases by enacting rent controls targeted to those with the most need; this should include providing alternative subsidized housing or rental vouchers to those who are evicted;
- developing and supporting programs in which tenants are paid to maintain their housing and serve as on-site ombudsmen who monitor the regulation of evictions, tenant harassment, corruption, and inefficiency on the part of public and private landlords; they should also monitor changes in private landlords' tax-delinquency strategies in order to detect early signs of gentrification, so that measures can be taken early to protect the

tenants who these strategies would displace;

- registering all SRO housing and restricting its conversion except when the vacancy rate for this type of housing is normal;

- requiring developers to replace low-income rental housing converted to condominiums or torn down for new construction, and allotting the replacement housing to low-income individuals and families in exchange for their labor on its construction;

- protecting vulnerable, low-income tenants from the market-driven effects of secondary home development in resort, vacation, and other low-income communities by requiring developers to construct low-income housing units on a one-to-one basis for those who are displaced;

- protecting mobile-home tenants from displacement through the conversion of their rented sites to more profitable uses by requiring developers to secure alternative sites for their relocation;

- developing zoning regulations in consultation with local residents to preserve mixed-use districts by allowing conditional reinvestment in some zones while protecting others from gentrification;

- offering case management and legal or other proactive counsel to those on the brink of eviction from their homes or from the second or more double-up where they have been staying within the same twelve-month period; and,

- granting lifetime tenancies to tenants over sixty-five, regardless of the fate of their buildings.

#2. Preventing Homelessness by Helping Homeless People Move into Other Existing Housing

These recommendations presuppose that there is existing housing into which homeless people can move. To help realize this goal which depends on action in both the shorter and longer term, the federal government should:

- enable more people to pay rent in the private market by providing them Section 8 and other rental supplements;

- require that federal loan programs for the homeless include support to meet the start-up costs of moving into a new home, and give tax credits to utility companies which connect their electric, gas, and phone services at no cost;

- stop awarding public housing subsidies to localities on a per-unit basis, and subsidize only occupied units in public housing; and,

- redirect federal involvement in the secondary mortgage market to support the efforts of public housing tenants to move out and become homeowners.

The three levels of government should collaborate to:

- enforce the Community Reinvestment Act, which requires banks to provide low-interest loans in the communities where they do business;

* require banks to provide nondiscriminatory mortgages and home equity loans that encourage family-based housing strategies;

* enforce laws against housing discrimination, particularly those that affect members of social-racial and ethnic minorities and families with children;

* support the implementation of low down payments on conventional mortgages, government-issued mortgages, cooperative ventures, and the refinancing of multifamily units to decrease rents;

* redesign homeowner loan and grant programs to meet the cash flow limitations of low-income people;

* examine the anti–home ownership policies of the welfare system;

* require the rehabilitation of apartments in public housing that are unoccupied because of poor management;

* require land-use regulations such as large-lot zoning and restrictions on mobile homes to be more inclusionary so as to provide opportunities for home ownership by low-income people; and,

* remove more housing from the speculative market and into the social sector.

Local governments should:

* promote the development of financing packages that enable low-income residents to purchase homes in economically depressed communities where population exodus has left a glut of inexpensive housing;

* modify housing codes and land use regulations to allow for the legal reuse of abandoned buildings, while assuring that health and safety standards are maintained;

* seize tax-delinquent buildings quickly and make them available to nonprofit housing providers for renovation and rental or sale to low-income residents; and,

* encourage "sweat equity" programs, which enable low-income residents to own and renovate buildings seized through tax default.

#3. Preventing Homelessness through Construction of New Low-Income Housing

Maintaining a healthy democracy depends on the active participation of all citizens. People unable to work or educate themselves and their children due to lack of stable housing exert a downward drag on the society, its economy, and its competitiveness in the global marketplace. The following recommendations presuppose that the prevention of homelessness depends also on increasing the supply of permanent low-income housing through new construction. The realization of this longer term goal is therefore in the society's best interest. The federal government should:

- develop and act upon a comprehensive national housing plan based on actual need and an improved census count of the homeless which includes the street-count; includes day-time counts in public places like soup kitchens; increases the categories of persons enumerated face-to-face; acknowledges the limitations of the sheltered homeless count; accepts a definition of homelessness which includes those who stay in unstable, over-crowded double-ups; improves the enumeration of doubled-up families to produce questions that more adequately capture the reality of this form of temporary shelter; and, is based on a stronger preparation of the census takers;

- expand public housing in rural areas in small-scale, scattered-site housing as suitable to the needs of particular communities; and,

- restore federal funding for the construction of permanent housing to earlier levels.

The three levels of government should collaborate to:

- expand loans and tax-abatements for those who create private-sector rental housing for low and moderate-income residents to levels that enable them to realize reasonable profits;

- give higher priority to developing plans and timetables for the more effective use of federal funds for the construction of low-income housing, with oversight from citizen advisory boards;

- increase the supply of new SRO housing for homeless adults;

- permit squatters on selected tracts of public land or buildings and ensure secure tenancies and sanitary services for those who establish homes; and,

- change the negative image of public housing by educating the general public about the successful projects in which tenants play an active role in maintenance, security, and social programs for youth and the elderly.

ADEQUATE INCOME

These recommendations presuppose that the prevention of homelessness depends on having enough stable income to maintain one's own housing. To help realize this goal, the federal government should:

- index the minimum wage to changes in the cost of living to enable those who work to earn a living wage, restore funding for subsidized job and job-training programs to 1980 levels, and increase the employment opportunities available to marginal workers;

- implement community development programs which increase the employment opportunities in low-income areas;

- renew the spirit of the 1934 Housing Act by creating new jobs in the construction of subsidized housing; and,

- restore auxiliary services which provide skills development, community organizing, and empowerment training to tenants of public and other low-income housing.

Federal and state governments should collaborate to:

- fulfill their obligation to oversee the local administration of public assistance programs to ensure that recipients receive the payments, food stamps, and housing vouchers to which they are legally entitled;
- index public assistance shelter allowances to HUD's fair-market rent levels; and,
- index other public assistance payments to changes in the cost of living.

ADEQUATE HEALTH

These recommendations presuppose that the prevention of homelessness depends on levels of individual and public health which enable people to work and maintain an adequate income to pay for their own housing. To help realize these goals, which are both short and long-term, the federal government should:

- require local housing and health authorities to enforce existing health and housing codes as they apply to private and public low-income housing;
- conduct a national assessment of the prevalence of malnutrition among those on public assistance, working for the minimum wage, and the homeless; and,
- enact a universal health care program.

Local governments should:

- develop methods based on existing housing and health codes for evaluating which double-ups can accommodate healthy family life on a short or long-term basis;
- require public health workers to make home visits and apply these methods as the basis for deciding when to encourage individual families who are being denied emergency shelter to live doubled-up; and,
- provide public assistance, food stamps, and supportive services to the two or more families who are eligible and being encouraged to remain doubled-up, based on the findings from the home visit evaluation.

To conclude these recommendations, there should also be more private and public support for the multidisciplinary, applied research needed to document local and regional variation in the rates and causes of poverty and homelessness, and the social resources and informal strategies low-income people employ to combat them. More also needs to be known about the impact of poverty and homelessness on family stability, child development, and life expectancy at all ages. This information would provide the basis for much more effective responses to the current low-income housing crisis and homelessness.

DISCUSSION

Most of the above recommendations depend on the wider, more effective implementation of existing laws and social programs, particularly the Social Security and
Housing laws enacted during the Great Depression of the 1930s. The New Deal was
based on the idea that the flaws of capitalism, especially the monopolistic practices
of big business, "needed to be eliminated by vigilant, intrusive government, not by
changing the system but by trying to regulate it through fiscal policy and the
creation of welfare programs for people in trouble" (Bernstein 1995). As Thurow
(1996) writes, "The free market economies that existed in the 1920s imploded in the
Great Depression and had to be rebuilt by government. . . . The social welfare state
was not implemented by wild-eyed leftists. Its midwives were always enlightened
aristocratic conservatives (Bismarck, Churchill, Roosevelt) who adopted social
welfare policies to save, not destroy capitalism by protecting the middle class."
Similarly, most of the above recommendations do not call for the more radical change
needed to resolve the inherent contradictions between capitalism and democracy,
but for a renewal of what worked before—at least until the United States is willing
to more effectively address the problems of falling real wages, rising inequality, and
the widest gap between rich and poor among western industrialized nations
(Bradsher 1995a, 1995b).

Since 1970, the loss of millions of jobs to slower economic growth, technological
change, and globalization have compounded earlier challenges to the capitalist
welfare state, resulting in a much lower standard of living for all but the wealthiest.
This in turn led eventually to scapegoating of the poor and resentment of the
programs designed to protect them. By the time the federal government acknowledged that the scope of homeless destitution was much wider than had been thought
before (DeParle 1994), this resentment—which might be better targeted against the
rich—had been increasing for some time. However, most of the middle and lower-
middle income people who feel this way probably do not realize that the gap between rich and poor in the United States is widening at an unprecedented rate
(Thurow 1996). The richest one percent of American households now hold nearly
40 percent of the nation's wealth, and the top 20 percent hold more than 80 percent
(Herbert 1995). America's poor youth are the worst-off of those in eighteen western
industrialized nations (Bradsher 1995c), and the proportion of wealthy voters rose
while that of low-income voters fell in the 1994 midterm elections (*New York Times*
1995a). The apathy in that election among middle and lower-income voters and the
much more generous funding of conservative candidates in both major political
parties swept the extreme right into office at all three levels of government. But, of
the 44.6 percent of registered voters who participated, barely more than half gave
the conservatives what they claimed was a "landslide." Given the proposals now in
Congress to lower the federal budget deficit by gutting social programs for the poor
when inflation since the mid-east oil embargo of 1973 and the 1980s budget cuts has
already reduced them to their lowest levels since 1970, the recommendations in this

book sound utopian.

But the proposed budget cuts also mount assaults on other programs which protect the quality and future of American life. For example, "Scientific research, science training, and American research universities that are the envy of the world" will suffer badly (*New York Times* 1995b; Broad 1995). Nor does it appear that the damage wrought by earlier cuts in the budgets of important agencies that guard public health and safety will be rectified: the Center for Disease Control and Prevention, once "the U.S. Agency on the front line of the Disease War internationally . . . [is] overcrowded, understaffed, and overwhelmed" (Altman 1995); and, recent blackouts in the radar which directs air traffic above and around New York City were attributed to "a combination of inadequate staff and aging equipment" (*New York Times* 1995c; Wald 1995a, 1995b).

There are, however, some rumbles of dissent (Baker 1995; Fram 1995; Havemann and Vobejda 1995; Holmes 1995; *New York Times* 1995d, 1995e; Pear 1995a, 1995b). For example, even though many states (including Connecticut, the nation's wealthiest [*New York Times* 1995f]) are trying to "crack down" on the poor, appeals are also made for the removal of farm price supports (Cook 1995; *New York Times* 1995g), equalizing the proposed tax cuts, requiring the "Department of Defense to absorb its fair share of the budget cuts" and "eliminating the huge, unjustified Federal subsidies and tax breaks doled out every year to wealthy companies and other special interests" (Kasich 1995; Lueck 1995; *New York Times* 1995h, 1995i, 1996).

Nevertheless and despite the demise of the Soviet Union, the President and conservatives in Congress support exempting from cutting the half of all controllable budgeted spending that is for military uses. In fact, they want to give the Department of Defense several billions more than it asked for (*New York Times* 1995j; Schmitt 1995) at a time when it and the Department of Commerce already gave "hundreds of millions of dollars a year to help the [arms] industry win new export markets" (Sennott 1996) in the ferociously competitive global marketplace.

In the world's richest nation there ought to be enough to pay for defense and for the educational and social programs needed to develop and maintain its human capital. But this would require a massive shift in political priorities, including increased tax enforcement. For example, the internal revenue service estimates that Americans cheat the government out of about $150 billion a year in unpaid taxes— enough to cover three-fifths of the federal budget deficit" (Hershey 1993). Seymour Melman, Chairman of the National Commission for Economic Conversion and Disarmament, also suggests an alternative way of conducting government business: "Altogether, cuts in valueless military parts of the proposed 1996 to 2002 budgets would save at least $875.7 billion. With these savings we could improve America's infrastructure while creating two million–plus new jobs—more than enough to offset the jobs lost ending military programs . . . [and] almost half the nation's badly damaged housing could be rebuilt for $98 billion. Education would be vastly improved by spending the $100 billion needed for public school building maintenance. And $44 billion could be spent to fully finance major Federal education programs; for $15 billion, we could raise the financing of higher education to the same annual per student rate as Japan's" (1995).

But instead, the United States continues to fall behind the other western industrialized nations in education, family policy, health, housing, and employment programs (Dehavenon 1997; Kammerman 1995; the Luxembourg Study 1995); the country's competitiveness in the global economy lags (*New York Times* 1995j); and another generation of its human capital is sacrificed to greed. As the Secretary of the Treasury, Robert E. Rubin, argued in response to the Luxembourg Study, the "rising economic inequality [is] a threat to the nation's social fabric and economic growth" (Bradsher 1995d).

The findings in this book suggest that if the kinds of proposed cutbacks in education and social programs continue to be enacted, the human and social costs will be devastating, long-lasting, and likely to rise, since no one can reliably predict the unintended consequences of piecemeal reforms in complex bureaucratic systems (Myers 1995; Toner 1995). The potential tragedy of such misplaced priorities is uniquely American, since the United States is still the world's wealthiest, most industrialized nation. Today, when the need to prepare more effectively for the challenges of a very different world are greater than before, the United States as a democracy can no longer "politically afford to permit [our] citizens to sleep on the street" (cf. Preface). The authors of this book collaborated in the hope that their work would contribute to a wider acknowledgment of the urgent need for "social change of an ineluctably moral character . . . to redress the gross injustice of inequality . . . " (cf. Introduction).

Epilogue: A Perilous Bridge

Marvin Harris
(*With apologies to Thornton Wilder*)

Imagine a bridge that spans a deep gorge. Thousands walk across the bridge every day and cross over safely. But the bridge has been constructed with a special device that prevents it from becoming overloaded. Every so often trap doors in the roadway drop open, and a number of people fall through and are dashed to pieces on the rocks below. Then the doors automatically swing up, and traffic resumes. Although everyone knows that the bridge has this defect, they do nothing to correct its design but continue to use it. They have been told that the doors drop open only when stepped on by people who have just never learned to walk right. Indeed, whenever someone falls through, the crowd shouts insults as the miscreants hurtle downward: "Don't ever try to use this bridge again!" In reality, however, the doors drop open at random intervals, regardless of who steps on them.

I contend that there is a great deal of resemblance between this nightmarish bridge and the circumstances that create and perpetuate homelessness and poverty in the USA. Our social engineers have in fact built an economy that depends on dumping millions of people through the trap door of unemployment onto the rocks of homelessness and poverty. The standard explanation for this punitive system is that if there is no unemployment, the labor market becomes too tight, the prices of goods and services rise without corresponding increments in productivity, and inflation rates soar to dangerous, runaway levels. Crucial to an etic analysis of the causes of poverty and homelessness is the fact that the government regularly manipulates the unemployment rate to prevent inflation. It does this through the authority vested in the Federal Reserve System to raise or lower interest rates (high interest rates, less investment, more unemployment).

At the end of World War II, the achievement of "full employment" was accorded the highest priority among the goals of democratic societies. It was written into the United Nations Charter and was implicit in Franklin Roosevelt's "Four Freedoms," as "Freedom from Want." But during the 1970s and 1980s the goal of full employment gradually disappeared from the political spotlight. At the same time the level of what was technically deemed an "acceptable" or even a necessary amount of unemployment rose from 2 percent to 6 percent, where it stands today.

Dozens of studies confirm that the root cause of poverty and homelessness is unemployment. It is not that people do not want to work, or even that they do not know how to work: it is rather that decent jobs are just not there. The current assault against welfare entitlements has unfolded virtually without acknowledging that the government itself is an accomplice in the creation of poverty and homelessness—by setting quotas on the number of people who must not find jobs, at all costs. In backing away from the obligation to support people who are in dire need of help, the government is acting exactly like the deadbeat fathers that it is forever condemning.

I join Dehavenon in emphasizing the importance of etic- and macro-level viewpoints applied to the task of understanding the causes of poverty and homelessness. Far too much effort has been expended (and much of it obfuscatory and counterproductive) in trying to figure out why certain people with such-and-such biographies, advantaged or disadvantaged as they may be, fall through the trap doors. What we need is a new bridge.

References

Action Research Project on Hunger, Homelessness, and Family Health. 1989. The Tyranny of Indifference: A Study of Hunger, Homelessness, Poor Health and Family Dismemberment in 818 New York City Households with Children in 1988–89. New York.

———. 1990. The Tyranny of Indifference: A Study of Hunger, Homelessness, Poor Health and Family Dismemberment in 1,325 New York City Households with Children in 1989–90. New York.

———. 1991. No Room at the Inn: An Interim Report with Recommendations on Homeless Families with Children Requesting Shelter at New York City's Emergency Assistance Units in 1991. New York.

———. 1992. Promises! Promises! Promises! The Failed Hopes of New York City's Homeless Families in 1992. New York.

———. 1993. Out of Sight! Out of Mind! or, How New York City and New York State Tried to Abandon the City's Homeless Families in 1993. New York.

———. 1994. No Room at the Inn: Or How New York City Abandoned Homeless Families to Public Places in 1994. New York.

———. 1995. Out in the Cold: The Social Exclusion of New York's Homeless Families in 1995. New York.

———. 1996. The Giuliani Administration and Doubled-Up Families at New York City's Emergency Assistance Unit in 1996. New York.

Adams, Carolyn Teich. 1986. Homelessness in the Postindustrial City: Views from London and Philadelphia. *Urban Affairs Quarterly* 21 (4):527–549.

Adams, Richard N. 1960. An Inquiry into the Nature of the Family. In *Essays in the Science of Culture in Honor of Leslie A. White*, eds. Gertrude Dole and Robert Carneiro, 30–49. New York: Thomas Y. Crowell.

Altman, Lawrence K. 1995. U.S. Agency on Front Line of Disease War: Crowded, Understaffed and Overwhelmed. *New York Times*, May 20.

Altshuler, Alan A. 1970. *Community Control*. New York: Pegasus.

Appelbaum, R., and P. Dreier. 1990. Recent Developments in Rental Housing in the United States. In *Government and Housing*, eds. William van Vliet and Jan van Weesep. New York: Sage Publications.

Arensberg, C., and Kimball, S. 1965. *Culture and Community*. New York: Harcourt, Brace and World.

Atlanta Task Force for the Homeless. 1988. Facts about Atlanta-Area Homelessness. Monthly fact sheet for November.

————. 1990. Homelessness in Metro Atlanta II. Atlanta: Task Force for the Homeless.

Automotive News. 1991. Chrysler Plant Takes the Labor Out of Labor, December 9.

Axinn, J., and H. Levin. 1982. *Social Welfare: A History of the American Response to Need*. White Plains, N.Y.: Longman, Inc.

Baker, Russell. 1995. Those Vital Paupers: Welfare Is Part of Capitalism. *New York Times*, January 17.

Balmori, D., and Morton, M. 1994. *Transitory Gardens, Uprooted Lives*. New Haven: Yale University Press.

Banfield, Edward C. 1958. *Moral Basis of a Backward Society*. New York: Free Press.

————. 1970. *The Unheavenly City—The Nature and Future of Our Urban Crisis*. Boston: Little, Brown.

Barak, Gregg. 1992. *Gimme Shelter*. New York: Praeger.

Bassuk, Ellen. 1984. The Homelessness Problem. *Scientific American* 251:40–45.

Baxter, Ellen, and Kim Hopper. 1981. *Private Lives/Public Spaces: Homeless Adults on the Streets of New York City*. New York: Community Service Society.

Beauregard, Robert A. 1986. The Chaos and Complexity of Gentrification. In *Gentrification of the City*, eds. Neil Smith and Peter Williams, 35–55. Boston: Allen and Unwin.

Belcher, John R., and F. DiBlasio. 1990. *Helping the Homeless: Where Do We Go from Here?* Lexington, Ky.: Lexington Press.

Bender, Donald R. 1967. A Refinement of the Concept of Households: Families, Co-Residence and Domestic Function. *American Anthropologist* 69:493–504.

Bernard, H. Russell. 1988. *Research Methods in Cultural Anthropology*. Newbury Park, Calif.: Sage Publications.

Bernstein, Richard. 1995. The Backlash against New Deal Liberalism. *New York Times*, March 29.

Bingham, Richard D., Roy E. Green, and Sammis B. White, eds. 1987. *The Homeless in Contemporary Society*. Newbury Park, Calif.: Sage Publications.

Blake, Angie. n.d. History, Community and Public Space: Historic District Designation in Mount Pleasant, Washington, D.C., 1982–1987. American University, Department of History. Manuscript.

Boissevain, Jeremy, and J. Clyde Mitchell, eds. 1973. *Network Analysis: Studies in Human Interaction*. The Hague: Mouton.

Bolger, Rory. 1979. *Recession in Detroit: Strategies of a Plantside Community and the Corporate Elite*. Ann Arbor, Mich.: University Microfilms.

Bond, Patrick. 1991. Alternative Politics in the Inner City: The Financial Explosion and the Campaign for Community Control of Capital in Baltimore. In *Hollow Promises*, eds. Michael Keith and Alisdair Rogers, 140–168. London: Mansell Publishing

Borgos, Seth. 1986. Low-Income Homeownership and the ACORN Squatters Campaign. In *Critical Perspectives on Housing*, eds. R. G. Bratt, C. Hartman, and A. Meyerson, 428–446. Philadelphia: Temple University Press.

Boujouen, Norma, and James R. Newton. 1984. The Puerto Rican Experience in Willimantic Windham Regional Community Council.

Bradsher, Keith. 1995a. Gap in Wealth in U.S. Called Widest in West. *New York Times*, April 17.

―――. 1995b. Widest Gap in Incomes? Research Points to U.S.: Study Covered Industrial Nations in 1980s. *New York Times*, October 27.

―――. 1995c. Low Ranking for Poor American Children. *New York Times*, August 14.

―――. 1995d. Ideas and Trends: More on the Wealth of Nations. *New York Times*, August 20.

Brager, George, Harry Specht, and James L. Torczyner. 1987. *Community Organizing*. New York: Columbia University Press.

Brannigan, Martha. 1991. Mortgage Requests by Blacks, Hispanics, Denied by NCNB at Twice Rate of Whites. *Wall Street Journal*, 13 September.

Bratt, Rachel G. 1986. Public Housing: The Controversy and Contribution. In *Critical Perspectives on Housing*, eds. R. G. Bratt, C. Hartman, and A. Meyerson, 335–361. Philadelphia: Temple University Press.

Breckenfeld, Gurney. 1977. It's Up to the Cities to Save Themselves. *Fortune*, March.

―――. 1977. Business Loves the Sunbelt (and Vice Versa). *Fortune*, June.

Brickner, P. W., et al., eds. 1985. *Health Care of Homeless People*. New York: Springer Verlag.

Broad, William J. 1995. G.O.P. Budget Cuts Would Fall Hard on Civilian Science. *New York Times*, May 22.

Brown, Susan E. 1977. Housing in Bogotá: A Synthesis of Recent Research and Notes on Anthropological Contributions to the Study of Housing. *Urban Anthropology* 6 (3): 249–267.

Buckley, Walter. 1967. *Sociology and Modern Systems Theory*. Englewood Cliffs, N.J.: Prentice-Hall.

Burnham, L. 1987. Hands across Skid Row. *The Drama Review* 32:126–150.

Burns, Leland S. 1987. Third World Solutions to the Homeless Problem. In *The Homeless in Contemporary Society*, eds. Richard D. Bingham, Roy E. Green, and Sammis B. White, 231–248. Newbury Park, Calif.: Sage Publications.

Burt, M. R. 1992. *Over the Edge: The Growth of Homelessness in the 1980s*. New York: Russell Sage Foundation.

Butterworth, Douglas S. 1980. A Study of the Urbanization Process among Mixtec Migrants from Tilantongo in Mexico City. In *Urban Place and Process*, eds. Irwin Press and M. Estellie Smith, 241–256. New York: Macmillan.

Buttimer, Anne, and David Seamon, eds. 1980. *The Human Experience of Space and Place*. New York: St. Martin's Press.

Cameron, Stuart. 1992. Housing, Gentrification and Urban Regeneration Policies. *Urban Studies* 29 (1): 3–14.

Cernea, Michael M. 1990. *Internal Refugees and Development-Caused Population Displacement*. Cambridge: Harvard University, Harvard Institute for International Development.

City of Atlanta. 1989. *Comprehensive Homeless Assistance Plan*. Atlanta: City of Atlanta.

Cohen, C. I., and J. Sokolovsky. 1981. A Reassessment of the Sociability of Long-Term Skid Row Residents: A Social Network Approach. *Social Networks* 3:93–105.

―――. 1989. *Old Men of the Bowery: Strategies for Survival among the Homeless*. New York: Guilford Press.

Connecticut Census Data Center. 1988. *Connecticut Population and Per Capita Income Estimates, August*. Hartford, Conn.: State of Connecticut, Office of Policy and Management.

―――. 1991. *Data Release, February 14*. Hartford, Conn.: State of Connecticut, Office of

Policy and Management.

Conquergood, Dwight. 1992. Life in Big Red. In *Structuring Diversity*, ed. Louise Lamphere. Chicago: University of Chicago Press.

Cook, Kenneth A. 1995. Subsidizing the Farm Bureaucracy. *New York Times*, July 14.

Cooper, Mary A. 1987. The Role of Religious and Nonprofit Organizations in Combating Homelessness. In *The Homeless in Contemporary Society*, eds. R. D. Bingham, Roy E. Green, and Sammis B. White. Newbury Park, Calif.: Sage Publications.

Cordova, Teresa. 1991. Community Intervention Efforts to Oppose Gentrification. In *Challenging Uneven Development*, eds. P. Nyden and W. Wiewel, 25–48. New Brunswick, N.J.: Rutgers University Press.

Cress, D. M. 1990. Lookout World, the Meek Are Getting Ready: Implications of Mobilization among the Homeless. Paper presented at the 1990 American Sociological Association conference, Washington, D.C.

Crouse, Joan M. 1986. *The Homeless Transient in the Great Depression: New York State, 1929–1941*. Albany: State University of New York Press.

Crystal, S. 1982. *New Arrivals: First Time Shelter Clients*. New York: New York City, Human Resources Administration.

————. 1984. Homeless Men and Homeless Women: The Gender Gap. *Urban and Social Change Review* 17 (2): 2–6.

Davenport, J. A., J. Davenport III, and D. H. Newett. 1990. A Comparative Analysis of the Urban and Rural Homeless. Paper presented at 15th National Institute on Rural Social Work, Fredonia, New York.

Dear, M., and J. Wolch. 1987. *Landscapes of Despair: From Deinstitutionalization to Homelessness*. Princeton, N.J.: Princeton University Press.

De Certeau, M. 1984. *The Practice of Everyday Life*. Berkeley: University of California Press.

Dehavenon, Anna Lou. 1987. *Toward a Policy for the Amelioration and Prevention of Family Homelessness and Dissolution: New York City's After-Hours Emergency Assistance Units in 1986–87*. New York: East Harlem Interfaith.

————. 1990. Charles Dickens Meets Franz Kafka: The Maladministration of New York City's Public Assistance Programs. *New York University Review of Law and Social Change* 17 (2).

————. 1995. Cultural Materialism and the Causes of Hunger and Homelessness in New York City. In *Science, Materialism and the Study of Culture*, eds. Maxine L. Margolis and Martin F. Murphy. Gainesville: University of Florida Press.

————. 1997. Households and Families: North America. In *The Women's Studies Encyclopedia*. Hemel Hempstead: Prentice Hall/Harvester Wheatsheaf. Forthcoming.

DeParle, Jason. 1994. Report to Clinton Sees Vast Extent of Homelessness. *New York Times*, February 17.

Dewalt, B., and P. Pelto, eds. 1985. *Micro and Macro Levels of Analysis in Anthropology: Issues in Theory and Research*. Boulder and London: Westview Press.

Domhoff, William G. 1967. *Who Rules America?* Englewood Cliffs, N.J.: Prentice-Hall.

Doughty, Paul L. 1970. Behind the Back of the City: "Provincial" Life in Lima, Peru. In *Peasants in Cities*, ed. William Mangin, 30–46. Boston: Houghton Mifflin.

Downey, Kirstin. 1988. Study Finds D.C. Area Is One of Few Strong Investment Markets. *Washington Post*, November 5.

————. 1990. Renters Called Vulnerable in Downtown. *Washington Post*, December 29.

————. 1991. The Real Price of Housing Fraud. *Washington Post*. September 2.

Drake, St. Clair, and Horace R. Cayton. 1945. *Black Metropolis: A Study of Negro Life in a Northern City*. New York: Harcourt, Brace.

Dreier, Peter, and Richard Appelbaum. 1991. American Nightmare: Homelessness. *Challenge* (March-April):46–52.

Duncan, James S., Jr. 1976. Landscape and the Communication of Social Identity. In *The Mutual Interaction of People and Their Built Environment*, ed. Amos Rapoport, 391–401. The Hague: Mouton.

Eames, Edwin, and Judith Granich Goode. 1968. The Culture of Poverty: A Misapplication of Anthropology to Contemporary Issues. In *Urban Life*, eds. George Gmelch and Walter P. Zenner. Second edition. Prospect Heights, Ill.: Waveland Press.

———. 1977. *Anthropology of the City: An Introduction to Urban Anthropology*. Englewood Cliffs, N.J.: Prentice-Hall.

Edgerton, Robert B. 1985. Sick Societies: Rules, Exceptions, and Social Order. Berkeley, Calif.: University of California Press.

Epstein, David G. 1972. The Genesis and Function of Squatter Settlements in Brasilia. In *The Anthropology of Urban Environments*, eds. T. Weaver and D. White, 51–58. Boulder, Colo.: The Society for Applied Anthropology.

Ewen, Lynda Ann. 1978. *Corporate Power and Urban Crisis in Detroit*. Princeton, N.J.: Princeton University Press.

Fallis, G., and A. Murray. 1990. *Housing the Homeless and Poor: New Partnerships among the Private, Public, and Third Sectors*. Toronto: University of Toronto Press.

First, R. J., B. G. Toomey, and J. C. Rife. 1990. *Preliminary Findings on Rural Homelessness in Ohio*. Columbus: Ohio State University School of Social Work.

Fisher, P., and W. Breakey. 1986. Homelessness and Mental Health: An Overview. *International Journal of Mental Health*, 14 (4): 6–41.

Fitchen, J. M. 1981. *Poverty in Rural America: A Case Study*. Boulder, Colo.: Westview Press.

———. 1991a. *Endangered Spaces, Enduring Places: Change, Identity, and Survival in Rural America*. Boulder, Colo.: Westview Press.

———. 1991b. Homelessness in Rural Places: Perspectives from Upstate New York. *Urban Anthropology* 20 (2): 181–84.

———. 1992. On the Edge of Homelessness: Rural Poverty and Housing Insecurity. *Rural Sociology* 57 (2): 173–93.

Foucault, M. 1977. *Discipline and Punish: The Birth of the Prison*. New York: Pantheon Books.

———. 1980. *Power/Knowledge*. New York: Pantheon Books.

Fram, Alan. 1995. Clinton Opposes Compromise Cuts. *Albuquerque Journal*, March 30.

Frazier, E. Franklin. 1939. *The Negro Family in the United States*. Chicago: University of Chicago Press.

Friedrichs, J. 1988. *Affordable Housing and the Homeless*. New York: Aldine de Gruyter.

Gale, Dennis E. 1984. *Neighborhood Revitalization*. Lexington, Ky.: Lexington Press.

———. 1989. The Impact of Historic District Designation in Washington, D.C. Occasional Paper no. 6. Washington, D.C.: George Washington University, Center for Washington Area Studies.

Georgia Residential Finance Authority. 1990. *Georgia Housing Goal Report*. Atlanta: Georgia Residential Finance Authority.

Giachello, Aida L., et al. 1983. Uses of the 1980 Census for Hispanic Health Services Research. *American Journal of Public Health* 73 (3): 266–74.

Giamo, Benedict. 1989. *On the Bowery: Confronting Homelessness in American Society.* Iowa City: University of Iowa Press.

Giddens, A. 1981. *A Contemporary Critique of Historical Materialism.* Berkeley: University of California Press.

———. 1984. *The Constitution of Society.* Berkeley: University of California Press.

Gilderbloom, J., and R. P. Appelbaum. 1988. *Rethinking Rental Housing.* Philadelphia: Temple University Press.

Glasser, Irene. 1988a. Lives in Poverty: A Study of General Assistance. Unpublished report to State of Connecticut, Department of Income Maintenance.

———. 1988b. *More Than Bread: Ethnography of a Soup Kitchen.* Tuscaloosa: The University of Alabama Press.

———. 1991. *An Ethnographic Study of Homelessness, Connecticut.* Ethnographic Exploratory Research Report no. 17. Washington, D.C.: Center for Survey Methods Research, Bureau of the Census.

———. 1994. *Homelessness in Global Perspective.* New York: G. K. Hall Reference, Macmillan.

Gmelch, George, and Walter P. Zenner, eds. 1988. *Urban Life.* Second Edition. Prospect Heights: Waveland Press.

Goffman, E. 1959. *The Presentation of Self in Everyday Life.* New York: Doubleday.

———. 1961. *Asylums.* New York: Doubleday.

———. 1963. *Behavior in Public Places.* New York: Free Press.

———. 1971. *Relations in Public: Microstudies of the Public Order.* New York: Harper & Row Publishers.

Gorham, L., and B. Harrison. 1990. *Working below the Poverty Line.* Washington, D.C.: The Aspen Institute.

Gottdiener, M. 1984. Debate on the Theory of Space: Toward an Urban Praxis. In *Cities in transformation,* ed. M. P. Smith, 199–218. Beverly Hills, Calif.: Sage Publications.

———. 1985. *The Social Production of Urban Space.* Austin: University of Texas Press.

Gottdiener, M., and A. Lagopoulos. 1986. *The City and the Sign: An Introduction to Urban Semiotics.* New York: Columbia University Press.

Graves, Nancy B., and Theodore D. Graves. 1974. Adaptive Strategies and Urban Migration. In *Annual Review of Anthropology* 29:117–51.

Green, Constance M. 1976. *Washington: A History of the Capital.* Princeton, N.J.: Princeton University Press.

Greenberg, M. R., F. J. Popper, and B. M. West. 1990. The TOADS: A New American Urban Epidemic. *Urban Affairs Quarterly* 25:435–54.

Greenlee, Richard W. 1991. The Rural Working Poor and Their Strategies for the Prevention of Homelessness. Paper presented at the Rural Sociological Society Meetings, Columbus, Ohio, August 20.

Gross, B. M. 1980. *Friendly Fascism: The New Face of Power in America.* New York: M. Evans.

Hall, P. D. 1992. *Inventing the Nonprofit Sector; And Other Essays on Philanthropy, Voluntarism, and Nonprofit Organizations.* Baltimore: Johns Hopkins University Press.

Hannerz, Ulf. 1969. *Soulside.* New York: Columbia University Press.

———. 1992. *Cultural Complexity: Studies in the Social Organization of Meaning.* New York: Columbia University Press.

Hansen, Art, and Anthony Oliver-Smith, eds. 1982. *Involuntary Migration and Resettlement: The Problems and Responses of Dislocated Peoples.* Boulder, Colo.: Westview.

Harris, Marvin. 1964. *The Nature of Cultural Things*. New York: Random House.

———. 1983 *Cultural Anthropology*. New York: Harper and Row.

Hartman, Chester, Dennis Keating, and Richard LeGates, with Steve Turner. 1981. *Displacement: How to Fight It*. Berkeley, Calif.: National Housing Law Project.

Harvey, D. 1989. *The Condition of Postmodernity*. New York: Basil Blackwell.

Havemann, Judith and Barbara Vobejda. 1995. Senate Is Toning Down House's Welfare Reforms. *International Herald Tribune*, April 14.

Hays, William C., and Charles H. Mindel. 1973. Extended Kinship Relations in Black and White Families. *Journal of Marriage and the Family* 35 (1): 51–57.

Heider, Karl G. 1988. The Rashomon Effect: When Ethnographers Disagree. *American Anthropologist* 90:73–81.

Henderson, Nell. 1993. D.C. Agency Owes U.S., Audit Says. *Washington Post*, August 13.

Herbert, Bob. 1995. The Issue Is Jobs. *The New York Times*, May 6.

Hersey, Jr., Robert D. 1993. I.R.S. Raises Its Estimate of Tax Cheating. *New York Times*, December 29.

Hobsbawm, E.J. 1981. *Bandits*. Revised edition. New York: Pantheon.

Hoch, C., and R. Slayton. 1989. *New Homeless and Old: Community and the Skid Row Hotel*. Philadelphia: Temple University Press.

Holmes, Steven A. 1995. Clinton Says He May Veto Welfare Bill. *New York Times*, April 9.

Hopper, Kim. 1989. Not Just Passing Strange. *American Ethnologist* 15 (1): 155–67.

———. 1991. A Poor Apart: The Distancing of Homeless Men in New York's History. *Social Research* 58:107–32.

Hopper, Kim, and Jim Baumohl. 1994. Held in Abeyance: Rethinking Homelessness and Advocacy. *American Behavioral Scientist* 37 (4): 522–52.

Hopper, Kim, and J. Hamberg. 1986. The Making of America's Homeless: From Skid Row to the New Poor, 1945-1984. In *Critical Perspectives on Housing*, eds. R. G. Bratt, et al., 12–40. Philadelphia: Temple University Press.

Hopper, Kim, Ezra Susser, and Sarah Conover. 1985. Economies of Makeshift: Deindustrialization and Homelessness in New York City. *Urban Anthropology* 14:183–236.

Ignatieff, M. 1984. *The Needs of Strangers*. New York: Vintage.

Jackson, Anthony. 1976. *A Place Called Home: A History of Low-Income Housing in Manhattan*. Cambridge, Mass.: MIT Press.

Jakle, J. A., and D. Wilson. 1992. *Derelict Landscapes: The Wasting of America's Built Environment*. Lanham, MD: Rowman & Littlefield.

Johnson, Charles S. 1941. Growing Up in the Black Belt. Washington, D.C.: American Council on Education.

Jordan, Joseph. 1990. *. . . You'll Never See Those Days Anymore*. Washington, D.C.: Institute for the Preservation and Study of African-American Writing.

Kammerman, Sheila B. 1995. Child and Family Policies: an International Overview. In *Children, Families and Government: Preparing for the 21st Century*, eds. Edward Zigler, Kagan and Hall. New York: Cambridge University Press.

Kasich, John R. 1995. Get Rid of Corporate Welfare. *New York Times*, July 9.

Keith, Michael, and Alisdair Rogers. 1991. *Hollow Promises? Rhetoric and Reality in the Inner City*. London: Mansell Publishing.

Kemper, Robert Van. 1980. Migration and Adaptation: Tzintzuntzenos in Mexico City. In *Urban Life*, eds. George Gmelch and Walter P. Zenner, 90–8. New York: St. Martin's Press.

Kennedy, Shawn G. 1995. Riot Police Remove 31 Squatters from Two East Village Buildings. *New York Times*, May 31.

Knickman, James R., and Beth C. Weitzman. 1989. *A Study of Homeless Families in New York City: Risk Assessment Models and Strategies for Prevention.* Vols. 1–4. New York: Health Research Program of New York University.

Kozol, Jonathan. 1988. *Rachel and Her Children: Homeless Families in America.* New York: Crown Publishers.

———. 1991. *Savage Inequalities.* New York: Crown Publishers.

Kusmer, K. L. 1987. The Underclass in Historical Perspective: Tramps and Vagrants in Urban America, 1870–1930. In *On Being Homeless: Historical Perspectives*, ed. R. Beard, 20–31. New York: Museum for the City of New York.

Landis, Kenesaw M. 1948. Segregation in Washington. A Report of the National Committee on Segregation in the Nation's Capital, Washington, D.C..

Lamb, R. H., ed. 1984. *The Homeless Mentally Ill.* Washington, D.C.: The American Psychiatric Association.

Lang, M. H. 1989. *Homelessness amid Affluence: Structure and Paradox in the American Political Economy.* New York: Praeger Publishers.

Lawrence, B. 1989. *Defenders of God: The Fundamentalist Revolt against the Modern Age.* San Francisco: Harper & Row.

Lazere, E. B., P. A. Leonard, and L. L. Kravitz. 1989. *The Other Housing Crisis: Sheltering the Poor in Rural America.* Washington, D.C.: Center on Budget and Policy Priorities.

Lebowitz, Barry D., Jacob Fried, and Cynthia Madaris. 1973. Sources of Assistance in an Urban Ethnic Community. *Human Organization* 32 (3): 267–71.

Lee, Barrett, and David C. Hodge. 1984. Social Differentials in Metropolitan Residential Displacement. In *Gentrification, Displacement, and Neighborhood Revitalization*, eds. John Palen and Bruce London, 140–69. Albany: State University of New York Press.

Leeds, Anthony. 1969. Significant Variables Determining the Character of Squatter Settlements. *America Latina* 12 (3): 44–86.

Leeds, Anthony and Elizabeth. 1970. Brazil and the Myth of Urban Rurality: Urban Experience, Work, and Values in the 'Squatments' of Rio de Janeiro and Lima. In *City and Country in the Third World*, ed. A. J. Field, 229–85. Rochester, Vt.: Schenkman Publishing Company, Inc.

———. 1976. Accounting for Behavioral Differences: Three Political Systems and the Responses of Squatters in Brazil, Peru, and Chile. In *The City in Comparative Perspective*, eds. J. Walton and L. H. Masotti, 193–248. New York: Sage Publications.

Lefebvre, H. 1976. *The Survival of Capitalism.* London: Allison & Busby Ltd.

———. 1979. Space: Social Product and Use Value. In *Critical Sociology*, ed. J. W. Freiberg, 285–95. New York: Irvington Pubishers, Inc.

———. 1991. *The Production of Space.* Oxford: Blackwell.

Legates, Richard T., and Chester Hartman. 1986. The Anatomy of Displacement in the United States. In *Gentrification of the City*, eds. Neil Smith and Peter Williams, 178–200. Boston: Allen and Unwin.

Lemert, Charles C., and Garth Gillan. 1982. *Michel Foucault: Social Theory and Transgression.* New York: Columbia University Press.

Lett, James. 1990. Emics and Etics: Notes on the Epistemology of Anthropology. In *Emics and Etics: the Insider/Outsider Debate*, eds. Thomas N. Headland, Kenneth L. Pike and Marvin Harris. Newbury Park, Calif.: Sage Publications.

Lewis, Oscar. 1959. *Five Familes: Mexican Case Studies in the Culture of Poverty*. New York: Basic Books.

———. 1961. *The Children of Sanchez*. New York: Random House.

———. 1966. The Culture of Poverty. *Scientific American* 215:19–25.

———. 1966. *La Vida: A Puerto Rican Family in the Culture of Poverty—San Juan and New York*. New York: Random House.

———. 1968. *A Study of Slum Culture: Backgrounds for La Vida*. New York: Random House.

———. 1970. The Culture of Poverty. In *Anthropological Essays*, ed. O. Lewis, 67–80. New York: Random House.

Liebow, E. 1967. *Tally's Corner*. Boston: Little, Brown and Company.

Lobo, Susan. 1982. *A House of My Own: Social Organization in the Squatter Settlements of Lima, Peru*. Tucson: University of Arizona Press.

Lombardi, John R. 1976. Reciprocity and Survival. *Anthropological Quarterly* 48 (4): 245–54.

Lovell, A. M. 1984. Marginality without Isolation: Social Networks and the New Homeless. Paper presented at the 83rd annual meeting of the American Anthropological Association, Denver, Colorado.

Lovell, B. 1985. *Report of the Orange County Coalition for the Homeless*. Balboa, Calif.: Orange County Coalition of the Homeless.

Lueck, Thomas J. 1995. Lower Budgets Don't Cut Flow of Tax Breaks. *New York Times*, July 5.

Luloff, A. E. 1993. Homeless Children in New Hampshire. Paper presented at Rural Sociological Society Meetings, Orlando, Florida. August 9.

Lynch, Timothy, and Paul Leonard. 1991. *A Place to Call Home: The Crisis in Housing for the Poor—Detroit, Michigan*. Washington, D.C.: Center on Budget and Policy Priorities.

Mair, A. 1986. The Homeless and the Post-Industrial City. *Political Geography Quarterly* 5:351–68.

Mangin, William. 1967a. Latin American Squatter Settlements: A Problem and a Solution. *Latin American Research Review* 2:65–98.

———. 1967b. Squatter Settlements. *Scientific American* 217 (4): 21–29.

Marcuse, Peter. 1985. Gentrification, Abandonment, and Displacement: Connections, Causes, and Policy Responses in New York City. *Journal of Urban and Contemporary Law* 28:107, 195–240.

———. 1988. Neutralizing Homelessness. *Socialist Review* 18:69–96.

Mariano, Ann. 1989. Anacostia Has a New Vitality. *Washington Post*, September 9.

Marsden, G. M. 1980. *Fundamentalism and American Culture: The Shaping of Twentieth-Century Evangelicalism 1870–1925*. New York: Oxford University Press.

Martins, M. R. 1982. The Theory of Social Space in the Work of Henri Lefebvre. In *Urban Political Economy and Social Theory*, eds. R. Forrest et al., 160–85. London: Gower Publishing Company, Ltd.

Maxwell, Andrew H. 1993. The Underclass, 'Social Isolation'and 'Concentration Effects': 'The Culture of Poverty' Revisited. *Critique of Anthropology* 13 (3): 231–45.

Melman, Seymour. 1995. Preparing for War (against Ourselves). *New York Times*, June 26.

Merton, Robert K. 1968. *Social Theory and Social Structure*. Glencoe, Ill.: Free Press.

Miao, Greta. 1974. Marital Instability and Unemployment among Whites and Nonwhites, the Moyhnihan Report Revisited—Again. *Journal of Marriage and the Family* 36:1–

77.

Michigan Employment Security Commission. 1978. *Annual Planning Report—Fiscal Year 1979*. Detroit: Michigan Employment Security Commission.

Mingione, E. 1983. Informalization, Restructuring and the Survival Strategies of the Working Class. *International Journal of Urban and Regional Research* 7:311–39.

Mitchell, J. C. 1987. The Components of Strong Ties among Homeless Women. *Social Networks* 9:37–47.

Mithun, Jacqueline. 1973. Cooperation and Solidarity as Survival Necessities in a Black Urban Community. *Urban Anthropology* 2 (1): 25–34.

Mollenkopf, J. H., and M. Castells, eds. 1991. *Dual City: Restructuring New York*. New York: Russell Sage Foundation.

Momeni, J. A., ed. 1989. *Homelessness in the United States*. Vol. 1, *State Surveys*. Westport, Conn.: Greenwood Press.

Morales, Julio. 1986. *Puerto Rican Poverty and Migration*. New York: Praeger.

Myrdal, Gunnar. 1944. *An American Dilemma: The Negro Problem and Modern Democracy*. New York: Harper & Row.

Myers, Steven L. 1995. Comptroller Says Cuts May Prove Costly. *New York Times*, May 17.

Myrdal, Gunnar. 1944. *An American Dilemma: The Negro Problem and Modern Democracy*. New York: Harper and Row.

National Law Center on Homelessness and Poverty. 1994. No Homeless People Allowed: Anti-Homeless Laws, Litigation and Alternatives in 49 U.S. Cities. Washington, D.C., December.

Newman, Katherine. 1985. Declining Fortunes: Anthropological Perspectives on Deindustrialization. *Urban Anthropology* 14 (1–3): 5–19.

Newman, Maria. 1991. Homeless Found to Go Slowly to Shelters: Report Disputes Mayor's View That City Policy Adds to Problem. *New York Times*, December 23.

New York City Commission on Homelessness. 1992. The Way Home: A New Direction in Social Policy.

New York Times. 1986. U.N. Film on Homeless Will Omit U.S. Scenes. *New York Times*, December 29.

———. 1992a. Public Housing Ills Lead to Questions About HUD. *New York Times*, July 20.

———. 1992b. Coalition Asks Court to Force Newark Housing Authority to Build. *New York Times*, August 19.

———. 1995a. Low–Income Voters' Turnout Fell in 1994, Census Reports. *New York Times*, June 11.

———. 1995b. Crippling American Science. *New York Times*, May 23.

———. 1995c. How to Fix Air Traffic Control. *New York Times*, June 16.

———. 1995d. Welfare's Vital Core. *New York Times*, March 29.

———. 1995e. Hit the Poor. Reward the Rich. *New York Times*, March 12.

———. 1995f. Connecticut Lawmakers Approve Strict New Welfare Rules. *New York Times*, June 4.

———. 1995g. A Fair Farm Bill. *New York Times*, June 17.

———. 1995h. Alms for the Affluent. *New York Times*, April 7.

———. 1995i. Go after Corporate Welfare. *New York Times*, January 18.

———. 1995j. The Pentagon Jackpot. *New York Times*, July 10.

———. 1995k. I.M.F. Sees Global Growth But Slower Pace for the U.S. *New York Times*,

April 24.

———. 1996. Unjustified Shipping Subsidies. *New York Times*, March 12.

Nyden, Philip W., and Wim Wiewel. 1991. *Challenging Uneven Development: An Urban Agenda for the 1990s*. New Brunswick, N.J.: Rutgers University Press.

O'Hare, W. P. 1988. *The Rise of Poverty in Rural America*. Washington, D.C.: Population Reference Bureau.

Ohio Department of Mental Health. 1985. *Homelessness in Ohio: A Study of People in Need*. Columbus: Department of Mental Health.

Orange County Homeless Issues Task Force. 1990. *Demographic Profile and Survey of Homeless Persons Seeking Services in Orange County*. Garden Grove, Calif.: Orange County Homeless Issues Task Force.

Palen, J. John, and Bruce London. 1984. *Gentrification, Displacement and Neighborhood Revitalization*. Albany: State University of New York Press.

Palen, John, and Chava Nachmias. 1984. Revitalization in a Working Class Neighborhood. In *Gentrification, Displacement, and Neighborhood Revitalization*, eds. John Palen and Bruce London, 128–39. Albany: State University of New York Press.

Partridge, William L. 1989. Involuntary Resettlement in Development Projects. *Journal of Refugee Studies* 2:373–84.

Paschke, B., and D. Volpendesta. 1991. *Homeless Not Helpless*. Berkeley, Calif.: Canterbury Press.

Patton, L. T. 1988. The Rural Homeless. Appendix C. In *Homelessness, Health, and Human Needs*. The Committee on Health Care for Homeless People, 183–217. Washington, D.C.: National Academy Press.

Paul, Ellen F., Fred D. Miller, Jr., and Jeffrey Paul. 1992. *Economic Rights*. New York: Cambridge University Press.

Pear, Robert. 1995a. Republican Squabble Delays Welfare Debate. *New York Times*, June 16.

———. 1995b. G.O.P. Governors Urge Big Changes for Welfare Bill. *New York Times*, April 12.

Pellow, Deborah. 1981. The New Urban Community: Mutual Relevance of the Social and Physical Environments. *Human Organization* 40 (1): 15–26.

Pelto, Pertti J. 1970. *Anthropological Research*. New York: Harper & Row.

Pelto, Pertti J., and Gretel H. Pelto. 1978. *Anthropological Research: The Structure of Inquiry*. Cambridge: Cambridge University Press.

Piven, Frances Fox, and Richard A. Cloward. 1971. *Regulating the Poor: The Functions of Public Welfare*. New York: Vintage, Random House.

Plumb, Stephen E. 1991. Assembling the Future at Jefferson North. *Ward's Auto World*, November.

Porter, K. H. 1989. *Poverty in Rural America: A National Overview*. Washington, D.C: Center on Budget and Policy Priorities.

Powell, Michael. 1991. Homeless Sleight of Hand? Study: City Bases Plan on Inflated Numbers. *Newsday*, December 23.

Rapoport, Amos. 1982. *The Meaning of the Built Environment: A Nonverbal Communication Approach*. Beverly Hills, Calif.: Sage.

Reid, W. 1977. Sectarian Agencies. In *Encyclopedia of Social Work*, vol. 2, ed. J. B. Turner, 1244–54. Washington, D.C.: National Association of Social Workers.

Rivlin, Leanne G., and Josephine E. Imbimbo. 1989. Self–Help Efforts in a Squatter Community: Implications for Addressing Contemporary Homelessness. *American Journal of Community Psychology* 17:705–28.

Robbins, Tom. 1984. New York's Homeless Families. *City Limits* (Nov.): 1, 7–12.

Robertson, M. 1987. *Homelessness in Albuquerque: Population and Conditions.* Albuquerque: City of Albuquerque, N.M., Department of Human Services.

———. 1991. *Interpreting Homelessness: The Influence of Professional and Non-Professional Service Providers. Urban Anthropology* 20 (2): 141–54.

Robertson, M., R. Richard, and R. Boyer. 1985. *The Homeless of Los Angeles County.* Document no. 4, Basic Shelter Research Project. Los Angeles: School of Public Health, University of California Los Angeles.

Rodman, Hyman. 1971. *Lower Class Families and the Culture of Poverty in Trinidad.* New York: Oxford University Press.

———. 1973. Social Forces: The Lower-Class Value Stretch. In *The Urban Scene,* ed. Joe R. Feagin, 150. New York: Random House.

Ropers, R.H. 1988. *The Invisible Homeless: A New Urban Ecology.* New York: Human Sciences Press.

Rosenthal, Rob. 1989. Worlds within Worlds: The Lives of Homeless People in Context. Paper presented at the 1989 American Sociological Association Conference, San Francisco, California.

———. 1991a. Straighter from the Source: Alternative Methods of Researching Homelessness. *Urban Anthropology* 20:109–26.

Ross, P. J., and E. S. Morrissey. 1989. Rural People in Poverty: Persistent versus Temporary Poverty. In *Proceedings of National Rural Studies Committee,* 59–73. Corvallis, Ore.: Western Rural Development Center.

Rossi, P. H. 1989. *Down and Out in America: The Origins of Homelessness.* Chicago: University of Chicago Press.

Rossi, P. H., J. D. Wright, G. A. Fisher, and G. Willis. 1987. The Urban Homeless: Estimating Composition and Size. *Science* 235:1336–41.

Rousseau, A. M. 1981. *Shopping Bag Ladies: Homeless Women Speak about Their Lives.* New York: Pilgrim Press.

Rowe, Stacy. 1989. Panhandlers and Sidewalk Encampments: Social Networks for the Homeless in Los Angeles. *Practicing Anthropology* 11 (1): 14–16.

Rowe, Stacy, and Jennifer Wolch. 1989. Social Networks in Time and Space: The Case of Homeless Women in Skid Row, Los Angeles. School of Urban and Regional Planning, University of Southern California, Los Angeles, California. Unpublished manuscript.

———. 1990. Social Networks in Time and Space: Homeless Women in Skid Row. *Annals of the Association of American Geographers* 80:184–204.

Rubenstein, Richard E. 1970. *Rebels in Eden: Centralism vs. Decentralism.* Boston: Little, Brown.

Ruddick, Susan. 1990. Heterotopias of the Homeless: Strategies and Tactics of Placemaking in Los Angeles. *Strategies* 3:184–201.

Ryan, William. 1976. *Blaming the Victim.* New York: Random House.

Sachar, Rajindar. 1994. The Realization of Economic, Social and Cultural Rights: The Right to Adequate Housing. Second Progress Report to the United Nations Economic and Social Council Commission on Human Rights: Sub-Commission on Prevention of Dicrimination and Protection of Minorities. E/CN4/Sub.2/1994/20.

———. 1995. Housing—A Human Right. Paper presented at Seminar of Swedish Non-Governmental Organizations and Networks. Stockholm, Sweden.

Sahlins, Marshal D. 1972. *Stone Age Economics.* Chicago: Aldine.

Sante, Luc. 1995. New York's Attack on Itself. *New York Times*, June 4.

Sassen-Koob, S. 1987. Growth and Information at the Core: A Preliminary Report on New York City. In *The Capitalist City*, eds. M. P. Smith and J. R. Feagin, 138–54. Cambridge: Basil Blackwell.

Schill, Michael H., and Richard Nathan. 1983. *Revitalizing America's Cities*. Albany: State University of New York Press.

Schmitt, Eric. 1995. G.O.P. Would Give Pentagon Money It Didn't Request. *New York Times*, July 5.

Sennott, Charles M. 1996. A Special Report, Armed for Profit: The Selling of U.S. Weapons. *The Boston Globe*, February 11.

Shapiro, I. 1989. *Laboring for Less: Working But Poor in Rural America*. Washington, D.C.: Center on Budget and Policy Priorities.

Shields, R. 1990. The System of Pleasure: Liminality and the Carnivalesque at Brighton. *Theory, Culture and Society* 7:39–72.

———. 1991. Places on the Margin: Alternative Geographies of Modernity. New York: Routledge Press.

Singelakis, Andrew Thomas. 1990. Real Estate Market Trends and the Displacement of the Aged. *The Gerontologist* 30 (5): 658–65.

Smith, Neil. 1991. Mapping the Gentrification Frontier. In *Hollow Promises*, eds. Michael Keith and Alisdair Rogers, 84–109. London: Mansell Publishing.

Smith, Neil, and Michele LeFaivre. 1984. A Class Analysis of Gentrification. In *Gentrification, Displacement, and Neighborhood Revitalization*, eds. John Palen and Brude London. Albany: State University of New York Press.

Snow, D. A., and L. Anderson. 1987. Identity Work among the Homeless: The Verbal Construction and Avowal of Personal Identities. *American Journal of Sociology* 92:1336–71.

Snow, D. A., S. G. Baker, and L. Anderson. 1989. Criminality and Homeless Men: An Empirical Assessment. *Social Problems* 36:532–49.

Soja, E. A. 1989. *Postmodern Geography: The Reassertion of Space in Critical Social Theory*. New York: Verso.

Southall, A. W. 1994. The Crisis of the City: The Future in the Present. Paper presented at the Conference of the International Commission on Urban Anthropology (I.U.A.E.S.), University of Lodz, Lodz, Poland, July.

Southard, Dee. 1993. Homeless Families in the National Forest: An Ethnographic Study. Paper presented at Pacific Sociological Association, Portland, Oregon, April 1.

Spayd, Liz. 1993. D.C. Coalition Endorses New Convention Center. *Washington Post*, August 14.

Spradley, James. 1979. *The Ethnographic Interview*. New York: Holt, Rinehart and Winston.

Stack, Carol. 1970. The Kindred of Viola Jackson: Residence and Family Organization of an Urban Black American Family. In *Afro-American Anthology: Contemporary Perspectives*, eds. N. Whitten and J. Szwed. New York: The Free Press.

———. 1974. *All Our Kin—Strategies for Survival in a Black Community*. New York: Harper and Row.

Staples, Robert. 1971. *Black Family Essays and Studies*. Belmont, Calif.: Wadsworth Publishing.

State of Connecticut. 1988. Report to the General Assembly on the General Assistance Program. Hartford, Conn.

Stefl, Mary E. 1987. The New Homeless: A National Perspective. In *The Homeless in Contemporary Society*, eds. Richard D. Bingham, Roy E. Green and Sammis B. White, 46–63. Newbury Park, Calif.: Sage Publications.

Stegman, Michael A. 1993. *Housing and Vacancy Report New York City, 1991*. New York: NYC Department of Housing Preservation and Development.

Steiner, Henry J., and Philip Alston. 1996. *International Human Rights in Context: Law, Politics, Morals*. New York: Clarendon. Oxford University Press.

Stoner, M. R. 1983. The Plight of Homeless Women. *Social Service Review* 57 (4): 565–81.

Tabb, William K. 1977. *The Political Economy of the Black Ghetto*. New York: Norton.

Task Force on Homelessness of the Manhattan Borough President's Office. 1987. A Shelter Is Not a Home. New York.

Thurow, Lester C. 1996. The Future of Capitalism: How Today's Economic Forces Shape Tomorrow's World. New York: William Morrow and Company.

Toner, Robin. 1995. When Health Care Cuts Cost More. *New York Times*, June 6.

Trainor, Theresa. 1992. We Are Not Weeping Willow Trees: A Study of Old Southwest. Non-thesis option paper, American University, Department of Anthropology, Washington, D.C.

Trancik, R. 1986. *Finding Lost Space: Theories of Urban Design*. New York: Van Nostrand Reinhold Company.

Tropman, John E. 1989. *American Values and Social Welfare: Cultural Contradictions in the Welfare State*. Englewood Cliffs, N.J.: Prentice-Hall.

Tucker, Maggie. 1993. Applying Water Pressure in DC. *Washington Post*, July 14.

Urban Collaborative. 1972. Jefferson-Chalmers Report Number Four—Household Survey. Detroit, Michigan.

U.S. Department of Housing and Urban Development. 1994. *Priority: Home! The Federal Plan to Break the Cycle of Homelessness*. U.S. Printing Office. HUD-1454-CPD(1).

Valentine, Charles A. 1968. *Culture and Poverty: Critique and Counter-Proposals*. Chicago: University of Chicago Press.

———. 1971. The Culture of Poverty: Its Scientific Significance and Its Implications for Action. In *The Culture of Poverty: A Critique*, ed. Eleanor B. Leacock, 193–225. New York: Simon & Schuster.

———. 1973. Models and Muddles Concerning Culture and Inequality: A Reply to Critics. In *The Urban Scene*, ed. Joe. R. Feagin, 166–79. New York: Random House.

Van Dyne, Larry. 1989. The House Game. *The Washingtonian*, April, 167–96.

Van Vliet, W., and J. van Weesep. 1990. *Government and Housing: Developments in Seven Countries*. Newbury Park, Calif.: Sage Publications.

Wallis, B. 1991. *If You Only Lived Here: The City in Art, Theory, and Social Activism, a Project by Martha Rosler*. Seattle: Bay Press.

Wald, Mathew. 1995a. Aging Control System Brings Chaos to Air Travel. *New York Times*, August 20.

———. 1995b. Report Faults Staffing Level of Controllers. *New York Times*, October 6.

Walzer, M. 1983. *Spheres of Justice*. New York: Basic Books.

Watson, S., and H. Austerberry. 1986. *Housing and Homelessness*. Boston: Routledge and Kegan Paul.

Watts, Lewis G., et al. 1964. *The Middle-Income Negro Family Faces Urban Renewal*. Boston: Commonwealth of Massachusetts, Department of Commerce and Development.

Wheeler, Linda. 1993. DC Council Restricts Begging. *Washington Post*, June 2.

Whyte, W. 1955. *Street Corner Society*. Chicago: University of Chicago Press.

Wilhelm, Sidney M. 1971. *Who Needs the Negro?* Garden City, NY: Doubleday Anchor.

Williams, Brett. 1988. *Upscaling Downtown.* Ithaca, NY: Cornell University Press.

Wilson, William Julius. 1980. *The Declining Significance of Race.* Chicago: University of Chicago Press.

———. 1987. *The Truly Disadvantaged.* Chicago: University of Chicago Press.

Winchester, H. P. M., and P. E. White. 1988. The Location of Marginalized Groups in the Inner City. Environment and Planning D. *Society and Space* 6:37–54.

Wirth, Louis. 1938. Urbanism as a Way of Life. *American Journal of Sociology* 44:1–24.

Wolch, J. R., M. Dear., and A. Akita. 1988. Explaining Homelessness. *Journal of the American Planning Association* 54 (4): 443–53.

Wolfe, A. 1981. *America's Impasse: The Rise and Fall of the Politics of Growth.* New York: Pantheon.

Wright, James D. 1989. *Address Unknown: The Homeless in America.* New York: Aldine de Gruyter.

———. 1992. Special Issue on Counting the Homeless. *Evaluation Review: A Journal of Applied Social Research* 16 (4).

Wright, T. and A. Vermund. 1990. Small Dignities: Local Resistances, Dominant Strategies of Authority, and Suburban Homeless. Paper presented at the 1990 Annual American Sociological Association, Washington, D.C.

Yanagisako, Sylvia. 1979. Family and Household: the Analysis of Domestic Groups. *Annual Review of Anthropology* 8:161–205.

Zeitz, Eileen. 1979. *Private Urban Renewal: A Different Residential Trend.* Lexington, Ky.: Lexington Press.

Zukin, S. 1988. The Postmodern Debate over Urban Form. *Theory, Culture and Society* 3:431–46.

———. 1991. *Landscapes of Power: From Detroit to Disney World.* Berkeley: University of California Press.

Index

Contributors

M. RORY BOLGER is instructor of anthropology at Wayne County Community College in Detroit, Michigan, and Social Planner V with Detroit's City Planning Commission. He received his Ph.D. in anthropology from Wayne State University, where he concentrated on urban kinship and community, cultural ecology, and Mesoamerica. He is principal author of Detroit's ordinances defining and regulating emergency shelters for the homeless and single room occupancy housing. *Recession in Detroit: Strategies of a Plantside Community and the Corporate Elite* summarizes his doctoral research. An article, "Ethnic Identity and Assimilation—7 Generations of an Irish-Canadian Lineage," was published in *Central Issues in Anthropology*, May 1985.

ANNA LOU DEHAVENON received her Ph.D. degree in anthropology from Columbia University in 1978. She serves as project director for the Action Research Project on Hunger, Homelessness, and Family Health in New York City which she founded, as adjunct assistant professor of anthropology in community medicine at the Mount Sinai School of Medicine, City University of New York, Research Associate in the Department of Anthropology at City College (CUNY), and Visiting Professor of Anthropology at the Center for the Study of Administration of Relief in New Delhi, India. Her research on New York City's oppressed classes extends over two decades. Dehavenon has published widely in scholarly and popular venues concerning the causes of poverty in the United States. In 1988, she convened the Task Force on Poverty and Homelessness of the American Anthropological Association with Delmos Jones.

JANET M. FITCHEN received her Ph.D. in cultural anthropology from Cornell University in 1973. She was professor and chair of the Department of Anthropology at Ithaca College until her untimely death after a brief illness with brain cancer in

1995. She concentrated on the study of the contemporary United States, with a primary research focus on poverty and on rural America, which led to the book *Poverty in Rural America: A Case Study*. Her most recent book, *Endangered Spaces, Enduring Places: Change, Identity, and Survival in Rural America*, describes agricultural, economic, demographic, social, and cultural changes that are now transforming rural communities. She also published articles on community response to environmental problems. During 1990–92 she conducted additional research on rural poverty in upstate New York, with a grant from the Ford Foundation, through the Aspen Institute's Rural Economic Policy Program. During the 1992–93 academic year, she spent a sabbatical year as a "roving researcher in rural poverty" supported by the W. K. Kellogg Foundation and under the auspices of the Western Rural Development Center in Corvallis, Oregon, in which she conducted exploratory scoping research in nine other states. She was a consultant and trainer for a variety of human service programs in New York state and around the nation, including community action programs, social service agencies, and Cooperative Extension. She worked with Head Start programs and rural school districts, helping them to understand effects of poverty on children and to develop strategies for working effectively with low-income families.

IRENE GLASSER received her Ph.D. in anthropology at the University of Connecticut in 1968 and an MSW from the University of Connecticut in 1970 and is a professor in anthropology at Eastern Connecticut State University, where she teaches anthropology and Canadian Studies. Her background in social work helped her understand the social welfare institutions that surround issues of urban poverty in North America. Her publications include *More Than Bread: Ethnography of a Soup Kitchen* and *Homelessness in Global Perspective*. She is also a frequent contributor to *Practicing Anthropology*, and she has guest edited the Fall 1994 issue on "Anthropology and Welfare." Dr. Glasser's most recent research focuses on a comparison of homelessness in one U.S. city (Hartford, Connecticut) and one Canadian city (Montreal, Québec) in order to better understand the forces that both prevent and cause homelessness.

SUSAN HAMILTON received an M.A. in applied anthropology from Georgia State University and is a doctoral candidate in development anthropology at Syracuse University. Her research, conducted in Argentina, Bolivia, Mexico, and the United States, centers around housing, homelessness, settlement, and resettlement. She currently works as a community organizer with Syracuse United Neighbors and volunteers with the Mad Housers when visiting Atlanta.

MARVIN HARRIS, after more than thirty years of association with Columbia University, presently holds the position of graduate research professor of anthropology at the University of Florida. Harris has been a leading force in anthropological theory and methodology for more than four decades. He is the author of fifteen books addressing numerous facets of general anthropology, including *The Nature of Cultural Things* (1964a), *The Rise of Anthropological Theory: A History of Theories of Culture* (1968d), *Culture, Man and Nature: An Introduction to General Anthropology* (1975), *Cultural Materialism: The Struggle for a Science of Culture* (1979a), and *Our Kind* (1989).

KIM HOPPER received his Ph.D. in sociomedical studies from Columbia University and is now research scientist at the Nathan S. Kline Institute for Psychiatric Research. He has taught anthropology and epidemiology at Columbia University, Rutgers University, the City University Medical School, and the New School for Social Research. Since 1979, he has done ethnographic and historical research on homelessness, chiefly in New York City. He was a cofounder of both the New York Coalition for the Homeless and the National Coalition for the Homeless, and served as president of the latter organization from 1991–93. As an anthropologist and advocate, he is especially interested in cultural struggles to define the terms and debate the merits of rights and reciprocities—and the often poorly articulated notions of equity they rest on—as they take shape in poverty practice and policy.

ANDREW H. MAXWELL is an assistant professor of anthropology at Montclair State University. Formerly he was assistant Professor of Sociology and African-American Studies at the State University of New York at Binghamton. His previous work includes articles on the underclass and the culture of poverty, the community studies model, gentrification and African-American communities, and general systems theory.

AMY PHILLIPS received her B.A. in anthropology from Georgia State University, Atlanta, Georgia, in 1984. She is a charter member of the Mad Housers. Her initial involvement with the Mad Housers began in 1987 at the first organizational meeting and continued on a full-time basis through June 1992. In addition to being a Mad Housers volunteer, she has served as an officer of the of the Mad Housers (corporate secretary 1988–90, Executive Director 1991) and a member of the board of directors (1988–92). She is currently self employed as a contract archaeologist working throughout the continental United States and Hawaii.

MICHAEL ROBERTSON received his Ph.D. in anthropology from the University of New Mexico and is currently a member of the clinical faculty of the Department of Psychiatry Human Services Program at the University of New Mexico. He developed and directed the first program of street outreach to the homeless mentally ill in New Mexico and continues to work as a program development consultant for the New Mexico Division of Mental Health and the New Mexico Division of Vocational Rehabilitation. Since 1984 he has worked extensively with homeless people and investigated the circumstances of homelessness in New Mexico. During five separate periods between 1986 and 1992 he lived as a homeless man on the streets of Albuquerque. He has written a variety of articles and research studies about the conditions of street life and the structure of homeless services.

ANITA VERMUND received her Master's in Social Work from Columbia University and currently works for the Health Care Agency of the County of Orange, Costa Mesa, California, as a licensed social worker. She worked in the Mentally Disabled Homeless Program from 1986 through 1988.

BRETT WILLIAMS is Director of the American Studies Program and Associate Professor of Anthropology at American University in Washington, D.C., where she has been involved in ethnographic research and community projects for the last twenty years. Her publications include *Upscaling Downtown*, *John Henry*, and the edited collection *The Politics of Culture*, as well as many articles. She is currently writing (with Robert Manning) a book about credit and debt in the contemporary United States. She has long been active in issues concerning urban poverty, working on cultural events such as festivals and films, and activist projects in neighborhoods and schools. She is currently working in two public housing projects in Washington, D.C., collaborating with residents to record oral histories and organize for social change.

TALMADGE WRIGHT is assistant professor in the Department of Sociology and Anthropology, Loyola University, Chicago, where he is engaged in research on homeless mobilizations, housing, social space and urban built environments. He has also undertaken research on marketing and popular culture publishing work on design, marketing and the built environment from a critical sociological perspective. Between 1986 and 1989 he worked for the Fair Housing Council of Orange County as an Urban Housing analyst.

ISBN 0-89789-484-7

9 780897 894845

90000>

EAN

HARDCOVER BAR CODE